Infrastructure Development – Theory, Practice and Policy

Sustainability and Resilience

2021 Conference Compendium

Edited by

Rachna Gangwar
Adani Institute of Infrastructure Management, Ahmedabad

Astha Agarwalla
Adani Institute of Infrastructure Management, Ahmedabad

Sandhya Sreekumar
MIT World Peace University, Pune

Infrastructure Development – Theory, Practice and Policy

Sustainability and Resilience

2021 Conference Compendium

Edited by

Rachna Gangwar
Adani Institute of Infrastructure Management, Ahmedabad

Astha Agarwalla
Adani Institute of Infrastructure Management, Ahmedabad

Sandhya Sreekumar
MIT World Peace University, Pune

ROUTLEDGE
Routledge
Taylor & Francis Group

First published 2022
by Routledge
4 Park Square, Milton Park, Abingdon, Oxon OX14 4RN

and by Routledge
605 Third Avenue, New York, NY 10158

Routledge is an imprint of the Taylor & Francis Group, an Informa business

British Library Cataloguing-in-Publication Data
A catalogue record for this book is available from the British Library

ISBN: 9781032114668 (pbk)
ISBN: 9781003311157 (ebk)
DOI: 10.4324/9781003311157

Contents

Section III: Measuring the Outcomes – Focusing on the 'How' to Ensure 'Why'

Lists of Figures

List of Tables

About the Authors

Rachna Gangwar is Associate Professor & Head, Centre for Surface and Air Transport at Adani Institute of Infrastructure Management Ahmedabad. She has more than 20 years of experience working across industry and academia in India and Germany. Her teaching and research interests are in transport policy, public-private partnerships, urban transport systems, and logistics and supply chain management. She has written many case studies and published several refereed papers on contemporary issues in the Indian context. She has been a part of research projects undertaken for the erstwhile Planning Commission, Asian Development Bank, and Railway Board on private container train operations, railway turnaround, and PPPs in railways.

Prior to joining Adani Institute of Infrastructure Management, she held teaching and research positions at the University of Karlsruhe Germany, Indian Institute of Management Ahmedabad, Institute of Management Technology Ghaziabad, and TAPMI School of Business Jaipur. Her industry experience includes working for PTV AG, one of the largest German consulting firms in transport and logistics where she handled several European projects for government clients.

She is a Chartered Member of the Chartered Institute of Logistics Transport, and a Member of Transportation Research Group of India, and The World Conference of Transport Research Society.

Astha Agarwalla is an Associate Professor in Economics and Public Policy, at Adani Institute of Infrastructure Management, Ahmedabad, where she also heads the Centre for Urban and Real Estate Development. A Masters in Economics, She has done her Ph.D. from IIM-Ahmedabad in Public Systems. She has worked with government utilities and infrastructure division of Deloitte and taught courses in Urban Infrastructure Management and Public Policy at IIM-Indore. Her current research interests include urban infrastructure management, urban and regional development, macroeconomics, public finance, and public policy and governance.

Sandhya Sreekumar, Ph.D., is an Assistant Professor at the Maharashtra Institute of Technology World Peace University (MIT WPU), India. She received her Ph.D. in Public Administration from Pandit Deendayal Petroleum University, India. She has worked as a Research Officer at the Adani Institute of Infrastructure Management, India. She served as a Research Associate while contributing to two projects, at the Indian Institute of Management Ahmedabad (IIMA). Her research focuses on urban governance, water and sanitation services and local administration.

Foreword

Infrastructure is an important indicator and substratum of growth of any nation. Infrastructure is a transdisciplinary domain, which involves domain experts from all disciplines for a common cause. A conference with focus on Infrastructure that brings domain experts on one platform is of paramount importance. The International conference on infrastructure development (ICID) – Theory, Practice and Policy is an endeavor in this light.

ICID provided a platform, not only for inter-disciplinary discussions, translating engineering solutions to managerial practices, but also for inter-sectoral dialogue, covering the broad spectrum of transport, energy, real estate, and social infrastructure. The intersectoral perspective, transcending the sectoral boundaries, provides opportunities for development of hybrid models of infrastructure, addressing needs and creating end-to-end value.

The conference provides a platform for confluence of theory, practice, and policy, in the domain of infrastructure. Adani Institute of Infrastructure (AII) has always envisioned itself as a leading institution generating knowledge and ideas based on sound theoretical base, aimed to benefit business practice, and contributing to policy formulation cum implementation. ICID series envisages to become a channel for the same.

The theme for first occurrence of this conference was 'Sustainability and Resilience'. There could not have been a time more apt for exploring the intricacies of human interaction with nature and measuring the tenacity of human response to challenges whether natural or man-made. Sustainability dialogue is crucial for infrastructure development, since infrastructure is for long term, and the realization of intergenerational parity, leaving as many resources for future generations, as enjoyed by us, leads our way to development of sustainable infrastructure.

Technology has an important role to play, both in creating newer, disruptive, sustainable solutions, and to measure the impact of sustainability related regulations on business productivity and outcome. Technology is a necessary enabler and shall have more presence in times to come than ever before.

The compendium brings together the papers presented at the conference and covers this interdisciplinary, inter-sectoral dialogue. This is just a beginning, and AII is resolved to play an instrumental role in facilitating such dialogues in future.

M Muruganant
Director
Adani Institute of Infrastructure, Ahmedabad

Preface and Acknowledgements

In the fast-changing landscape of the infrastructure sector in India, the opportunities are mammoth and so are the challenges. With emerging and disruptive technologies, conventional management practices and regulatory mechanisms are becoming ineffective, and policymakers are faced with numerous challenges. The new technologies such as autonomous electric vehicles are blurring the traditional sectoral boundaries and emphasize the need for greater integration and convergence between sectors and disciplines. Academia and research organizations have an important role to play in understanding the nuances of the changing business environment and provide innovative solutions. While several academic conferences and events bring experts from a particular infrastructure domain together, the conference that not only addresses the sectoral issues but also the intersectoral and convergence issues was missing. The conference 'Infrastructure Development: Theory, Practice, and Policy is an attempt in that direction. We endeavor to establish this initiative as a regular event that brings the researchers, practitioners, policymakers, and other stakeholders from all infrastructure sectors and disciplines together and provides a platform for knowledge creation and dissemination.

The first conference was conceived amid the unprecedented COVID 19 pandemic and the resilience of the existing infrastructure systems was being tested like never before. In addition, the challenges emerging from the current development model that viewed the world as a global village became evident when the international borders had to be closed and the trade was interrupted. This pandemic has forced us to rethink the current infrastructure development, further emphasizing the need for holistic sustainable infrastructure development and not just the economic viability and low carbon. The theme 'sustainability and resilience of the first conference held on April 29-30, 2021, was selected to deliberate on some of these issues.

The conference was organized in four-panel discussions on the themes of (i) making sustainability mainstream, (ii) transport sustainability during the pandemic, (iii) Moving ESG from 5-Star Conferences to the Board Rooms, and (iv) vision for the future, and five sectorally organized technical sessions, (i) sustainable urban and real estate infrastructure, (ii) transportation and mobility systems, (iii) energy and green infrastructure, (iv) social infrastructure and sustainability, and (v) financing sustainable infrastructure.

In addition to research papers presented during the conference, 25 senior experts from industry, academia, and government deliberated on the most pressing issues around sustainability and resilience across infrastructure sectors in various panels, or as keynote speakers in technical sessions. We are thankful to each one of them for their commitment (amidst COVID 19 second wave), valuable insights, and perspectives. We are grateful to Dr. Malay Mahadevia, Whole-time Director, Adani Ports & SEZ and Trustee, Adani Institute of Infrastructure; Prof. G Raghuram, Former Director, IIMB and Academic Advisor, NRTI; Prof. Sebastian Morris, Former Professor, IIM Ahmedabad; Prof. Arun Kumar Sharma, Queensland University of Technology; Prof. Shailesh Gandhi, IIM Ahmedabad; Prof. Wouter Dewulf, Antwerp University; Mr. Shailesh Pathak, CEO, L&T Infrastructure Development Projects Limited; Prof. Richard Thakor, University of Minnesota; and Dr. Satyam Shivam Sundaram, Partner, EY for their valuable guidance as advisory members and speakers. We are especially thankful to Prof. Sebastian Morris, Prof. Arun Sharma, and Prof. G Raghuram for their valuable contribution to this compendium too.

We sincerely thank Mr. Anil Sardana, CEO, Adani Transmission Ltd; Mr. Manish Agrawal, Partner, Infrastructure Advisory, PwC India; Mr. Ben Zandi, CEO, Adani Airports; Prof. Anil Gupta, Former Professor, IIM Ahmedabad and Founder, HoneyBee Network; Dr. Prasad Modak, Executive President, Environmental Management Centre LLP; Mr. Suhas Tuljapurkar, Director, Legasis Service; Mr. Mukund Rajan, Chairman, ECube Investment Advisors Private Ltd; Mr. Sankar Chakraborti, CEO, Acuité Ratings, Chairman, SMERA Gradings & Ratings & Chairman, ESG Risk Assessments & Insights; Mr. R V Shahi, Ex-Secretary to Government of India. Chairman, Energy Infratech; Mr. Ajay Shankar, Ex-Secretary to Government of India. Expert – TERI; Mr. Anish De, Director, KPMG; Mr. Kuljit Singh,

Director, EY; Mr. Sunil Shrivastava, Ex DMD, SBI & Advisor - World Bank; Dr. Veni Mathur, Vice-Chairperson, Chartered Institute of Logistics and Transport India; Dr. Kamal Kishore Sharma, Director General, Taxila Business School; Prof. Ashwini Kumar, CEPT University; Prof. Amit Garg, IIM Ahmedabad for their valuable contribution in the panel/technical sessions.

At the Adani Institute of Infrastructure Management (AIIM), the then Director Prof. A.V. Thomas, Dean Mr. Devang Desai, and Registrar Mr. Ketan Doshi provided support to the endeavor. Heads and members of the five Centers of Excellence in Infrastructure at AIIM, namely, Centre of Excellence in Surface and Air Transport, Centre of Excellence in Energy, Centre of Excellence in Urban and Real Estate Development, Centre of Excellence in Social Infrastructure, and Centre of Excellence in Finance and Risk Management, provided wholehearted support in organization of the conference. Organizing a virtual event with international and national participation right in the middle of the pandemic was not possible without the untiring support from the administrative and service teams from the Institute. We are thankful to Mr. Hiren Mandaliya, Mr. Keshav Bhatia, Mr. Saurin Gandhi, Mr. Ritesh Soni, Ms. Shreyansi, Mr. Yogender, Mr. Manu, Mr. Deepan Rawal, Ms. Devika Mathur, Mr. Kartik Vadgama, Ms. Nisha Gupta, Mr. Chandresh, Ms. Neha Rawal, Mr. Purvish Shah and all the administrative staff members of AIIM for their kind and tireless support.

It was heartening to observe that the pandemic and the standstill it had brought the world to, could not affect the enthusiasm of participants. The Conference received original research studies being conducted in national and international institutions of repute. The originality of research culminated in emergence of three broad themes, leading paradigms for future research in fields of infrastructure and sustainability.

The first theme that highlights the future direction sustainability research and discourse is going to take, brings out the importance of localized infrastructure and solutions. Close connect with the stakeholders, reliance on local resources, and quick feedback and rectification mechanisms, along with easy enforceability make local solutions more effective and efficient in achieving sustainable infrastructure solutions. A more humane focus is needed further, as the distribution of negative externalities of climate change is lopsided, with those who are poor and vulnerable facing greater challenges.

The second theme centered around the need for technological innovations to achieve desired outcomes in an efficient and cost-effective manner. One of the biggest highlights of the conference was to bring to the fore the need for and importance of interdisciplinary research and development effort to find scientific and engineering solutions and to design economic and managerial models around them to make them feasible. Another challenge is that of financing such models to develop sustainable infrastructure. Newer models of risk assessment and sharing and utilization of resources have to be worked out to find ways and means to address the infrastructural challenges.

The third theme highlights the importance of measuring outcomes and developing the feedback loops for sustainability related initiatives. Methods to measure the impact of economic and business activities on climate have received enough interest and coverage. What is needed next is methods to measure the differential impact of sustainable practices vis-à-vis the usual default practices, to clearly bring out the gains in terms of economic and social welfare. Also, there is a need to devise methods to study the impact of environmental regulations on business productivity and long-term sustainability. Research has provided evidence that ad-hoc regulatory mechanisms based on piecemeal information often led to more harm than good. Resorting to sustainable solutions has huge economic trade-offs, and inefficiently designed regulations can make people pick the wrong side of these trade-offs.

This compendium is a culmination of the conference deliberations. It brings together the select papers from the conference and other contributions from experts and researchers. The compendium puts together the research under the three themes, and we hope that the theoretical findings will impact the practice and policy in the future, as well as pave the way for future research in the direction of achieving more efficient, and more humane infrastructure.

Rachna Gangwar

Astha Agarwalla

Sandhya Sreekumar

The Quest for a Green Economy in India – The Policy Quagmire

Sebastian Morris[1]
Senior Professor
Goa Institute of Management

1. INTRODUCTION

In this brief, we review India's commitment to reduce the emission of green house gases (GHG). We also argue that India in unique among the large countries for having sacrificed its own national interest in committing to an emission reductions that would in all likelihood make the average emission per Indian lower than that of most countries. This magnanimous commitment imposes large unwarranted costs on the economy, since it comes at too early a stage of development of the economy, and its achievement is based on the continuing exclusion of large masses of its people from the process of economic development. It would also most likely stand in the way of the country being able to penetrate the middle income barrier.

Many of the policy initiatives are laudable and can be considered successful in terms of their own narrow objective of reducing GHG emitting energy. We review the more important of these developments.

However, what is being ignored, is the large potential to reduce GHGs by removing the allocative price distortions of energy, and water embodying energy in its use in the agricultural sector. The expensive, electric vehicle strategy can be justified on ensuring that India does not miss the technology and manufacturing of EVs, and less on the GHG emission over the medium term. There can be significant reductions in GHG if the modal of surface transport increases for rail, as it would be the simple action of correctly pricing rail freight, which may well be even above the revenue maximizing rate! There are many low hanging fruits, which are ignored by both policy makers and much of the academia.

2. INDIA'S COMMITMENT AND NATIONAL INTEREST

India is almost unique in having pursued highly visible policies for a green economy, when at a level of income that is one of the lowest in the world. Unlike most middle income countries, and in sharp contrast to the east Asian tigers, its commitment happens at a very early stage in its transformation where the inclusion of the masses into the development process has yet to take place. The commitments have come from popular leaders and has been a top down process. Indian prime ministers have almost without exception committed to GHG reductions and have upped the targets in recent years. India's own commitment to reduce GHGs is indeed very ambitious and altruistic. Thus "*India has maintained that it is not a polluter and cause of climate change and has voluntarily committed to reducing greenhouse gas emission intensity of its GDP by 33-35 per cent below 2005 levels by 2030*" (Economic Times, 2021). In contrast China which is the largest emitter of GHGs in its recent very aggressive reduction targets would peak at 2030 with a zero emission by 2060. Similarly, "China's emission projections from current policies have been revised downward during the ongoing COVID-19 pandemic. If implemented, current policies would result in GHG emission levels of 12.9-14.7 $GtCO_2e$/year in 2030. With these policies, China is expected to achieve its 2020 pledge and 2030 NDC targets" (Climate Action Tacker, 2021).

[1] Former Professor at Indian Institute of Management, Ahmedabad (email: morris@iima.ac.in)

The difference is best indicated by the per head emission in 2030. India in all likelihood has committed itself to a target that is just about a fifth that of China. This is a tremendous sacrifice of the interests of the Indian people when we recognise that a democratically elected government has made this commitment. We have forecasted India's GDP to grow from 2014 at six percent as also China's. China's ability to hold on to a GDP growth of 6%, even with a massive top-down induced change in its production structure, towards a green economy is beyond doubt. The Indian economy had slowed down to under 4.5% even before the COVID Crisis and is likely to recover at a slower rate. These would imply that the gap between the two in 2030 may be even larger than the forecasted 5:1 (Morris, 2020). And worse than what the table below since a considerable part of India's GHG current estimates are based on its substantial methane emissions from its large cattle population[2]. In reality, methane should not be counted at its greenhouse value which is around 10 times for CO_2 but only at 1 or a little more since the half-life of methane is around 12 years, which means that its impact is temporary and would not cumulate unlike for CO_2, methane's contribution should be adjusted for its half-life. When global warming is known to be the result of accumulation over the last two centuries or more the value of a molecule becomes close to that of carbon and no more.

GHG Emissions of China and India (Actual and Targets) in Relation to Population and GDP

		2005	2014	2030
China	CO_2e emissions (million tonnes)	7000	13000	14700
	GDP in 2019 USD (trillion)	2	10	27
	Emission intensity (tonne per million USD)	3057	1240	537
	Population (million)	1307	1367	1450
	Emission intensity per person (tonne)	5.36	9.51	10.14
India	CO_2e emissions (million tonnes)	1643	2306	3915
	GDP in 2019 USD (trillion)	1	2	5
	Emission intensity (tonne per million USD)	1226	1130	735
	Population (million)	1150	1296	1514
	Emission intensity per person (tonne)	1.43	1.78	2.59

More importantly, India would still be in the early stages of its economic transition and just at lower to middle income levels, with the major task of overcoming the so called "middle income barrier", which has dogged nearly all the Latin American economies. Given the inequity of the development process in India – it has one of the lowest labour participation rates – that barrier is real. It would require major reorientation of the development process towards inclusion – by an employment oriented high-speed growth – to have any chance of breaking this "barrier". Emission reduction at an early stage of development when capital is scare is expensive, and reduces the potential of the country growing beyond middle income levels, and may reduce the prospects of overall ultimate reduction in energy use per person. Today when the internal income distribution is highly iniquitous in India, the energy consumption is even more so. That means that the per head consumption of the vast majority of Indians even in 2030 would be abysmally low in comparison to much of humanity. Africa with its land and resource endowment would then have overcome the levels of the median consumer in India.

3. CORE POLICIES TO REDUCE GHGS

Be that as it may, this statesmanship by India's prime ministers, and widely lauded by its intelligentsia, gives direction to the economy. We bring out the principal policy thrusts of the government which are important in this drive to reduction of energy use intensity in production from the 2014 level of around 1200 tonnes per million 2019 US$ to about 735 by 2030.

3.1 BEE and white goods

India is one of the few countries that has a ministry of environment and non-conventional energy. It has over the years deployed large budgets to incentive the shift to solar, wind and non-conventional hydro power. It has also set in motion

[2] C.2015 its overall emissions at 2.7 tonnes per capita was lower than that of Indonesia (9.2), UK (7.8) a post industrial society, US (20.4), Brazil (5.6) an economy in the middle income trap for long, China (9.0), and EU (8.1). The world average was (7.0). The share of methane in India's GHGs was a high 23% while for the world as a whole it was around 15.5% (Timperley, 2019).

programmes like subsidizing the adoption of LEDs in lighting use, which have been quite successful. Others in the same vein have been star rating of equipment, laying out better standard in the use of energy and in overall performance of refrigerators, air conditioners and in electrical equipment in general. Given the Bureau of Energy Efficiency (BEEs) approach of interacting with industry, and with a scientific orientation, the standards have spread with little cost to the economy. There has much success in bringing down the GHG emissions from white goods of a wide variety. The subsidization of CFLs and now LEDs has led to near total adoption of LEDs, high efficiency vapour lamps, which should have reduced the emission per lumen almost proportionately with the reduction in energy input. The dynamism of technology and the fast growth of the Indian white goods markets have also helped.

3.2 Buildings

However, when the actors are dispersed and are numerous its success have been meagre. This for instance has been the case with regard to construction. Architectural approaches in India remain extremely energy inefficient over the life cycle and heavy in the use of materials as well. The archaic standard designs of PWDs, the fact that the architectural profession does not have an engineering approach, and are paid on a percentage of construction cost, and functionality in contrast to "form and fashion" being of less value in "premier" high profile housing and institutional construction, are all parts of the problem. "Green" designs that are in the limelight, are almost entirely "small", and veer to the romantic and traditional, are land intensive, have entirely bypassed multistory construction, and are out of question in densely populated urban locales. This set of factors limits the actual impact of a large number of highly motivated "green" architects, whose works remain small and more the exception. Lack of standard designs (the contrast with the town house innovation in the Western World during the middle of their economic transformation) also contributes. Independent house owners have to depend upon on an architect (with all his idiosyncrasies) or on masons and their "designs". Low FSI with which Indian cities plan also impede functional architecture, and add to the inefficiency, for the same standard of living since the volume covered to surface area tends to be very small making air-conditioning very inefficient, when the need for air-conditioning is the highest in India. It is only the very low incomes of people that has kept the unit demand low for electricity for household cooling. In some of the richer cities like Delhi, the AC demand has been growing despite the very prices for households using ACs[3].

3.3 Wind power

Perhaps the most important success has been in the areas of wind and solar power generation. In the case of wind the potential had been underestimated, because the CEA had worked with tower heights of only 50 mts, and with highly restrictive assumptions on the land availability. With higher 100m towers and with more realistic assumptions the potential went up and there has been significant development of wind power. Today the constraint is more in terms of scheduling, since often even wind generation has to be backed down, given the grid and demand limitations, not to speak of idling of thermal power plants.

3.4 Solar

In the case of solar, the developments have been quite remarkable. The first big push came with high feed-in tariffs which was almost at double the levels at which California at the same time procured solar power. Some 3000 MW may have been added at these unnecessarily high tariffs. The episode, though, may have had the benefit of bringing world attention to the commitment to solar in India. When the same gave way to bid-in tariffs with the NTPC acting as the procuring arm for the Government, and institutionalization of the policy, the development of solar power skyrocketed with the addition of more than 30,000 MW of capacity. Solar scrips allowed transferability of produced solar power across the country and targets to procure solar power, proportional to their demand, imposed on states and a professional organization through which the policy was implemented worked very well.

However thereafter it slowed down, as the government realized that much of the capacity had been added by using imported solar panels and the opportunity of using the heighted demand to create local capability in photovoltaic manufacturing. The government also ran into problems with the WTO when it tried to restrict imports, and lost its case, since the arguments were on flimsy grounds, when the government itself had bound the tariffs at near zero

[3] AC demand is the fastest growing component of household today, as it should be.

levels. The arguments of state procurement, "interruption in supply", or a deep commitment to solar, which were made sequentially, were not acceptable to the WTO panels (WTO, 2016; Karttunen et al., 2018). Clearly the capacity of the government to put its case was in question, and the contradictions created by lack of coordination between the MNRES and the Commerce Ministry was sorely visible. Since then, as Trump's "America First" trampled over the WTO, India found an opportunity to raise tariffs marginally and now with the world industry trying to find a second location for manufacturing outside of China there is renewed hope that manufacture of modern solar panels will happen to push the solar capacity additions.

3.5 Electric vehicle

The electric vehicle progamme of the government is also ambitious but has suffered from over enthusiasm as well. Government's deep commitment was interpreted by the market to mean that there would be a ban on diesel from 2025 which froze the entire investment process in 2019. The auto sector was on the verge of completing its investments to meet the Bharat VI norms when talk of this ban was in the air. Given the government's penchant for knee jerk reactions, and for "governance by bans" the prospect was taken seriously. Coming along with a sharp rise in the insurance fees (because of bunching of three years payment into one payment at the time of purchase), rises in fuel prices, and slow down of the economy, the growth of the auto sector went into a negative 25% or so from the peak achieved in 2018. The COVID only helped to mask this decline. Today the industry hopes for a recovery to reach the 2018 levels by end of 2021-22, on the back of an enhanced demand for personal mobility. The government in order to bring down the perceived uncertainties had to reiterate many times that it had no intention to ban diesel vehicles. Today with better appreciation of the potential for penetration of EVs in India's vast two-wheeler market, and incentives which are significant enough to make the shift to EVs by two/three wheelers in dual use (commercial) and by commercial utility vehicles, the EV programme is slated to make rapid strides. The thruput subsidy programme (now called the Production Linked Subsidy Scheme (PLI)) for many sectors, with the favourable wind in the form of a desire of global production networks to have a second foot outside China, has begun to work in EVs and would perhaps begin to bite in the area of advanced chemistry cells (which includes lithium ion batteries). The policy with regard to battery manufacture in India is realistic and recognizes the potential not only in mobility but also in grid and subgrid power storage. Thus, it is quite likely that India would make rapid strides in EV, though at higher unit cost given the small size of the market in relation to leaders like China and the US. These countries along with Japan and Germany are likely to drive the core technologies, the standards for components and their interconnect, besides the evolution of the "standard design".

The existence of some of the leading auto firms in the Indian market, and an adequate global footprint of some of the leading Indian firms gives much hope. In auto, the policies having been functional very early in the mid-eighties, had served to create a competitive auto industry in India. Now the strengths of the industry allows for a push into EVs with a high chance of success.

Electricity Capacity in China and India 2018 (million KW)

	Total	Hydro	Solar	Wind	Pumped	Per capita capacity
China	1917	322	175	184	30	1382
		(16.8)	(9.1)	(9.6)	(1.6)	
India	411	45	27	35	3.8	305
		(10.9)	(6.6)	(8.5)	(0.9)	

Source: EIA (2021a; 2021b)

3.6 Natural gas

Other important initiatives have been the push towards natural gas. Natural gas in industrial and bulk applications have increased, replacing largely oil, but their role could have been greater had a well designed market been in place, which would have brought out the value of gas in allowing the grid to schedule more solar and wind. Today when there is an overall excess capacity in the electricity sector there not all the renewable power can be scheduled efficiently. However natural gas in retail applications have been slow. Pricing distortions (vis-à-vis LPG) hampered its development during the first decade and half, and it is only now with the LPG subsidies having gone away that natural gas use can increase. There is a case for true market delivery of gas with the design of a market mechanism on the lines of the market centered around Henry hub in the US. In the case of both electricity and markets the current long and medium term contracts need to go financial, allowing for delivery to be based on price discovery by the minute in markets.[4]

4. DISTORTIONS AND AVOIDABLE EMISSIONS

Despite these major positive developments, we would argue that India's search for environmentally sustainable development has been non-inclusive, and low hanging fruits for saving on GHG emissions through energy use efficiency has been woefully inadequate. Most important in the waste has been the reluctance to correct allocative prices for energy in its various embodiments – water, and electricity. Distortions in pricing have cumulated and the economy is today very far from efficiency in such areas as transportation, agriculture.

4.1 Railways

Thus the price of electricity for the railways is very high and well above the cost to serve. This along with the high administered prices for freight makes the demand for freight shift on to roads, pounding the roads by an overly large population of trucks, and imposing very high emissions per tonne mile that so shifts. C. 2000 when the size of the conventional rail capacities in China and India were similar, the Chinese railways carried more than 4 times the freight that the Indian did. In 2018, the it was nearly 5, though on relatively better capacities of the Chinese railways.

The Railways used the capacity, inappropriately, to carry short and medium distance passengers where the comparative advantage of the railways is least in relation to road. Buses, especially as the roads have improved could have carried a great deal more of the passengers, to a relative reduction in the population of trucks. Indeed ever since the political process of tariff setting by the rail, truck demand has grown at rates that have given a high artificial elasticity of truck capacity demand close to 3 (!) to reduce the modal share of rail to a low under 30% (perhaps it is more correctly around 23%). India had a modal share of nearly 60% in the 60s. Indeed the cross over point where rail is seen as being cheaper by users have been pushed to over 1500 km when in India with a high density of habitat it should have been no more than 500 kms. With rail having an energy use intensity that is incomparably lower than of trucks, the unnecessary GHG emissions on this score is enormous. The trucks alone emitted 70289 Gg of CO_2 (alone) in 2008 (Ramachandra & Shewatmala, 2009). A hypothetical 10% savings by a shift back to rail means 70 Million MTs of CO_2 less emitted. Today, it could be more than double this figure.

The Ministry's intent to increase its modal share to 45% over the next decade, would certainly be a pipe dream if the pricing distortions are not corrected, and sufficient coordination for intermodal operations are not made, whatever are the proposed supply side measures.

4.2 Urban mess and GHGs

The best estimate of EV penetration by 2025 or so, is unlikely to be more than 10% when the weighting is done with CO_2 emissions. In contrast, the avoidable waste of energy in city transportation is very large. In almost all cities, but especially in the bigger metros and submetros, due to ill-design and poor maintenance of roads, lack or impossibility of coordinated signaling given the non-grid network topology that is usual, poor traffic management approaches, ill-conceived lane divisions traffic is slowed down to a crawl. Most city roads operate, even on arterials, at the lower portion of the service – carrying capacity graph. Time spent at cross-roads, and there are far too many given the absurd geometry of road networks, is relatively very large in India[5]. Hence, despite high designed fuel efficiencies in Indian vehicles, and the world class quality of Indian refining, this entirely avoidable emission load continues. And it is barely recognized by policy makers as an issue. Unnecessary movement necessitated by lack of investments in crucial intra-city links further compounds the problem. Public transport development weaknesses have created a huge demand for personal transport (much larger than

[4] For a review of the regulatory and policy developments till 2009, as also for a workable design of day ahead and balancing markets see Pandey & Sebastian Morris (2009). Since then, the policy problems have remained largely unaddressed. The appropriate structure of the market that could work for India, given the fragmentation of the market, and the need to grow rapidly and to schedule solar and wind, is a design that provides for markets in capacity and in energy that are linked.

[5] This shows up easily in Google Maps Traffic lines, which tend to be red before a crossing. So crossing is possible without a substantial stop, except during the few off-peak hours.

in other countries at similar levels of development) further compounding the problem. Thus, metros carry far less than what they could have since built up densities are regulated at low levels around them, and land use restrictions from times without the metro would continue. Metros are likely to a disaster in India, since due to lack of interconnect, absence of multimodality and poor integration with land use planning they are unlikely to carry the loads that would make a significant dent in its modal share, except perhaps in Delhi.

All these distortions are likely to continue since overcoming them would require major changes to the approach of city planning, and to heightened coordination across many authorities, which in itself major administrative reform[6]. Although not a low hanging fruit, the issues here need to be flagged, since these if unaddressed can constrain the very development of the country, and impose unnecessary hardship on its people.

4.3 Emotive environmentalism

An emotive environmentalism exhibited by a vociferous middle and upper class that stands in the removing trees from roads is also to be noted. Every tree left on the side and in the middle of the road, due to pressure from these "environmentalists" with courts acting in cohoots, actually results in additional emission of a approx. 2000 times[7] more CO_2 than what the tree could have captured, due to the slowing down of traffic! How many such trees obstruct in Indian cities? It is anybody's guess but working with a million trees[8], the emotional emission is of the order of 5 million tonnes of CO_2.

Add to that other obstacles that seem to be very "important" to our identity conscious society to have - little temples and tombs. Besides these, other protrusions and obstructions by not only unregulated hawkers and squatters, but due to uncoordinated construction by departments like electricity, police, telephone, PWD, railways, gardens and parks contribute to the mess that are city roads in India. Movement necessarily becomes a crawl. But then, everybody including planners believe that all problems are due to increasing population of vehicles! The herding of traffic to a few roads result in perpetual congestion on these roads, which then has to be "overcome" by building ill-designed flyovers!

We can most conservatively assume all of these result in a 25% slowdown in traffic in urban areas. By overcoming these, the overall reduction in CO_2 possible in urban transportation is about 30% of the share of fuels used in the urban areas. Even at an assumption that 20% of the fuels are used in urban areas where there is such slowdown, we get a figure of 52.8 million tonnes of CO_2[9] which is only a very conservative estimate of the avoidable emissions.

4.4 Agriculture

Perhaps the biggest waste of energy and hence of unnecessary CO_2 emissions in India is in agriculture in India. India pulls out about as much ground water as the rest of the world put together; when its share in world agricultural output is less than 10%,[10] its population being about 17% of the world's. That it nevertheless is a large net exporter of food, is because of the non-inclusive nature of its development[11] that have made many, perhaps even as much as 40% of the people consume far less nutrition measured on every one of its components, than the rest of the world.

Why does India use so much ground water? Government's pricing of electricity is the sole culprit. The subsidization of electricity takes the inane form of zero use price tariffs for electricity. This engenders very wasteful consumption, to

[6] For the horror that is urban India for its deep-rooted causes in faulty policy, planning and organization see Morris, S. (2017).

[7] A car or vehicle going an average of 20 km in a hour and giving 20 km per litre would consume 1 gm of fuel per metre. This is equivalent to 0.132 gms of CO_2 per metre. A loss of 10 metre per obstructive tree would mean that a car encountering such an obstacle would spew an additional 1.32 gms of CO_2. Over 10,000 cars having to pass the tree every day over 365 days this would be equivalent to 4.8 tonnes. In contrast the estimate for a tree of CO_2 capture is only 22.7 kgs per year. University of Michigan (2021).

[8] This million trees would mean one such obstructing tree per 400 people.

[9] Assumes that 90% of the emissions is in road transport and some 30% of the movement takes place in urban and near urban locales, where this slow down adding to the emissions, is prevalent.

[10] The FAO estimated that in 2014 world agricultural output was US$ 4771 b, and India's 367 b. See Business Standard (2017)

[11] Looking forward the malnutrition of children would be the first aspect of society that needs to improve if indeed there is a coherent engine of growth that is inclusive as well. The stark difference between India and much of East Asia is revealing. Thus, for China the malnutrition prevalent (weight for age) was around 3.5% of all children versus around 37% the rough average of the few years! Comparisons with other EA tigers would be even worse. Even in Vietnam at a level of income lower than that of India, some 10 years back, it was a low 20%.

rationing, to politicization and to non-revenue diversions of electricity. The agricultural demand for electricity had over a couple of decades from 1975 when it was made 'free to use' with the horsepower based tariff, rose at over 13% per annum to become the largest consumer of utility power when the agricultural output could not have risen at more than 3.2% per annum! The need to go deeper has left many dark zones in India's ground water resources, to salinity ingress, destruction of aquifers. The efficiency of water use out of ground water can easily improve by 100% if not more. Witness that the use of sprinklers and drip systems have been repelled by the zero price of electricity, bringing about its use only when the water resources are meagre. The problem is not the subsidization of electricity as much as the inane mode of doing so by making the allocative price zero. Direct endowment subsidies could enhance the private value of farmers considerably while reducing the power demand. Even if we take account for half of the power currently consumed by the agricultural sector, the wastage of power is a whopping 114086 Gwh of electricity in 2018-19 (CEA, 2020).

The CEA (2018) estimated, given the primary source mix and after considering in detail the efficiency of plants and transmission system, 0.82 MT of CO_2 emitted per MWH. The wastage in agriculture amounts to a whopping 93 million tonnes of CO_2. This is about 2.5% of the total emissions of the country, and probably about 10%[12] of the total emissions in the road transport sector in the country! And in the road transport sector, the EV push with all its incentives and costs, EV penetration is not likely to exceed 10% by 2027. And, that much can be realized in one go by correcting the perversities in the mode of subsidization. The same would also bring about large fiscal savings and avoidance of other environmental costs of over extraction and social value destruction. The shift to endowment subsidies, with tradability of the endowments and cost to serve pricing would also enhance the value to farmers and therefore would also be politically rewarding (Sebastian, 2017).

Add to that the waste in the use of water supplied by through canals. It is well known that India's water use efficiency is one of the lowest among large agricultural producers. Dharma Rao, (Dr.) Adviser National Water Mission, quoting Grail Research, brings out the water use in cubic metres for various crops in India, China and US as follows:

	India	US	China	Use Relative to China
Rice	4254	1903	1972	2.2
Wheat	1654	849	690	2.4
Corn	1937	489	801	2.4
Sugarcane	159	103	117	1.4

Source: Dharma Rao CV (undated)

Using a weighted average of 2.3, since these are the main crops, the enormous savings of water that includes canal water is to be noted. Inefficient use of canal water is also due to absurdly low prices. Here too politically it would be unfeasible to raise prices. However, this is not necessary. By casting the effective subsidy into endowments of water in volume terms, the distortions will go away. Key to the reform would be to fix the endowments, measure supplies volumetrically, and encourage tradability between farmers in an irrigation system. In addition, with tradability across systems, through very small investments, it is possible to recover the entire waste (Sebastian, 2017). In contexts where water is scarce, farmers with drip and sprinkler systems, show high efficiencies in water use. Again, the idea is in constrained tradability working to correct mispricing, as farmers discover prices among themselves for the water they now possess, with the direct endowment subsidies that we have proposed. (Morris, Sebastian 2002; 2007). Considering canal water, an additional 1.5% of savings in the CO_2 emissions is possible.

5. CONSTRAINTS ON HYDRO

It is interesting to note that while India has matched China in terms of solar and wind capacity shares at a much lower level of income, hydro development continues to be problematic. Hydro has potentially the highest benefit cost ratio, since it is power available on tap, and can be used in conjunction with relatively uncertain wind. It can also be used in peak demand after dusk and via pumped storage can store vast amounts of power not possible through batteries. It can also be used in ramping up of the grid up and down and its value in balancing is important to realize. Current long-term

[12] We base this on the observation that transportation is responsible for about 25% of the emission globally (Singh, et al 2021) and that 90% of the same is on account of road transport in India (op.cit). Use 25% of all emissions to be from road transport in India.

contracts in hydro power being based on deliveries, take away much of its high value. Its true high benefit cost ratio would in a fragmented electricity system (within a single grid) be revealed only in well-designed day ahead markets linked to balancing markets, with all contracts going financial as mentioned before. A loser's consensus has emerged among the intelligentsia that hydro is best avoided as it is going to be environmentally destructive. Examples of sound development elsewhere in the world with better government capacity, are drowned in the cacophony of a post-modernist support to these "emotional" environmentalists, who have successfully posed themselves as pro-people. Even the Ministry of Environment and Forests by resorting to outright bans has internalized the perspective. The real reason for this unholy alliance of romantic environmentalists with other segments of the intelligentsia who are concerned about the power, is the weak capacity of the government, to design and implement projects, and handle social cost and benefits in a better than pareto optimal way. The result is that while China develops the (cross) Himalayan river systems we at best nibble at the potential through a few expensive and underscaled run-of the river systems. Even these have proved to be failures due to poor design. (A few no doubt have been successful).

Pumped storage, given the existence of large number of dams with heads of under 600 feet in India, make it possible to install reversible turbines on many existing projects, and on irrigation projects as well, which can operate to store power. When combined with especially solar the evening peak can be easily met. However, the lack of a day ahead and balancing market for the electricity system with both markets for capacity and for energy prevent the joint efficiencies of solar, wind, hydro and pumped, and thermal coal. The approach should not be to combine them at the enterprise level but to do so through a well designed market at the economy or regional levels. But day ahead and balancing markets have been in the offing now for nearly 18 years, and other than the capacity of the think nothing stands in the way of development of day ahead and balancing markets.

If India can raise the role of hydro by another 5% of total primary energy, and move to create day ahead markets, there would be additional indirect effects which can operate on much of the existing hydro capacity. That could allow further creation of wind and solar. A benefit of 10% of current emission reduction in electricity production is possible thereby.

6. CONCLUSION

Initiatives of the government to reduce GHGs are laudable, but it is necessary to reexamine our penchant for making unilateral commitments. GHG reductions today as much as overall development process is not sufficiently inclusive. The drive to inclusion and rapid rise over the middle-income barrier should be the country's first priority. India would be making too large a sacrifice in voluntarily accepting a level of GHG per head that is a mere 1/5 th that of China. It should not agree to an emission level that is going to lower than the world's average reckoned in per capita terms, since the ethic of equality of all humans is unassailable.

Perversities in policy, but especially in pricing of energy result in large avoidable additions to GHGs in India. The opportunities here should attract the attention of policy makers, since thereby not only would there be reductions but also the removal of vast in-built inefficiencies and waste in the system. Transportation, agriculture, articulation within the city, enhanced hydro development, and dynamic day ahead and balancing markets can result in vast savings in emissions, besides greatly enhancing social and private benefits. Avoiding an "emotional environmentalism" and its knee-jerk reaction from the government in the form of bans has been the bane of the economy leaving vast numbers excluded and for the very high cost of whatever little environmental protection that has happened.

REFERENCES

Business Standard (2017). *India – An Agricultural Power House of the World.* https://www.business-standard.com/article/b2b-connect/india-an-agricultural-powerhouse-of-the-world-116051800253_1.html

CEA (2018). *CO_2 Baseline Database for the Indian Power Sector,* User Guide. Version 14.0. Central Electricity Authority. Government of India. https://cea.nic.in/wp-content/uploads/baseline/2020/07/user_guide_ver14.pdf

CEA (2020). *Growth of Electricity Sector in India from 1947-2020,* Central Electricity Authority. Government of India. https://cea.nic.in/wp-content/uploads/pdm/2020/12/growth_2020.pdf

Climate Action Tacker (2021). Data: China – Country Summary. Accessed on 27 July 2021. https://climateactiontracker.org/countries/china/

Economic Times (March 5, 2021). *India to meet its Paris agreement commitments ahead of 2030: PM Narendra Modi.* The Economic Times. https://economictimes.indiatimes.com/news/politics-and-nation/india-to-meet-its-paris-agreement-commitments-ahead-of-2030-pm-narendra-modi/articleshow/81351882.cms?utm_source=contentofinterest&utm_medium=text&utm_campaign=cppst

EIA (2021a). *China.* U.S. Energy Information Administration. https://www.eia.gov/international/data/country/CHN/electricity/electricity-capacity?pd=2&p=0000000000000000000007vo7&u=0&f=A&v=mapbubble&a=-&i=none&vo=value&&t=C&g=none&l=249--38&s=315532800000&e=1546300800000

EIA (2021b). *India.* U.S. Energy Information Administration. https://www.eia.gov/international/data/country/IND/electricity/electricity-capacity?pd=2&p=0000000000000000000007vo7&u=0&f=A&v=mapbubble&a=-&i=none&vo=value&&t=C&g=none&l=249--106&s=315532800000&e=1546300800000

Karttunen, M., & Moore, M. O. (2018). India–Solar Cells: Trade Rules, Climate Policy, and Sustainable Development Goals. *World Trade Review, 17*(2), 215–237.

Morris, S. (2007). Pricing Regulation and Financing Strategies. Chapter 9 in Briscoe, John and R.P.S. Malik (eds.) *Handbook of Water Resources in India - Development, Management, and Strategies*, Oxford University Press. New Delhi.

Morris, S. (2020). *Will the Stimulus of Rs. '20 lakh crore' Work to Arrest the Economic Crisis? An Assessment.* https://www.youtube.com/watch?v=RuckY8ABVvQ

Morris, S. (2002). The challenge to governance in India. *India Infrastructure Report.* Morris, S. & Shekhar, R. (eds.), India Infrastructure Report 2002 - Governance Issues for Commercialization, 3iNetwork, Oxford University Press, New Delhi. https://ssrn.com/abstract=2180148

Morris, S. (2017). The Horror of Urban Development in India–Identifying the Real Issues. *Indian Institute of Management, Ahmedabad, WP*, (2017-06), 01. https://ssrn.com/abstract=2995401 or http://dx.doi.org/10.2139/ssrn.2995401

Pandey, A. & Morris, S. (2009). *Electricity Reforms and Regulations - A Critical Review of Last 10 Years' Experience.* Indian Institute of Management Ahmedabad. http://forumofregulators.gov.in/Data/Reports/FOR_IIMA_STUDY%20ON%20ELECTRICITY%20REFORMS%20AND%20REGULATIONS%20-%20A%20CRITICAL%20REVIEW%20OF%20LAST%2010%20YEARS%20EXPERIENCE-%2017.06.2009.pdf

Ramachandra, T.V. & Shewtmala (2009). Emissions from India's Transport Sector : Statewise Synthesis. *Atmospheric Environment.* DOI:10.1016/j.atmosenv.2009.07.015. http://wgbis.ces.iisc.ernet.in/energy/paper/IISc_Emissions_from_Indias_Transport_sector/index.htm

Singh, N., Mishra, T., & Banerjee, R. (2021). Emissions inventory for road transport in India in 2020: Framework and post facto policy impact assessment. *Research Square.* https://assets.researchsquare.com/files/rs-297185/v1/16703c47-8a4f-45f2-b4ce-cd69e885ff98.pdf?c=1617380188

Timperley, J. (2019). *The Carbon Brief Profile: India.* https://www.carbonbrief.org/the-carbon-brief-profile-india

University of Michigan (2021). Accessed on 27 July 2021. https://www.unm.edu/~jbrink/365/Documents/Calculating_tree_carbon.pdf

WTO (2016). India - *Certain Measures Relating to Solar Cells and Solar Modules.* 24th February, WT/DS456/R, 15-2724. World Trade Organization.

SECTION I

Future Agenda and the Thrust Areas (What)

Sustainability and Economic Conflicts – Local Solutions with Global Direction can help in Juggling Act

Astha Agarwalla
Associate Professor, Economics and Public Policy
Adani Institute of Infrastructure Management, Ahmedabad

Evidence of climate change have started coming closer to us, from melting glaciers (Kaser, et al., 2004) to increasing daily temperatures (Hubler et al., 2008), from alterations in lifestyles of birds (Pearce-Higgins et al., 2015) to crop yield (Wei et al., 2014), the threats of harmful impacts of climate change are becoming a fast-approaching reality. Right from the Bruntland report (1987), the realization about needs of acting at the level of international community has helped in mobilizing national governments[1]. The subsequent international discourse led by United Nations Framework Convention on Climate Change (UNFCC) recognizes and puts common but differentiable responsibilities on countries for ensuring a safer environment in near future. Methods such as emission standards and clean development mechanism provide a strong framework to drive the policies and agendas of regulatory bodies of developed and developing countries around the world[2]. A big push to international agenda has come from the United Nation's sustainable development goals (SDGs), a menu of 17 items, clearly spelling out the actionable and achievable outcomes.

At the macro level these interventions have shaped the debate and policy formulation around sustainability across the world. Emergence of sectoral indices to track, regulatory mechanisms to enforce and incentives to plan are all designed and implemented across sectors, and business organizations have increasingly responded to these. However, the sufficiency and efficacy of these in achieving the desired outcomes has always been on a wanting side, as the difference between letter and spirit is reported to be huge in cases of top-driven sustainability agenda. Unless the enforcement mechanism is robust or the incentives are very high, behavioural change is difficult to come by, this increases the cost of achieving sustainability, making in unattractive to profit oriented businesses.

In terms of achieving measurable repetitive outcomes, in a cost-effective way, local solutions are found to be more effective (Baldo and Demartini, 2012). The debate between efficacy of Top-down versus bottom-up approaches of policy making and planning is not new. Lenses of efficiency of public administration and creation of public value are applied to assess the relative effectiveness of centralized (top-down) vs decentralized (bottom-up) approaches. Research has shown that the vantage of top-down policies and guidelines makes them distant from the local context, culture, resources, and environment, and hence make them less successful in addressing sustainability related issues.

Since the world level of urbanization has already crossed 50% and is expected to cross 68% by 2030, the world is more urban than rural, and hence our focus here is more on urban solutions. Cities generate 70% of world's waste and consume 80% of world's energy, hence the need to address the sustainability concerns is much larger for urban areas[3]. It is often said that the achievement of SDGs depends on how well cities can plan to achieve those, and hence SDG number 11, making cities more inclusive, safe, and sustainable gains more importance than the other goals.

We propose three hypotheses supporting the instances where local solutions might work better than macro level/national policies. We use the case of urban food supplies to substantiate the argument.

---

[1] *Source:* https://en.wikipedia.org/wiki/Our_Common_Future

[2] *Source:* https://unfccc.int/

[3] *Source:* http://www.fao.org/fao-stories/article/en/c/1260457/

Cities' demand for food cannot be met by the local production happening there. The peripheral areas must support the city system for food sufficiency. Cities, due to their densities are not suitable for agriculture[4]. Ganapathy (1983) has shown that only 5% of Ahmedabad city area was used for agriculture, indicating the dependency of the city on other areas for food. However, the same densities cause greater demand for food than rural areas. Food must travel to cities, increasing the demand for transport and energy, two of the most environmentally hazardous sectors[5]. With globalization, packaged food is becoming more prevalent increasing the energy intensity of food production. Add to that the use of chemical fertilizers and electricity for irrigation, agriculture becomes one of the leading sectors causing climate change.

Food production itself causes 25% of global emissions. Presence of hunger might suggest that food production is insufficient, which is a myth, as an estimate by Food and Agriculture organization suggests that the world produces more food than is needed. Another estimate suggests that as against the current world population of 7.6 million, the food produced is sufficient to meet the needs of 14 million people. One third of food produced gets wasted due to inefficient supply chains, unjust food distribution and unsustainable cities[6]. Food wasted lands in landfill sites, generating methane which is more hazardous to the environment than CO_2[7].

Romanticism in environmentalism often leads to expression of first order ideas only focusing on use of natural resources and disruption of current practices, completing ignoring the economic and market aspects, making the ideas commercially unviable and hence not practiced. What is desired is to think of local solutions, which are not only environmentally desirable, but also economically attractive and commercially viable.

We present below the three hypotheses supporting local solutions work better for sustainable urban food supply.

1. SUSTAINABILITY AS A LOCAL CONSTRUCT - SUSTAINABLE DEVELOPMENT RAISES QUESTIONS, ANSWERS TO WHICH CAN ONLY BE FOUND LOCALLY

One way of defining sustainability is ensuring availability of same level of resources to future generations to create similar level of well-being as us. This can be done in three ways (Daly, 2002)

(i) Use of renewable resources at a rate at which they can be regenerated,

(ii) Use of non-renewable resources at a rate at which close substitutes can be found for them, and

(iii) Use of pollutants at a rate at which the environmental sinks can absorb or recycle them.

In the context of food production, identifying local land parcels, or possibility of developing vertical farms is required to supplement food transported along long supply chains, creating larger carbon footprints. Any policy banning packaged food or forcing local supply of goods can not work in the context of all cities, as geographical and topographical differences are required to be considered for identifying the possibility of supplementing transported food with local food. Urban land rent is non-agricultural usage is very high, at least 4 to 5 times that in agricultural use. Hence allocation of such land for agriculture is highly infeasible economically, especially in developing countries, with low levels of overall urbanization and high densities in existing cities. However, some crops, like mushrooms, spices, condiments etc. can be grown on waste land/vacant land, based on local demand and availability conditions. This would not be sufficient to replace the urban food demand at all but would reduce the environmental impact to some extent and would provide green spaces in the cities.

Similarly, for pollutants, such as organic waste generated out of food, behavioural interventions work better than policy directives. Policy directives can generate revenue for the administration by the way of fees and fines, but often fail to achieve the outcome, i.e., segregation at source. Experiments by several cities have proven that involvement of stakeholders, creating local champions and awareness generation work better to achieve the outcome.

[4] Indian definition of urban areas includes places where more than 70% of male work force is engaged in non-agriculture activities, with other characteristics. See https://censusindia.gov.in/2011-prov-results/paper2/data_files/india2/1.%20data%20highlight.pdf

[5] *Source:* https://ecojungle.net/post/the-most-polluting-industries-in-2021/

[6] *Source:* https://www.deccanchronicle.com/lifestyle/environment/110419/sustainable-food-management-by-cities.html

[7] https://urbact.eu/sustainable-food-urban-communities-complete-overview

2. MACRO PRIORITIES AND LOCAL CONTEXT CAN BE CONFLICTING AT TIMES

At the macro level, food processing industry needs support as it creates employment and adds positively and significantly to output. Any national level policy banning processed food would produce undesirable consequences in terms of lost employment and commercial losses. A different approach, with local solutions, focusing more on demand side, by creating awareness and promoting organizations producing organic products will bring the change gradually. Research initiatives, finding out alternative methods of processing with local ingredients can work better, and then can be replicated at the higher levels for commercial success. A bottom-up approach in this case will therefore be more effective. Initiatives such use of functional packaging, removing all aesthetic requirements like colour, material appeal etc., to reduce the environmental impact might work at local level.

Similarly, use of chemical fertilizers is boosted by subsidies on urea-based fertilizers[8]. Fertilizer production is under the red category of polluting industries as per the Central Pollution Control Board (CPCB)[9]. Desirability of high productivity pushes the use of chemical fertilizers. At the policy level, the consequences of banning chemical fertilizers can be economically drastic, as these are the least cost fertilizers. On the other hand, a suitable mix of non-chemical fertilizers promoted at the local level, supported by local organizations using local organic waste can result in better balanced local outcomes.

3. MACRO POLICIES CAN PUSH PEOPLE TO CHOOSE WRONG SIDE OF TRADE-OFFS

International discourse to address the food issue is focused primarily on increasing intensity of food production, so that with the same size of land, more food can be generated. Intensity augmenting methods are likely to be energy intensive too, leading to more climate impact.

A bottom-up approach can work better here, where at each city level solutions are to be found based on the occupational composition and agricultural productivity of peripheral areas. The local solutions, designed to increase the efficiency of local supply chains and making the distribution better will certainly result in better outcomes locally. Initiatives such as recycling of food, by generation of compost from organic waste is one solution. Based on detailed analysis of waste composition at city level, suitable method of recycling can be adopted. Total segregation of waste is a distant possibility but use of kitchen waste for organic manure and other such uses can be promoted locally, reducing the burden on landfill sites and transport requirements for waste. Blockchain domes and vertical farms are another example of solutions to grow food organically in cities, lowering down the need to transport food from outer areas.

However, policy level intervention, mandating such initiatives might not result in successful implementation, due to inertia and difference in local conditions. A policy push towards building vertical gardens might lead people to ignore the opportunity costs of doing so, and the inherent requirement of energy to support such initiatives in cases where the environmental conditions are not conducive. In situ vertical farms are highly capital intensive and have a high opportunity cost, as they compete with light spaces.

4. CONCLUSION

Internationally cities are taking initiatives which are focused on local resources and promote sustainable practices among the citizens. For example, Amsterdam has introduced E-tricycles to transport food within the cities. Calgary Eats is a city level community owned initiative, targeting 5% increase in urban food production, 100% sustainable transportation of food and increasing consumption of local food by 30% by 2036. Portland is planning to provide a large space to local vendor market selling fresh organic food supplies, with first floor space used to house cooking demonstrations[10].

Some activities are better suited to be taken up at the local level, such as selection of indicators and measurement of outcomes. Stakeholder involvement in collection of data and construction of such indicators is an engaging exercise to ensure people's interest in achieving outcomes.

[8] *Source:* https://indianexpress.com/article/explained/explained-why-has-the-modi-government-increased-subsidy-on-dap-7323687/

[9] *Source:* https://www.downtoearth.org.in/news/agriculture/how-green-is-the-urea-sector-64836

[10] *Source:* https://foodtank.com/news/2014/11/ten-cities-leading-the-conversation-on-sustainable-eating/

Local solutions, which do not fit with the national/global direction are not scalable and hence not sustainable. Therefore, planning for local solutions should be aligned with the national/global sustainability agenda. Local solutions if proven to be successful and ably supported by policy interventions can create a bridge between centralized and decentralized approaches. For example, FAO is supporting development of vertical farms in Columbian cities, and success of the initiative has led the Government of Columbia to plan several political, and governmental intervention to spread the good practice to other cities[11].

A careful examination of material and energy need to work around local solutions also is needed. Often, in the euphoria of generating local solutions, the details around energy and material needed for that local solution to be successful and the contamination caused by such local solutions is ignored. A careful with and without approach is required to ensure that local solutions do not cost more.

REFERENCES

Del Baldo, M., & Demartini, P. (2012). Bottom-up or top-down: Which is the best approach to improve CSR and sustainability in local contexts? Reflections from Italian experiences. *Journal of Modern Accounting and Auditing, 8*(3), 381–400.

Herman, D. (2002). Five policy recommendations for a sustainable economy. *Sustainable Planet: Solutions for the Twenty-first Century*. 209–221. Beacon Press.

Ganapathy, R. S. (1983). Development of Urban Agriculture in India: Public Policy Option. IIM-A WP No. 482. http://vslir.iima.ac.in:8080/jspui/bitstream/11718/11190/1/WP%201983_482.pdf

Hübler, M., Klepper, G., & Peterson, S. (2008). Costs of climate change: the effects of rising temperatures on health and productivity in Germany. *Ecological Economics, 68*(1-2), 381–393.

Kaser, G., Hardy, D. R., Mölg, T., Bradley, R. S., & Hyera, T. M. (2004). Modern glacier retreat on Kilimanjaro as evidence of climate change: observations and facts. *International Journal of Climatology: A Journal of the Royal Meteorological Society, 24*(3), 329–339.

Pearce-Higgins, J. W., Eglington, S. M., Martay, B., & Chamberlain, D. E. (2015). Drivers of climate change impacts on bird communities. *Journal of Animal Ecology, 84*(4), 943–954.

Wei, T., Cherry, T. L., Glomrød, S., & Zhang, T. (2014). Climate change impacts on crop yield: Evidence from China. *Science of the Total Environment, 499*, 133–140.

[11] *Source:* http://www.fao.org/fao-stories/article/en/c/1260457/

Gender Representation in ESG Communication of Indian Companies: Observations and Insights

Diti Pundrik Vyas[1]
Associate Professor
Anant National University, Ahmedabad

Sushama Oza[2]
Advisor, Centre for Development Management and Communication
Mudra Institute of Communication, Ahmedabad

Abstract: As Environment, Social and Governance (ESG) is emerging as a popular reporting framework for sustainability by capturing extra-financial disclosures, it is vital to see how gender is represented in sustainability communication. This paper undertakes to study how gender plays out in these textual genres of selected Indian companies from top constituents of Nifty 100 Enhanced ESG Index through the study of visual imagery invoked to justify the sustainability claims. Our qualitative analysis demonstrates that though women have gained more visibility and are shown to be doing away with feminine stereotypes, they still abound in tradition and modernity paradox identified by feminist theorists. While the urban women are accepted as efficient co-workers and empowered consumers, the rural women are either locked in dependency or are projected as passive dependents on corporate favors. Images of rural women either elide over their struggles or shut out the struggle through a simplistic closure of corporate interventions. Also, though urban educated women are professionally "liberated" in the outside world, within the sphere of home, they are shown holding on to the traditional values. Within these reports the definitions of woman's beauty remain patriarchal in nature. We conclude by showing ways in which the representation of women can be reworked by embracing the tenets of equality and inclusion: building feminine strengths, upholding positive aspects about girls/women, focusing on female bonding and inclusion for all. We propose training and processes that support such progressive mindset which will be ultimately reflected in communication.

Keywords: **Gender, Representation, Sustainability Reports, ESG, Indian Companies**

1. INTRODUCTION

Businesses have long tried integrating sustainability in their business models: philanthropy, Corporate Social Responsibility (CSR) and creating shared value. In the recent years, Environment, Social and Governance (ESG) has emerged as a popular reporting framework for sustainability by capturing extra-financial disclosures and enabling the investors in particular and stakeholders in general to better assess the value of a corporation. With Global Reporting Initiatives (GRI), the United Nations Global Compact, Principles of Responsible Investing (PRI) and United Nations Environment Program, assets invested in ESG ETFs and ETPs increased by 7.3% setting a new record of US$88 billion by June 2020. (ETFGL, 2020). As a result of this, not only has there been a dramatic increase in the voluntary reports on sustainability (Palenberg et al.; Nielsen & Thomsen) but also in efforts to create frameworks for "identifying and quantifying the intangible value possessed by socially responsible, environmentally friendly firms with robust governance policies" (Nifty100 ESG Sector Leaders). There are number of indices for reporting ESG or Sustainability; the most accepted and popular ones are DJSI-Dow Jones Sustainability Index, GRI - Global Reporting Initiative, CDP - Carbon

[1] Former Associate Professor, Adani Institute of Infrastructure, Ahmedabad, diti.vyas@anu.edu.in

[2] Former Director, Strategy and Sustainability, Adani Foundation, sushamaa1@gmail.com

Disclosure Project, SASB - Sustainability Accounting Standards Board, GRESB, TCFD. In order to create a global ESG standard, the World Economic Forum 2020 has initiated working on one common framework with the big four. As Tensie Whelan and Carly Fink announce: "sustainability is going mainstream".

Whether in form of policy imperative and business initiative, along with the world at large, India too is realizing the fact that growth in business cannot be absolutely exclusive to sustainability. Ministry of Corporate Affairs' National Voluntary Guidelines (NVGs) in 2011, CSR Spending made mandatory in 2014-15, NITI Aayog's fine-tuning of the UNO's 17 Sustainable Development Goals (SDGs) in the form of Sustainable Development Framework in 2018, SEBI mandating publication of Business Responsibility Reports (BRRs) for 1000 top listed companies in 2019, the launch of the S&P, MSCI, Nifty and BSE Indices based on sustainability as a theme and the ongoing August 2020 proposal by Ministry of Corporate Affairs to revise the BRR formats to suit to the current environment, can all be looked at as historical milestones in this process. These policy level interventions bear witness to the journey of sustainability communication -- from its focus on compliance or creating social value in Corporate Social Responsibility (CSR) avatar to its strategic function of wooing the investors by integrating Environmental, Social and Governance (ESG) with risk mitigation and financial returns. Though India still lags behind in global share of ESG assets, in the face of growing investor demands and evolving regulatory requirements, ESG is emerging as a growing positive trend that can turn India into "ESG funding hotspot" (Economic Times, 2019). Therefore, this is an opportune time to examine the reporting in close quarters.

2. LITERATURE REVIEW

Research suggests variables such as firm size (Artiach et al., 2010), growth rate (Kyaw et al., 2017), the profitability of a firm (Artiach et al., 2010), representation of independent directors (Villiers et al., 2011). type of industry (Kumar et al., 2016), risk exposure (Wilkins et al., 2019) and diversity (Manita, R. et al., 2018; Mauro Romano, 2020) as variables in the ESG disclosures. Particularly, gender is often studied as a critical constituent of diversity along with age, ethnicity, religion culture, independence, professional expertise, industry experience, and career and life experiences. Various studies document the impact of gender diversity on ESG practices. The presence of female directors seen to have increased board effectiveness and bettered the governance through better monitoring (Adams and Ferreira, 2009), lead to more sustainable investment strategies (Pletzer et al., 2015) and resulted in fairer decisions (Birindelli et al., 2018).

3. MATERIALS AND METHODS

With growing interests and heightened expectations of stakeholder in ESG practices, it is vital to see how gender is represented in sustainability communication done by Indian companies. In their study of annual reports, Graves et al. (1996) state that the visual imagery forms an integral part in justifying the claims that the reports set out to prove. C. Squiecs (1989) postulates that the images in reports are a site where 'many kinds of problems ... be resolved, dissolved, dispersed or transformed depending on how pictures and design are handled' (p. 208). Drawing cues from these studies, the current piece aims to bring out insights about the representation of gender in highly regulated textual genres sustainability reports. Cutting across the genre conventions and standard parts, we look at how gender plays out in these textual genres of selected Indian companies from top constituents of Nifty 100 Enhanced ESG Index. It should be noted that the chosen list of Nifty100 ESG Enhanced Index is updated on 31st May 2021 and the weight of its constituents, are derived from a combination of free float market capitalization and ESG score as determined by Sustainalytics. The companies are selected on the basis of size, turnover/market capitalization, maturity in sustainability reporting and their representatives in sustainability reporting practices.

4. DISCUSSION

If one scans sustainability early reports of Nifty100 ESG Enhanced Index companies, women were underrepresented or stereotyped. They typically appear as the face of successful corporate initiatives for community development and feature as beneficiaries of the corporate interventions. Their presence in the board rooms and the office corridors was limited to women's day celebrations and training photos as evident in the Infosys Sustainability Report of the year 2017-18.

In contrast, the latest reports whether in the forms of Business Responsibility Reports (BRR) or Integrated Annual Reports, have come a long way in the representation of gender. In contrast to its 2017 sustainability report, Infosys' Integrated report

2019-20 represents more women in the workplace who are working hand in hand with their male counterparts. There is definitely temporal progression in the representation of gender as far as visibility of women is concerned as evident in these reports. However, we seek to investigate this perceived increase in gender parity by going beyond improved visibility and looking at representation qualitatively through the feminist lens.

Such an investigation necessitates an understanding of the historical foundations of the very notions of tradition and modernity in Indian feminist discourse. In his essay "The Nationalist Resolution of the Women's Question", P. Chatterjee lays down the historical framework for dealing with the issues of tradition and modernity in the construction of Indian women. Chatterjee finds that the strategy of nationalist discourse to create and widen the dichotomies between outer/ inner, world/home and material/spiritual on the pivot of modernity and tradition became central to the organization of gender in India in the 19th century. On the one hand, Chatterjee argues that patriarchy used "coercive authority with the subtle force of persuasion" to enforce 'feminine' virtues on the middle-class woman by appointing her as a custodian of the spiritual quality of the home, elevating her to the status of goddess and setting her apart from the vain western woman as well as the vulgar lower class Indian woman. On the other hand, Chatterjee observes that the Indian woman was allowed to be "modern" in the sense that she "could go to schools, travel in public conveyances, watch public entertainment programmes, and in time even take up employment outside the home" (248). However, Chatterjee also notes that this modernity was allowed only once her "femininity" was secured through "culturally visible spiritual qualities and manifested externally through spiritual signs of femininity" (247). This linking of the home and the world in the construct of 'new' Indian woman, created through restructuring of tradition and selective adaptation of western elements of modernity, was projected by the nationalist discourse as an alternative to both modern western society and patriarchal indigenous tradition. Rajeshwari Sunder Rajan further explores the shades of this complex relationship between tradition and modernity in the construction of the "new Indian woman" in the post globalization context. Sunder Rajan notes that advertisements and popular television serials like Rajani (1985) and Udaan (1989-91) foreground the 'modernity' element in the construction of the 'new Indian woman' but they do so without jeopardizing her connections with 'tradition'. She notes that though the woman might be shown as rebellious when young but she is essentially depicted as married, domesticated and exercising her financial and other independence for the well-being of her family when older. She further points out that though the new woman might be projected as professionally "liberated" and educated, she is also shown holding on to the traditional values of "husband-worship, family nurturance, self-sacrifice and sexual chastity" (Real and Imagined Women 135). She observes a reverse process in the representation of women in mythological, historical and religious programmes on the state-controlled television-programming channel which undertake the modernization of the traditional. The representation of mythological female characters such as Draupadi in the Mahabharata or historical figures such as Laxmibai are modernized as "liberated" in keeping with the "constitutional commitment to equal rights", but at the same time are valorized as "timeless" "symbols of 'our' 'national' culture" and "tradition" (Real and Imagined Women 134). As against these representations that she terms as 'imagined', juxtaposes the 'real' representation of women from sources as eclectic as Saoli Mitra's dance drama Nathbati Anathbati, Sheba Chachi's portfolio of photographs of women, Feminist Portraits, the eighteenth century Telugu poet Mudupalani's "Radhika Santwanam" and Ketan Mehta and Aruna Raje's films Mirch Masala and Rihaee. These representations of women across media are 'real' for Sunder Rajan because they neither gloss over the conflicts between tradition and modernity nor provide pseudo-solutions to it. According to Sunder Rajan, these representations reproduce "the dialectic of struggle" within the historical and social situations of the women represented (Real and Imagined Women 143). In line with this analysis of Indian women within the binary grid of tradition and modernity by Chatterjee and Sunder Rajan, it can be said that though certain sustainability texts display modernity in gender conception at a surface level, they reveal their entrenched leaning towards tradition deep down.

5. RESULTS

The women, in sustainability reporting, seem 'modern' as they employ strategies of feminist assertion by doing away with some feminine stereotypes. Through their centred position in the frame, posture, direct eye-contact, attire and activity, these office-going urban women extrude independence and agency. These images use one of the commonest methods of feminist revision that of gender role inversion. Termed as "simple stereotype switching" (5) by Seelinger Trites, this technique involves attributing patriarchal male roles like protector, provider, problem-solver or leader to the female characters and substituting traditionally feminine characteristics with those designated as traditionally masculine. Reliance

Industries Limited Integrated Report of the year 202-21 shows young female engineers brimming with confidence, dressed in masculine uniforms participating in the workforce as problem solvers in sectors that are traditionally associated with men. Hindustan Unilever Integrated Annual Report 2020-21 projects a traditionally clad Indian woman in assertive superwoman postures ready to take on the world whether it is household or workplace.

Throughout these reports women are represented profusely in the role of consumers: making purchase decisions, exercising their financial independence and consuming at their will. However, Maitrayee Chaudhuri in her essay "Feminism in Print Media" warns us as to how the corporate sector creates the concept of new womanhood apparently defined by "choice" and "consumption", focusing on the "high power consumer" and retreating from the issues of class and social justice (273). In line with these observations, the urban educated women in the visual representations are shown to be making purchase decisions for themselves Microsite and their families. Airtel Annual Report 2019-20 microsite shows young educated urban girl brandishing her newly purchased mobile phone.

However, their rural counterparts are still tethered in the dependency chain. Dependency is "a hierarchal model with one person more dependent on (and less powerful than) another" (Trites, 83). This 'dependency' is seen in the way empowerment through the corporate is mostly represented by a male. Kotak Mahindra Bank's Annual Report 2020-21 depicts a male figure donating a packet of 3ply masks and N95 masks in the covid times to a poor woman.

The images of sisterhood and female mentor-mentee appear rarely. Men in the beneficial position then become instrumental in bailing out the rural women respectively from their difficulties and are the reason behind their smiles thereby consolidating the power of patriarchal authority. These images either elide over what Sunder Rajan calls "dialectic of struggles" of the rural women or shut out the struggle through a simplistic closure of corporate interventions. Reliance Industries Limited Integrated Report 2020-21 portrays a rural woman with broad smile seemingly oblivious of the load on her shoulders.

Similarly, in HDFC Integrated Annual Report 2019-20, a female farm laborer despite her hardships is gazing at the eye of the camera in sheer happiness Further, one finds that the struggles of these rural women are whitewashed through the construction of the image of efficient poor woman. Commenting upon the difference between the differing images of women working in the informal sector as seen in the Shramshakti Report commissioned by the National Commission on Self-Employed Women and that of the World Bank in "Gender and Development in India, 1970-90s.", Mary John states that while the former showed women as exploited and working in vulnerable conditions, the latter created an image of the efficient poor woman. John elaborates on the idea of poor women as efficient poverty managers as evident in the World Bank report in the following words: The incredible range of tasks poor women perform, their often-greater contributions to household incomes despite lower wage earnings their ability to make scare resources stretch further under deteriorating conditions stand as proofs of efficiency (248). Reliance Industries Limited Integrated Report 2020-2 depicts a mother who in spite of her poor financial condition manages to produce abundantly from her farm.

A careful analysis of urban office going women also reveal a conflict between their modern feminist precepts and their feminine practices. Here the polarization between representations of younger and older women is worth commenting upon. In her essay "Real and Imagined Women: Politics and/of Representation" Sunder Rajan observes, "The younger woman, or more accurately a teenager, may enact actual rebellion, or even project sexual desire; whereas the older woman, invariably married, exercises her autonomy - her education, her earnings - on behalf of the family's well-being" (131). Young girls are typically depicted as carefree and are allowed to enact their freedom without bothering about anyone. However, as she grows up, in keeping with Sunder Rajan's observations, though professionally "liberated" and educated, she is also shown holding on to the traditional values of "husband-worship, family nurturance, self-sacrifice and sexual chastity" (Real and Imagined Women 135). Within the hierarchal familial structure represented by home, the responsibility of serving food rests with woman at the dinner table while the other family members enjoy their as depicted in Reliance Industries Limited Integrated Report 2020-21.

The attentive position in which the woman is standing and the relaxed smile on her husband's face seals the traditional gender codes back in place. Quite literally, the steering wheel goes to the man, when the couple is on a drive. There was actually only one exception to this gender-coded roles found in the 2019-20 Integrated report of Hindustan Lever Limited which shows a man nurturing an infant in contrast to the repetitive images of both rural and urban mothers engaging in child nurturance. These mother figures in the reports are stereotypically caring and always available for their children. The stress of managing their professional lives/household chores and motherly duties never come to the fore.

Though these women bask in the limelight in the workplace, they do so primarily in the presence of their peers. They can handle customers, make impressive points in group meetings and come up with effective solutions. However, they emerge as second leads in command temporarily in the absence of senior male leaders. Gender stereotypes reappear in the presence when male members in leadership positions surface in the frame.

Another aspect of patriarchal definitions of femininity is evident in the reports is the portrayal of feminine beauty and dress codes. The rural women are stereotypically made to bear the weight of religious and cultural signifiers of their marriage: bright *bindis* and vermilion on the forehead. Though within the office set-up urban educated women are devoid of such markers, as soon as they are transposed to familial home set-up the markers make a comeback. The modern office going women are depicted as chic and are couched in the visual phraseology that resonate with patriarchal ideas of beauty as represented in Larsen and Toubro Integrated Report 2019-20.

Some of these women are also opened up in the male-voyeurism. An image in Reliance Industries Limited Integrated Report 2020-21 depicts a women in provocative exercise pose wearing a body-hugging outfit.

6. CONCLUSION

While through sustainability communication, businesses have started reporting about the environmental, social and governance issues, they need to rework on the representation of women by embracing the tenets of equality and inclusion. In this process, the reports can build on the strengths traditionally associated with femininity by upholding some positive aspects about girls/women. These reports need to focus on female bonding whether in the form of mentor-mentee relationships or sisterhood by depicting women backing each other up and celebrating each other's strengths rather than depicting them at receivers' end. This is not to conclude that the reports need to reverse the equation of power dynamics by reversing it. The core of feminist thought is inclusion for all and this the reports must embrace. Sustainability reports must truly embrace the "social" of ESG communication and must treat everyone be it men, women or other gender, every ethnicity, colour, community as equal human beings. Visual representation being a powerful medium, ought to propagate the model of "interdependency" involving "mutual dependency that emphasises equality" (Trites 84). For achieving this kind of ideal representation, the culture of corporates/ businesses needs to be nurtured through training and processes that support the mindset and robust feedback mechanism in both directions. Only then will it be reflected in communication.

REFERENCES

Artiach, T., D. Lee, D. Nelson, and J. Walker, 2010. The determinants of corporate sustainability performance. Accounting & Finance 50: 31–51.

Adams, R. B., & Ferreira, D. (2009). Women in the boardroom and their impact on governance and performance. *Journal of financial economics, 94*(2), 291–309.

Bharati Airtel Limited (2020). *Annual Report Microsite.* https://www.airtel.in/airtel-annual-report-2019-20/

Birindelli, G., Dell'Atti, S., Iannuzzi, A. P., & Savioli, M. (2018). Composition and activity of the board of directors: Impact on ESG performance in the banking system. *Sustainability, 10*(12), 4699.

Chatterjee, P., Sangari, K., & Vaid, S. (1989). The nationalist resolution of the women's question.

De Villiers, C., Naiker, V., & Van Staden, C. J. (2011). The effect of board characteristics on firm environmental performance. *Journal of Management, 37*(6), 1636–1663.

ETFGL. (August 2020). ETFGI reports assets invested in ESG ETFs and ETPs listed globally broke through the US$100 billion milestone at end of July 2020. https://etfgi.com/news/press-releases/2020/08/etfgi-reports-assets-invested-esg-etfs-and-etps-listed-globally-broke

Graves, O. F., Flesher, D. L., & Jordan, R. E. (1996). Pictures and the bottom line: the television epistemology of US annual reports. *Accounting, Organizations and Society, 21*(1), 57–88.

Hemmings, D. R., Brennan, N. M., & Merkl-Davies, D. M. (2017). Explaining Communication Choices During Equity Offerings. *The Handbook of Financial Communication and Investor Relations*, 147.

HFDC Bank. (2020). *HDFC Integrated Annual Report 2019-20.* https://www.hdfcbank.com/content/bbp/repositories/723fb80a-2dde-42a3-9793-7ae1be57c87f/?path=/Footer/About Us/Investor Relation/annual reports/pdf/HDFC-Bank-Integrated-Annual-Report-2020-21.pdf

Infosys. (2020). *Navigate Your Next: Sustainability Report 2017-18.* https://www.infosys.com/sustainability/documents/infosys-sustainability-report-2017-18.pdf

Infosys. (2020). *Navigate Your Next: Sustainability Report 2019-20.* https://www.infosys.com/sustainability/documents/infosys-sustainability-report-2019-20.pdf

Kotak Mahindra Bank. (2021). *Never normal: Annual report 2020-21.* https://kapps.kotak.com/annualreport/pdf/kotak-annual-report-2020-21.pdf

Larsen and Toubro. (2020). *Integrated Report 2019-20. Technology for Sustainable Growth - L&T Integrated Report 2020 (windows.net).*

Kyaw, K., Olugbode, M., & Petracci, B. (2017). Can board gender diversity promote corporate social performance? *Corporate Governance: The International Journal of Business in Society.*

Manita, R., Bruna, M. G., Dang, R., & Houanti, L. H. (2018). Board gender diversity and ESG disclosure: evidence from the USA. *Journal of Applied Accounting Research.*

Nifty100 ESG Sector Leaders. (June 2020). Gaining Exposure to large cap companies with superior risk Management. https://www1.nseindia.com/content/indices/Whitepaper_Nifty100_ESG_Sector_Leaders.pdf

Nielsen, A. E., & Thomsen, C. (2007). Reporting CSR–what and how to say it?. *Corporate Communications: An International Journal, 12*(1), 25–40.

Palenberg, M., Reinicke, W., & Witte, J. M. (2006). Trends in non-financial reporting November 2006. *Prepared for the United Nations Environment Programme, Division of Technology, Industry and Economics (DTIE), Berlin.*

Pletzer, J. L., Nikolova, R., Kedzior, K. K., & Voelpel, S. C. (2015). Does gender matter? Female representation on corporate boards and firm financial performance-a meta-analysis. *PloS one, 10*(6), e0130005.

Reliance Industries Limited. (2019-20). *Integrated annual report 2020-21.* https://www.ril.com/ar2020-21/pdf/reliance-annual-report-21.pdf

Rajan, R. S. (2003). *Real and imagined women: Gender, culture and postcolonialism.* Routledge.

Romano, M., Cirillo, A., Favino, C., & Netti, A. (2020). ESG (Environmental, Social and Governance) Performance and Board Gender Diversity: The Moderating Role of CEO Duality. *Sustainability, 12*(21), 9298.

Squiecs C. (1989). The corporate year in pictures. In The Contest of Meaning Bolton R (ed.). Massachusetts Institute of Technology: Cambridge, 207–218.

Trites, R. S. (1997). *Waking Sleeping Beauty: Feminist voices in children's novels.* University of Iowa Press.

Whelan, Tensie, and Carly Fink. "The comprehensive business case for sustainability." *Harvard Business Review* 21.2016 (2016).

Wilkins, M., Burks, B., Charbon, R. C., Bastit, B., Cochelin, P., & Volland, E. F. (2019, May 13). The ESG Risk Atlas: Sector and Regional Rationales and Scores. https://www.spglobal.com/en/research-insights/articles/the-esg-risk-atlas-sector-andregional-rationales-and-scores

Need for an Alternative Approach to Housing for Industrial Workers – A Case of Morbi, Gujarat

Madhu Bharti
Professor
Centre for Environmental Planning and Technology University, Ahmedabad

Gargee Das
Assistant Manager, Planning and GIS
Rudrabhishek Infosystem, Noida

Abstract: With increasing urbanization and growth of real-estate sector the demand for ceramic tiles and sanitary wares has seen a significant surge. Due to easy availability of raw material *i.e.*, the local clay suitable for ceramic products, quartz, calcite, frits and glazes in Gujarat and neighbouring places like Rajasthan, uninterrupted power supply and availability of cheap labour, Morbi has emerged as a prominent centre for ceramic production. The ceramic industries situated near between Morbi and Wankaner accounts for 90% of total ceramic production in India and employs migrant labours. Ceramic Industrial units provide limited housing to the migrant workers, often with minimum level of amenities. Such housing is provided near the industrial unit, often on the campus. The spill over demand of labour housing is cratered by the local market.

This research aims to study the provision of industrial housing provided by ceramic industry, focuses on the condition of ceramic industrial labours' housing and proposed interventions to improve the housing supply for the migrant labour.

Keywords: Ceramic Industry, Industrial workers housing, Morbi, India

1. INTRODUCTION

Urbanization and industrialization have a direct impact on the population, employment and in-migration growth and affect spatial development and housing conditions of that area. In Europe, from early 18 century and in Asia, at the end of 20 century, industrialization has led to housing problem for the industrial workers, but limited attention is provided by the government and industries to this issue. It is very difficult for the workers to rent or own decent housing from their annual income (Conference, 1960). For most workers who come to a new town in search of employment opportunities, rental housing is the first step on the housing ladder. Later, when the migrants wish to settle down in the city with family, they prefer ownership housing to consolidate their position in the city.

Morbi district is situated in the state of Gujarat, India and it was formed on 15th August 2013 (Gujarat, Morbi District, 2019). Morbi, the industrial town is the second largest manufacturing cluster of ceramic tiles in the world (Indian Ceramics Industry, 2018). The Gujarat government has supported by installing industrial gas lines of Gujarat State Petroleum Corporation Ltd. which has increased the growth of ceramic productions as gas is one of the major uses in the manufacturing of ceramic products. Easy availability of raw material *i.e.* local clay suitable for ceramic products, quartz, calcite, frits and glazes in Gujarat and neighbouring places like Rajasthan and uninterrupted power supply from Gujarat Electricity Board made Morbi the prominent location for ceramic production. The major seaports, Mundra and Kandla are near to Morbi which has provided a boost to ceramic industry in Morbi. Ceramic industries in Morbi is spread along the National Highway 27 from Morbi to Wankaner.

To accelerate the industrialization government has taken various initiatives but there are no direct initiatives for the ceramic industrial labours and labours housing which cause the housing problem among the labours.

2. AIMS & OBJECTIVES

The aim of this research is to identify the issues and challenges faced by industrial workers in Morbi and to develop an approach to provide housing for the workers engaged in ceramic industry, so that decent affordable housing is available on rental and ownership basis in Morbi. The research will focus on the changing real estate situation in Morbi town and help in understanding how the housing problems can be mitigated that occur due to industrial development faced by the town. The study highlights the need for better qulity of housing for industrial workers.

This research is both descriptive quantitative and qualitative research to understand the housing conditions over time in ceramic industrial areas along with the prefernce of housing types for the industrial workers. Data is collected by systematic sampling of industrial workers living on industrial campus and nearby villages.

Limitation: Due to constrain the study area is limited only to the impact of ceramic industries in Morbi. The primary survey was carried out during January to March 2020 (just before the first lockdown was declared by government due to COVID-19).

3. LITERATURE STUDY

The literature study has divided in three parts with related case studies according to the housing condition of industrial workers, housing standard and preference of the workers and the recommendation for industrial workers' housing.

In Kanpur textile industry, a survey was conducted to study the living conditions of industrial workers during 1990 where random sampling of households was done. From the survey it was found that out of 64 survey houses, 67% houses were privately rented, 14% houses each were owned by the workers and provided by the state government and remaining 5% were provided by the factories. The rent is almost 15% of their average wage. The rooms were small, overcrowded and lack of adequate sunlight and ventilation. In some cases, there was no separate kitchen and the single room includes the cooking space too. The electricity was available but no running water. The cotton textile industry was coming to an end and thus the condition of the workers' houses was not maintained. The labour faced unemployment and the only hope was to get alternative employment in new industries for the textile workers.

In Indonesia, the preference of Industrial Workers was studied where data were collected by random sampling with low-income level. According to the study, the order of preference for workers' flat is the location followed by the quality of the building, condition of the surrounding environment and the availability of supporting facilities. Most of the workers preferred location of housing closer to their work than housing quality.

To understand the industrial workers' housing recommendation, a study was done in Socialist Republic of Vietnam where the industrial workers lived under poor housing condition. For the development of the residential area, site selection was done in three criteria to construct workers housing *i.e.* 1) From existing village or town, the site should be within 300m to have social facilities in walking distance. 2) From the industrial park within 500m for walkability. 3) Commuters who have a motorcycle or bicycle can be settled within 2km. For the recommendation, current legal policies were studied and analysed the current housing condition and thus to improve the workers' housing condition it was done for three different parts *i.e.* recommendation for spatial planning and building design, the recommendation for the institutional and legal system and recommendation for business and financial planning. The implementation of architectural regulations and constructions standards should be enhanced, and public facilities and infrastructure should be on sharing basis. Role of public housing entities should be enhanced and coordinate with a public-private partnership.

4. SITE PROFILE

The ceramic industrial area is spread in the eastern part of Morbi town and covers almost 90sq.km. located about 190km from Ahmedabad via NH947 and 75.2km from Rajkot via Rajkot-Morbi highway.

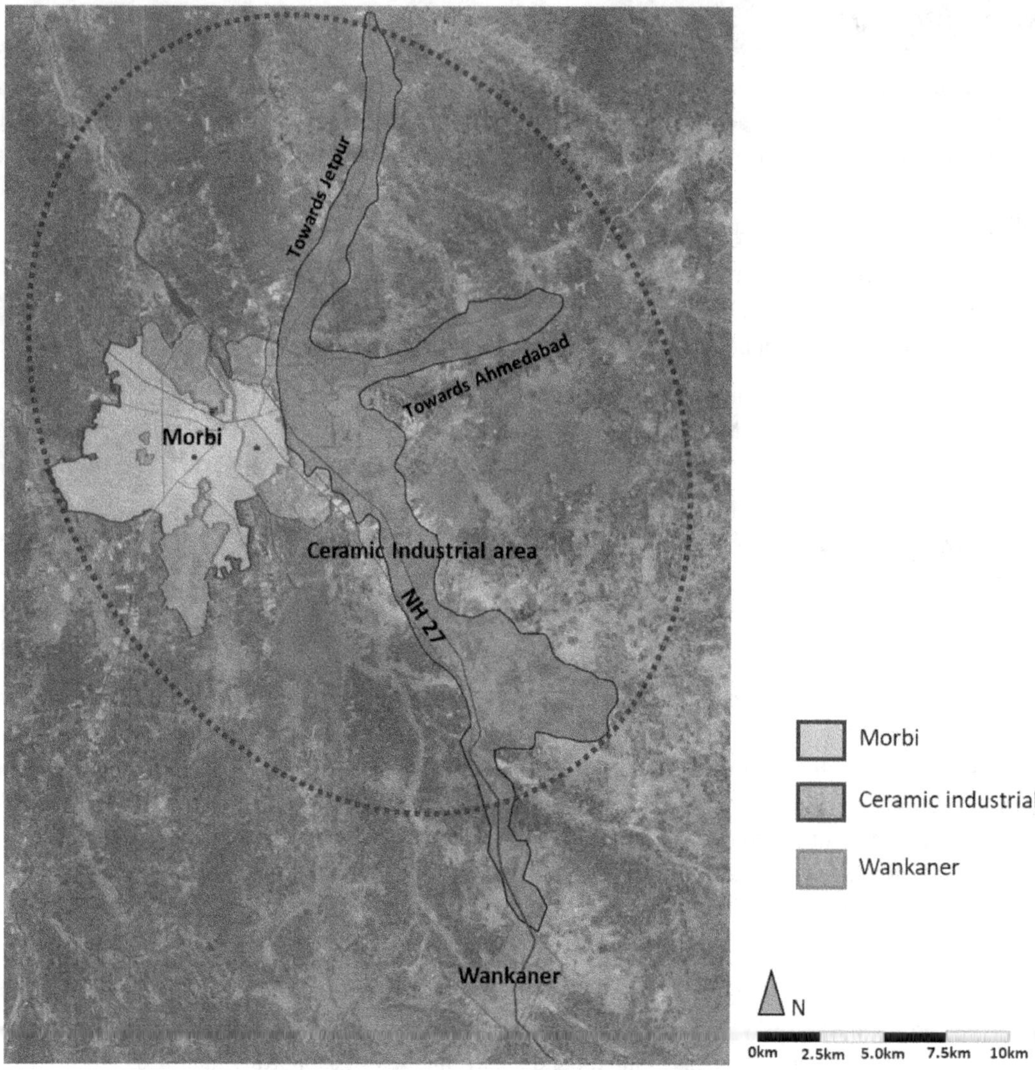

Map 4.1 Schematic location of study area

Source: Developed by author from primary survey & google image

(This image appears in colour at the end of the compendium).

Before 1979, Morbi was known for production of clocks and roof tiles. The Machchhu dam failure in 1979 flooded the town and thus many industries got destructed and huge financial loss occurred. Many residents migrated to work in diamond cutting industries. During 1980 to 1990 new mosaic tiles industry started to evolve in the western part of Morbi which was followed by setting up of ceramic industry in the eastern part of Morbi. Due to the boom in ceramic industry job opportunity and demand for labour has increased and thus in-migration started from nearby states of India.

4.1 Demography

While comparing the decadal population growth rate in Morbi Urban agglomeration and Morbi Municipality, it has been analysed that the decadal population growth rate of Urban agglomeration has reduced from 63% to 48% during 2001 but in Municipality area it has been increased from 23% to 61% since in 1991 the ceramic industry has started and the owners and other departmental staffs returned from Surat as discussed earlier and started residing in the Municipality area. With an increase in urbanization number of the nuclear family is increasing and thus the household size is decreasing with time. The decadal household growth of Morbi Urban agglomeration area is almost constant after 1991 till 2011 but in the municipality area, the household growth rate has increased from 23% to 73% during 2001 because of single migrants such as contractors increased after the establishment of ceramic industries and due to decrease in household size over time.

4.2 Real estate sector in Morbi town

After 1991, the ceramic industry started in Morbi and the owners, contractors and other departmental higher-level staff started residing in the municipality area due to which the growth rate of housing during 1991-2001 was on the peak.

The growth rate of ceramic industrial units from 2001-2011 was the highest *i.e.* 464% since the number of industries during 2010 started increasing. But when comparing this with the growth rate of housing units in the municipality area it has found that during 2001-2011 the growth rate has decreased from 73.38% to 47.62%. Thus, it can be analysed that the owners are the locals who are expanding their business and constructing a greater number of ceramic industries but not investing for extra housing. From Figure 4.1 and Figure 4.2, the relation between the growth rate of housing units in Morbi municipality and ceramic industrial units can be analysed.

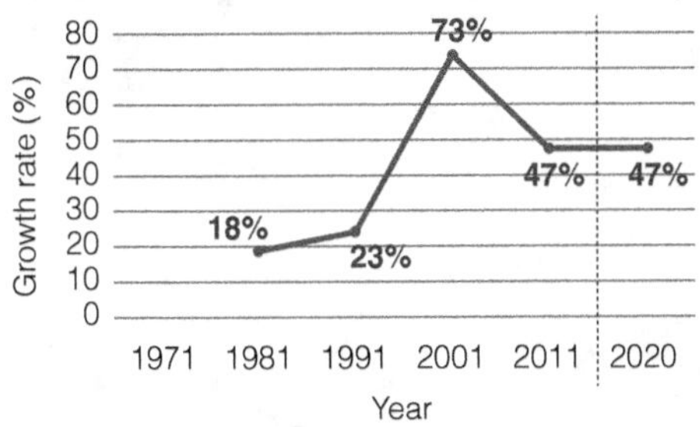

Fig. 4.1 Growth rate of housing units in Morbi municipality

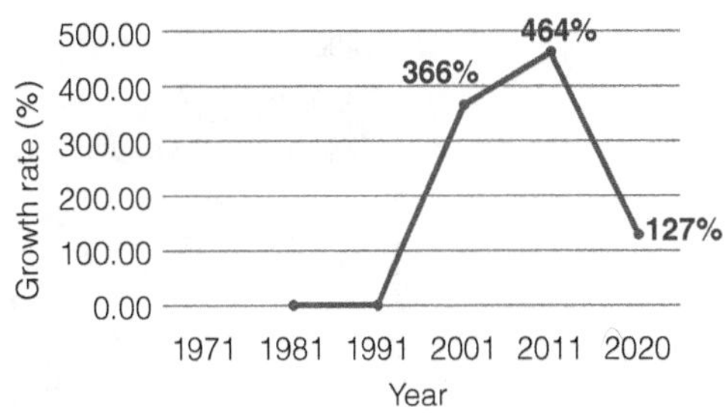

Fig. 4.2 Growth rate of ceramic industrial units

Source: Figure 4.1 Census data for 1971-2011; Primary survey for 2020. Fig. 4.2 Primary survey

The predominant land use in Morbi is residential. The different zone of the town *i.e.* North, East, South, West and Central has been divided according to the road network for easy understanding. As per the urbanization, the southern and southwestern part is the predominant area for real estate development since Rajkot is connected to Morbi from this side and people travelling from Morbi to Rajkot or vice versa for occupation prefers to reside in this area. Moreover, in the western part near the Morbi bypass road, the real estate sector is developing. But the eastern and northern part of town has lesser development due to community biased.

In the eastern part, new construction is coming up in Mahendranagar where mostly the Non-local/migrants resides, mainly the contractors of ceramic industries, providers of raw material for the ceramic industry reside. As compared to other zones, the market land price in the east zone is the least *i.e.* INR 11,000/sqm while in the south, west and north zone it is INR 1,11,000/sqm, INR 55,000/sqm and INR 22,000/sqm respectively.

Public housing *i.e.* Affordable Housing in Partnership (AHP) was started in 2016 near the bypass road in the western side of Morbi. According to the land price and demand of the area, the property price and rental value of the residential property is least in the eastern part of Morbi. Property price, unit size and rental value is described in Table 4.1.

Built up Area	North	East	South	West
2BHK	65 sqm	65 sqm	74 sqm	74 sqm
3BHK	92 sqm	92 sqm	111 sqm	111 sqm
4BHK	-	-	148 sqm	125 sqm
Average property price (INR/sqm)	28,000 (1.3 times of East)	21,000	35,000 (1.6 times of East)	33,000 (1.5 times of East)
Rental value/month 2BHK	INR 6,000-7000	INR 7,000-8000	INR 12,000-15000	INR 9,000-10000

Source: Primary survey

The lowest unit price of a new unit provided by the free market is INR 12lakhs having a built-up area of 65sqm for 2bhk and for a resale unit the lowest price is INR 6.25lakhs having a built-up area of 46sqm which is 1 room kitchen. The minimum rent of market rental property in the village area near the ceramic industries is INR 3000/month and in the urban agglomeration area, it is INR 6,000/month. With the increase in the land values and demand for housing in Morbi due to urbanization and industrialization the price of the residential property has escalated. With the growth of real estate sector, manufacturing of ceramic tiles and sanitary wares have increased but the labours who manufactures those, lives in very poor housing condition.

4.3 Evolution of ceramic industrial units, labours' housing over years in Morbi

As per the Morbi Ceramic Associations, initially (1991 to 2000), only small-scale industries were established where the average number of labours was 60per industry. In 2000, medium scale industries have started since the business of ceramic industry was booming and thus the growth rate of labours from 1995 to 2000 increased to nearly 400%. After 2002, the industrial units started to provide free housing to labours near the production units. In 2010, the growth rate of industrial units has increased to 163% from 114% and few large-scale industries have added in the market however the provision of housing has not kept pace with the growth in industrial units and jobs created. In Figure 4.3, the relation between the growth rate of industrial units, labour housing and labour population is shown.

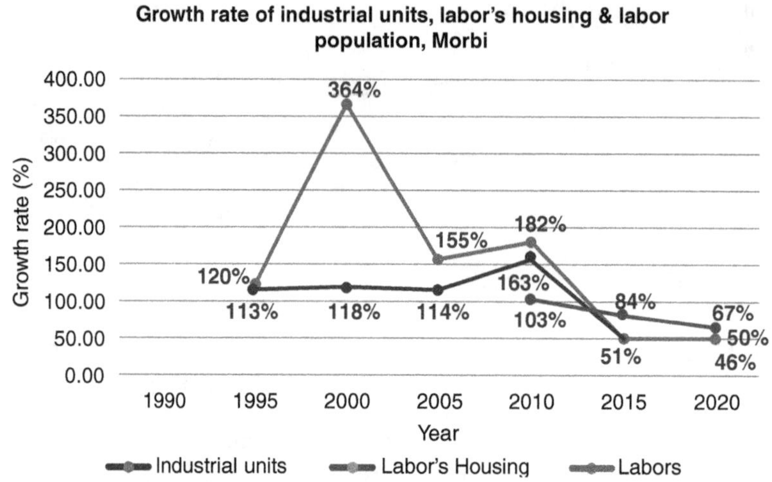

Fig. 4.3 Growth rate of industrial units, labour housing and labour population in Morbi

Source: Morbi Ceramics Associations

(This image appears in colour at the end of the compendium).

5. PROFILE OF LABOURS

Currently the ceramic industry in Morbi is heavily dependent on migrant labour, of which 95% are from Madhya Pradesh, Orissa, Rajasthan and Uttar Pradesh. The migrant labours come through social network and are mainly on contract basis. The contract is maintained by the contractor and there is no formal contract duration agreement. When there is labour need, the labours who are engaged for a longer period contact his known ones from his hometown and thus new labours join the market.

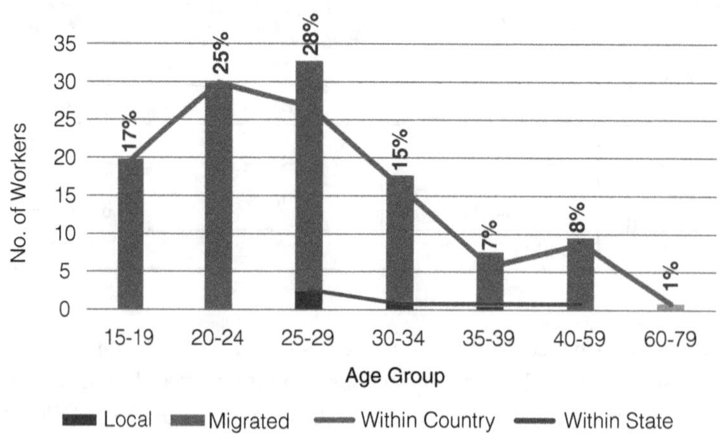

Fig. 4.4 Migration of labour by age group

Source: Primary survey

(This image appears in colour at the end of the compendium).

Out of the total labours in the ceramic industries, 70% falls under the age group of 15-29 who are define as Youth as per National Youth Policy 2014 and they are the major seekers of employment (Youth in India, 2017). Most of the younger labours are migrants and from the older age group there are local labours too, which indicates assimilation of the labour in Morbi.

Table 4.2 Labours migrated as family/single

Married status of labors →

Labors migrated as ↑	Single male worker	Married male worker	Married female worker	Single female worker	Total	Average HH income (INR/month)
Single male	39 (34%)	27 (23%)	-	-	66 (57%)	11,904
Family	-	35 (31%)	14 (12%)	-	49 (43%)	23,317
Single femal	-	-	0	0	0	0
Total	39 (34%)	62 (54%)	14 (12%)	0	115 (100%)	-
No. of labor for permanent stay	9 (43%)	11 (52%)	1 (5%)	0	21 (18%)	-

Source: Primary survey

In Table 4.2, the x-axis is the original married status of the labours *i.e.* 66% of the total labour population are married but only 43% of the total labour population has migrated as a family which is represented in y-axis. Thus, rest 23% of the married labours have migrated as single. The labours who migrated as family, both husband and wife use to work in the same ceramic industry and thus earn double than the labour who migrated as single. Moreover, married labours prefer to settle in Morbi for future than the single labour.

5.1 Monthly wages and location of residence

Out of the total workers, unskilled workers are the highest *i.e.* 78% whose monthly wage varies from INR 9,000-18,000 followed by semi-skilled 18% whose monthly wage varies from INR 12,000-20,000 and skilled 4% whose monthly wage varies from INR 18,000-25,000. According to Labour Law, Gujarat Minimum Wages per month for Tiles manufacturing in Unskilled is INR 8,278 Semi-skilled is INR 8,486 and Skilled is INR 8,720 (Labour Law Reporter, 2019).

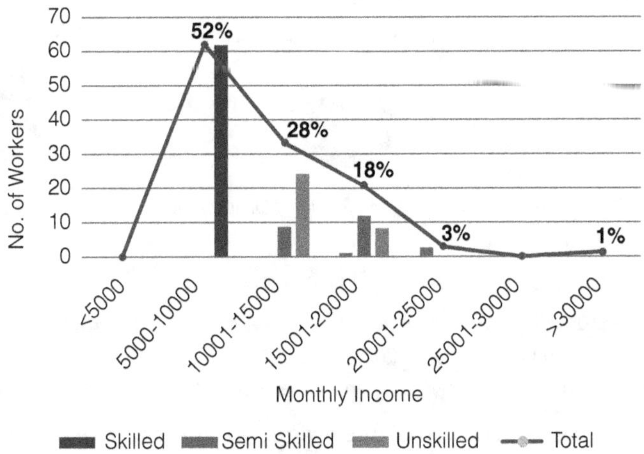

Fig. 4.5 Type of workers by monthly wages

Source: Primary survey

(This image appears in colour at the end of the compendium).

Out of the total workers, 92% resides in quarters provided by the industries, where 95% resides in free quarters and 5% pays rent from INR 100-700 per month. 4% of the labours who are locals stays in the Municipality. Rest 4% prefers to stay in nearby village area since the quarters are not clean and have an insufficient water supply. The workers residing in village areas are semi-skilled and skilled labours who can spend INR 1500-4000 per month on rent. The average monthly income of the labours residing in the village area is 1.2 times more than the average monthly income of the labours residing in the industrial area and thus the former can spend a higher amount in rent than the later.

Table 4.3 Area of resides, monthly wages & average rent for accommodation

Area of resides →

Different factors	Municipality area	Village area	Industrial area	Total labor
Average monthly income (INR)	16,800	14,400	11,795	-
Local	5 (100%)	1 (20%)	0	**6 (5%)**
Migrants	0	4 (80%)	110 (100%)	**114 (95%)**
Free accommodation	5 (100%)	1 (20%)	104 (95%)	**110 (92%)**
Paid accommodation	0	4 (80%)	6 (5%)	**10 (8%)**
Average rent for the accommodation (INR)	0	1,800	333	-
Total labor	**5 (4%)**	**5 (4%)**	**110 (92%)**	**120 (100%)**

Source: Primary survey

5.2 Condition of housing

To understand the housing condition of labour quarters, four factors are considered *i.e.* the physical structure of the housing unit, congestion factor, type of toilet and kitchen and availability of physical and social infrastructure. All the four factors are analysed and compared in different scale of industries for paid and free quarters.

Physical structure of housing unit

Out of the three different scales of industries, semi-permanent structure in small scale industries are highest *i.e.* 23% while in large scale and medium scale it is 10% and 6% respectively. The paid quarters in large scale industries are liveable and permanent structure while in medium scale industries those are 50% good and 50% liveable with permanent structures. Thus, the physical quality of the house in small scale industries is worse than large and medium scale industries while in large scale industries it is better than the other two.

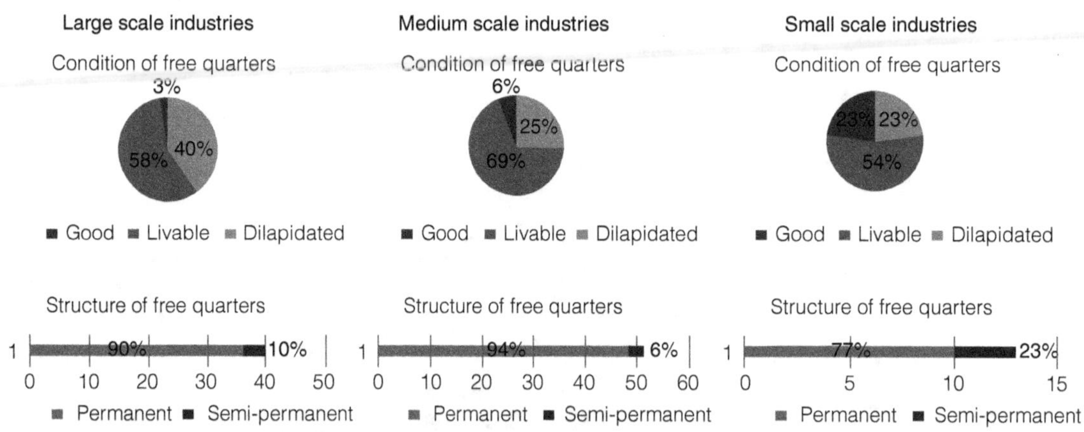

Fig. 4.6 Physical condition of free quarters in different scales of industry

Source: Primary survey

(This image appears in colour at the end of the compendium).

Congestion factor

According to (Neufert & Neufert, 2002) the minimum per capita area in dormitories is 3.16sqm but most of the rooms in the ceramic industrial quarters are congested having an area less than 3.16sqm per labour. The total congestion in large scale and small-scale industries is 45% while in medium scale industries it is 31%. In the quarters of ceramic industries, the congestion as per married couple is very less *i.e.* 6% which is in medium-scale industries. As the average number of labours in large scale industries is more than other two scale industries, they failed to provide enough number of units making it congested despite the physical condition of units is better than medium and small-scale industries.

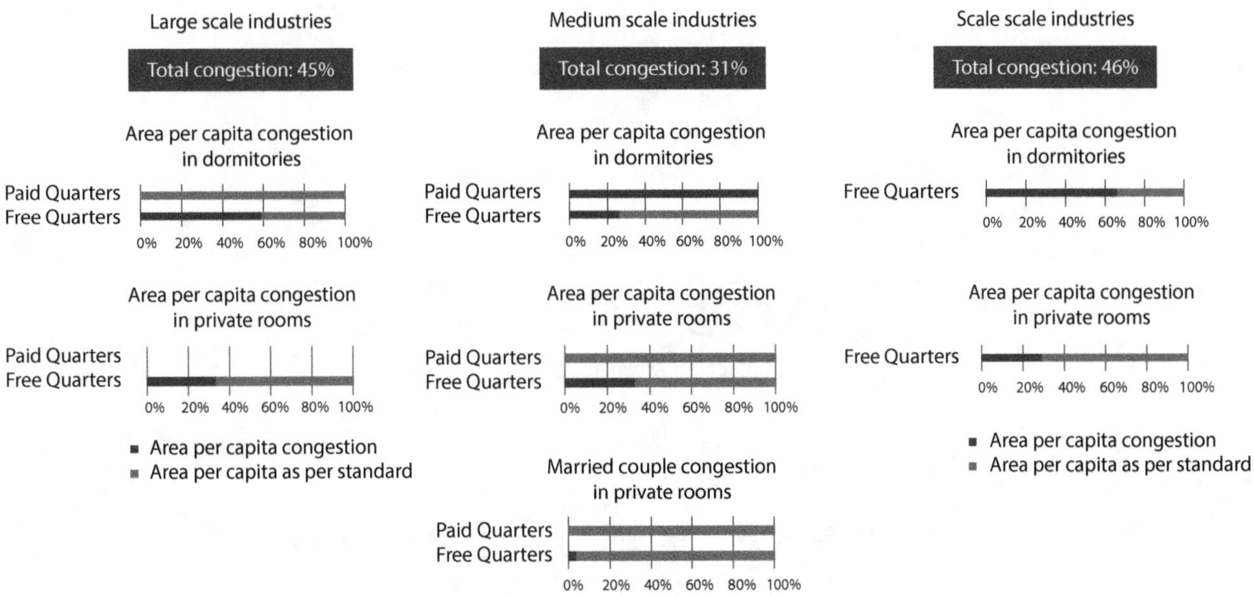

Fig. 4.7 Per capita area and married couple congestion for free and paid quarters in different scale of industries

Source: Primary survey

(This image appears in colour at the end of the compendium).

In Figure 4.7, the red mark shows congestion to compare in free and paid quarters for a different type of rooms *i.e.* dormitory and private rooms.

Type of toilet and kitchen

Almost half of residents reported lack of toilets due to which open defecation is practiced. In large industries in the paid quarters reported using common toilets and negligible open defecation, while in medium-scale and small-scale industries 50% practice open defecation. Nearly 89% of the living spaces do not have a kitchen,either the space with in the room is used for cooking or open space outside the room is used.

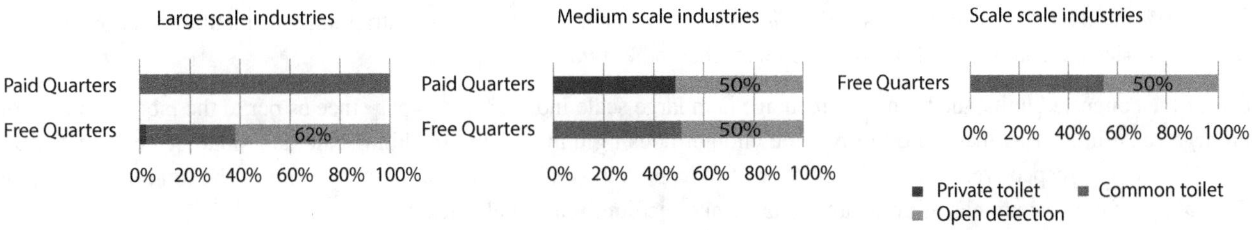

Fig. 4.8 Type of toilet for free and paid quarters in different scale of industries

Source: Primary survey

(This image appears in colour at the end of the compendium).

Availability of physical and social infrastructure

Interestingly in the region having shortage of water, 93% of households have reported to have access to water supply. Out of which 60% have supply from borewell, 38% have supply from water tankers that are bought by the industries and 2% have tube wells which are in small scale industries. In small-scale industries, 15% of households do not have running water supply and use tube well which is present near the accommodation area.

The social infrastructure that was considered during the survey is super-market, temple, garden, playschool, play area, clinic and ATM. Almost 73% of the social infrastructure is not present in the quarters. 15% of the social infrastructure are present within societies and 11% within the neighbourhood. Figure 4.9 shows the non-availability of social infrastructures in industrial areas. Only super-markets and neighbourhood shops are available which have come up due to private enterprise.

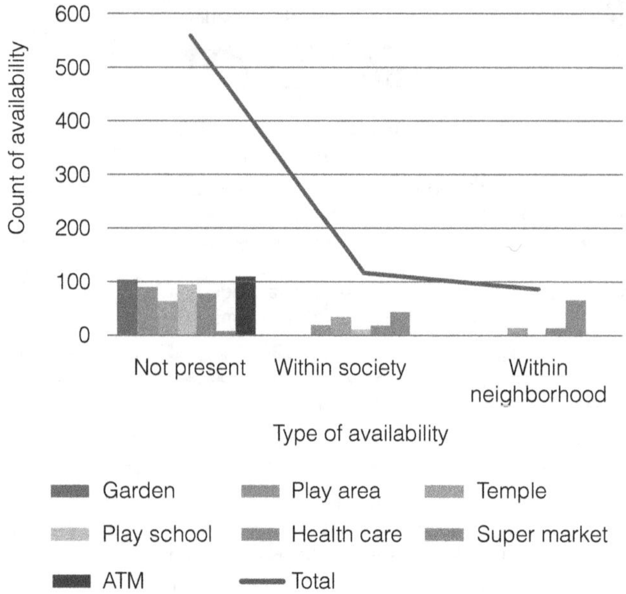

Fig. 4.9 Availability of social infrastructure
Source: Primary survey

(This image appears in colour at the end of the compendium).

5.3 Labours' housing shortage

The factors considered to calculate housing shortage are Obsolescence factor, Congested factor, Homeless and Non-serviceable kutcha housing units (Kundu, 2011). In the quarters of ceramic industries, every labour is provided with a housing unit to live and there are no homeless labours in this industry. The structure of the quarters is either permanent or semi-permanent though 53% are non-serviceable, none of the quarters is in a temporary structure. Thus, the factors homeless and non-serviceable kutcha housing units are not applicable to calculate housing shortage in the quarters of ceramic industries. Out of the total housing units, 6% are obsolescent and 38% are congested units. Out of the obsolescent units, 14% are in large scale industries and 43% are in medium and small-scale industries since as mentioned above in large scale industries the conditions of housing are better than other two industries.

Out of the congested units, the highest percentage is in large scale industries *i.e.* 45% since as per to the labour population in large scale industries they failed to provide enough housing units. In the medium-scale and small-scale industries, it is 40% and 14% respectively. Since the number of industries in small scale is less *i.e.* 16% out of the total industries, the percentage of congested units as compared to large and medium scale is also lesser.

While calculating the housing shortage in the labours quarters of ceramic industries according to obsolescence and congested factor, 22,341 housing units are in shortage. Out of which 47% are in medium scale industries since 6% of households have married couple congestion which requires one housing unit per couple while in large scale and small scale industries only area per capita congestion is present. Due to sharing of rooms in the dormitory, the housing units did not increase much.

6. HOUSING PREFERENCE AND AFFORDABILITY

Housing preference is a choice which is expressed as the desire or want for a particular form of housing (Preece, Crawford, McKee, Flint, & Robinson, 2019). To study the housing preference and affordability of the labours, it is important to understand their income and expenditure pattern. The major monthly expenditure of the labours is on food which is 73% of the total expenditure.

For the purpose of the study, permanent migrants are classified as those who want to own a house in Morbi, of which 58% falls under the age group of 20-29 are eager to earn, improve their living standard and settle in urban areas. Married migrants who are living in Morbi with their families are wanting to settle in Morbi while the single migrants come for employment opportunities. Municipality area is the most preferred area which is opted by 76% of the total permanent migrant labour as their future permanent location, due to greater opportunity and development of the area. However, 14% of the total permanent migrant labour prefer the surrounding villages area as it is less congested than Municipality area and rest 10% preferred industrial area so that the travel time and cost can be saved by residing near the workplace. The most preferred unit size is 4 rooms including kitchen *i.e.* 2bhk and carpet area of 30-60sqm.

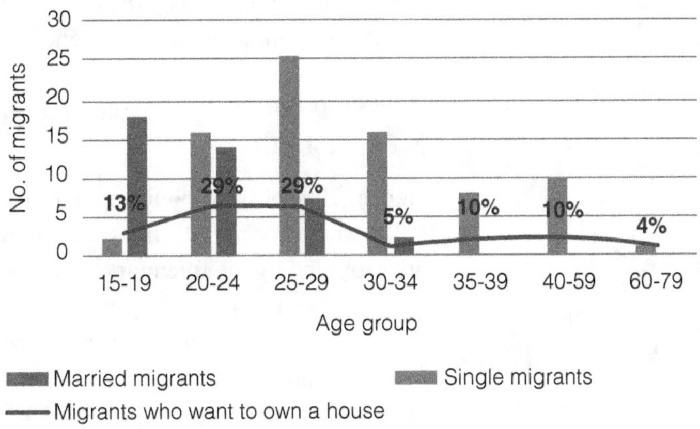

Fig. 4.10 Type of migrants as per age group
Source: Primary survey

(This image appears in colour at the end of the compendium).

The most preferred housing typology for the ceramic industrial labours is low rise apartment with 63% followed by row house and detached housing of 16% each and semi-detached of 5%. The housing typology preferred by the labours is also dependent on their household income. Figure 4.11 shows the preferred housing typology by the labours and amount want to spend on that housing. The labours earning a monthly household income of INR 5,000-15,000 preferred low-rise apartment while the household income of INR 25,000 to more than INR 30,000 per month preferred detached housing.

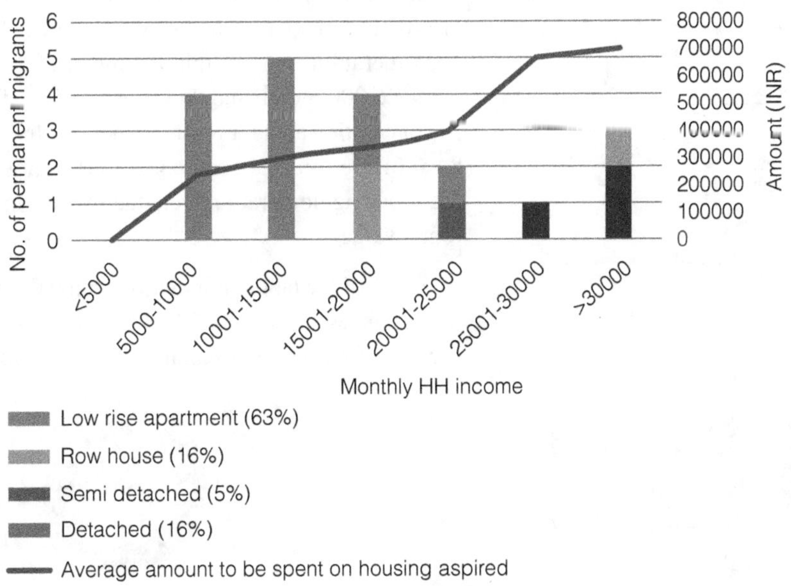

Fig. 4.11 Preferred housing typology as per HH income
Source: Primary survey

(This image appears in colour at the end of the compendium).

The amount that can be spent on housing by the labours varies from INR 3lakhs to INR 7lakhs as per affordability ratios based on their household incomes. As the property price has increased due to the scarcity of service land in urban areas, it is difficult for the labours to afford the housing provided by the free market as per their household income and amount that can be spent on housing.

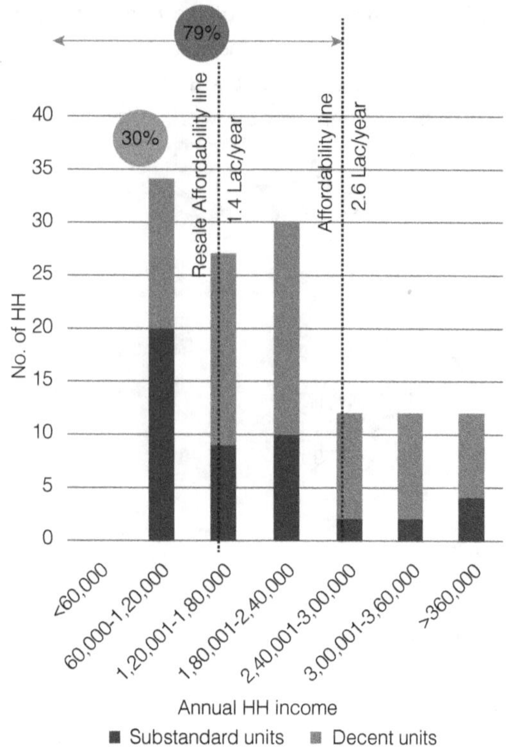

Fig. 4.12 Income pyramid for labour population

Source: Primary survey

(This image appears in colour at the end of the compendium).

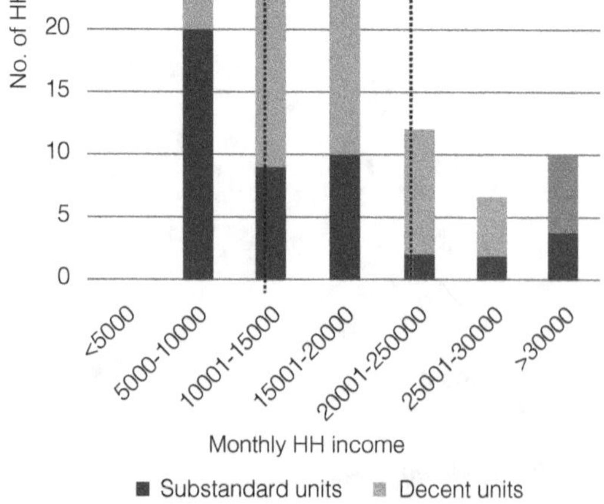

Fig. 4.13 Rental income pyramid for labour population

Source: Primary survey

(This image appears in colour at the end of the compendium).

As discussed above, in Morbi urban agglomeration area the lowest unit price of the new unit provided by the free market is INR 12lakhs. According to the Knight Frank affordability benchmark, one can afford a housing 4.5 times of their average household income (Nandan, 2019). Thus, the housing affordability for new units provided by the free market in Morbi is INR 2,66,666 *i.e.* the minimum annual household income one should earn to afford the new unit. Income pyramid for ceramic industrial labour population with the resale and new unit affordable line is shown in Figure 4.12.

Hence, 79% of the labour population of the ceramic industry falls below the affordability line and cannot afford the new units that are provided by the free market. Similarly, the lowest unit price of the resale unit provided by the free market is INR 6.25lakhs and thus, the housing affordability for resale units is INR 1,38,888 *i.e.* the minimum annual household income one should earn to afford the resale unit. Hence, 30% of the labour population falls below the resale affordability line and cannot afford the resale units in Morbi.

The minimum rent of market rental property in the village area is INR 3,000/month. Ideally, one can afford 25% of monthly household income in rent. Thus, the housing affordability for rental units is INR 12,000/month *i.e.* the one who earns less than INR 12,000/month cannot afford a rental housing even in the village area.

Figure 4.13 shows the income pyramid for rental units and 40% of the total ceramic industrial labour population in Morbi cannot afford the rental unit in the village area. Similarly, in the urban agglomeration area, the minimum rent of the market rental property is INR 6,000/month and thus, the housing affordability in the urban agglomeration area for rental property is INR 24,000/month. Almost 84% of the total labour population cannot afford a rental unit in the urban agglomeration area due to their lower-income and higher rental value.

The 56% of the labour population below the affordability line whose income is less than INR 12,000/month lives in substandard units and cannot afford resale or rental property in Morbi.

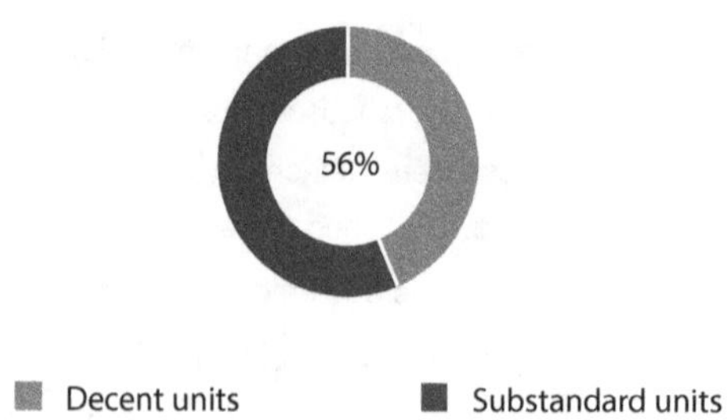

Fig. 4.14 Percentage of substandard units below affordable line

Source: Primary survey

(This image appears in colour at the end of the compendium).

If the single labours share the room for rental accommodation and we assume that the rental properties are available in the village or urban agglomeration area than the percentage of labour population who cannot afford the rental units in urban agglomeration area and village area will reduce to 27% and 2% respectively. Those labours who will not be able to afford the rental units are the labours with families. All the single labours can afford rental units since the rent gets shared by 3-4 people per room. In Morbi urban agglomeration area the minimum rent of the market rental property is INR 6,000/month which is for 2bhk with the built-up area of 65sqm. In this unit size, six labours can share the unit and thus the monthly rental share for each labour will be INR 1,000. Labour earning INR 4,000 per month can also afford this shared rental unit since 25% of the monthly income can be invested in rent. Similarly, for the village area, the minimum rent of the market rental property is INR 3,000/month which is for 1 room kitchen with a built-up area of 30sqm. Here, three labours can share one room excluding kitchen and thus the monthly share for each labour will be INR 1,000. In the ceramic industries of Morbi, the minimum wage of labour is INR 7,000/month and thus all the single labours can afford the shared rental units.

If all the single labours share the rental units than out of the total labour population lives in substandard units, only 4% will not be able to afford even rental or resale units provided by the free market. Out of the total labour population who cannot afford the units provided by the free market, 75% prefers to own a house and 25% want rental accommodation. Thus, the housing need is calculated according to affordability and the ownership and rental housing *i.e.* the preference of labours to own a house or to stay temporarily.

Table 4.4 Labours who cannot afford ownership nor rental properties provided by the free market

Type of stay →

Different factors ↑

Substandard	Permanent stay (75%)	Temporary stay (25%)
Large scale industry	33%	0
Medium scale industry	67%	100%
Small scale industry	0	0
Married labor	17%	100%
Bachelor labor	83%	0
Migrated as family	0	100%
Migrated as single	100%	0
Skilled labor	0	0
Semil-skilled labor	33%	50%
Unskilled labor	67%	50%
Age group	100% (15–29)	100% (25–29)
Engagement duration less than 1 year	50%	100%
Labors whose stay is more than engagement period	17%	0

Source: Primary survey

The maximum labour population who wants ownership and rental housing fall in medium scale industries since 56% of the total ceramic industries are covered by medium scale industries. As it has been assumed that if the single labours who do not want to own a house, shares the rental properties that are already provided by the free market, there is no need of additional shared units like dormitories as all the single labours can afford the free market rental units. Thus, the need for rental units is for the labours who reside with the family. Mostly the labours are unskilled and fall at the age group of 15-29 years *i.e.* the youth and only 17% of the total labour population have changed their job for 1-2 times. In Table 4.4, shows the type of stay in the x-axis and different factors in the y-axis. 83% of the total labours who want to own a house are bachelors and 100% have migrated as single. But since they want to own property the need only rental houses.

But all the labour population can afford the public housing since the AHP units under PMAY is available at INR 80,000 as discussed with the AHP department of Morbi municipality. There are already developing housing schemes through which the weaker section can afford decent housing, but the location of the public housing is far away *i.e.* 12km from the industrial area. The AHP units are present in the western side of Morbi and the industrial area is on the eastern side, so it is not attractive for the ceramic labours. Interventions are required so that public housing become affordable in different aspects for the ceramic industrial labours and thus improve the housing condition.

7. CONCLUSION

From this study the following conclusions are highlighted: the government policies and schemes provided for development of ceramic industry has accelerate the industrialization and growth of ceramic industry and consequent inflow of labour population, but there are no direct initiatives which focus to improvement of living conditions of the labours engaged in ceramic industrial. There is no initiatives to provide decent affordable housing for the industrial labours.

Real Estate sector in Morbi: The land price is least in east Morbi *i.e.* INR 11,000/sqm and thus the property price is lowest here *i.e.* INR 21,000/sqm with predominant of 2bhk and 3bhk apartments. The lowest unit price of a new and resale unit provided by the free market is INR 12 lakhs and INR 6.25 lakhs, respectively. The minimum rent of market rental property in the village area near the ceramic industries is INR 3000/month and in the urban agglomeration area, it is INR 6,000/month.

Labours' housing quality, amenities and physical condition: The structural condition of housing in small-scale industries is worst, as 23% of structures are dilapidated and semi-permanent. The total congestion in large scale and small-scale industries is 45% while in medium scale industries it is 31%. As the average number of labours in large scale industries is more than medium and small-scale industries, they failed to provide enough number of units making it congested, but the physical condition of units is better than medium and small-scale industries. In the free housing quarters of ceramic industries, about half of the workers use open defecation for the toilet while the other 45% use common toilets and rest private toilets. Open defecation is highest in the large-scale industries *i.e.* 62% since they do not provide enough toilets as per the labour population.

Public/social amenities are grossly missing in the area, with only the supermarket and temple available in the neighbourhood. The condition of labour housing of ceramic industries is poor, but while comparing the different scale of industries it can be analysed that the labour housing provided by the large-scale industries are better than medium and small scales of industries. This is because of the large scale and medium scale industries can invest 1.3 times and 1.1 times more in individual labour than small scale industries, respectively. Though the labour housing quality in small-scale industries is worst, the maximum housing need is in medium scale industries *i.e.* 47% since in medium scale industries married couple congestion is present which requires one housing unit per couple. The number of the housing shortage in the labours quarters of ceramic industries according to obsolescence and congested factor is 22,341 units.

Labours' housing aspiration and affordability: As per the primary survey, 82% of the labour population do not want to own a house in Morbi. Of these 63% prefer low rise apartment. As the property price has increased due to the scarcity of service land in urban areas, it is difficult for the labours to afford the housing provided by the free market. The total housing need of 4,957 units is divided as 75% for ownership and 25% for rental. The public housing currently being provided but Morbi Municipality is very far from the industrial areas thus does not serve the purpose.

8. RECOMMENDATION

Total requirement, units, land, and capital: The total housing need is 4,957 units and for the construction of those units, the suggested housing typology can be low rise apartments since 63% labours prefer this typology as their housing aspiration and the demand for the same in the real estate market is high due to high land price. For the ownership and rental housing 1BHK and 1RK units can be constructed. The minimum size of the unit for 1bhk with a carpet area of 30sqm is considered from EWS category of PMAY-AHP units since it is the minimum requirement for a standard 1bhk units and for 1RK the carpet area is 22sqm considered from per capita area of four members and minimum standard for kitchen and toilet.

The average market land price in Eastern zone is the lowest as compared to the other zones *i.e.* INR 11,000/sqm. Moreover, the ceramic industries are in the eastern part of Morbi and contractors and other departmental staffs of the ceramic industries reside in this zone. Hence, the residential area can be demarcated for the labours' housing in the same zone *i.e.* east but away from the contractors and other departmental staffs due to community difference.

For 4,957 private units, the built space required is 2,69,279sqm. The height of the apartments suggested is from 6-8 floors (as existing in east zone of Morbi). Hence, 141 numbers of blocks are required. If the FSI is considered as 3, the total land area required is 89,759sqm that is approximately 9 hectors and an equal area will be required for other land uses (as per general requirements of Master plans). As per the land cost in the east zone, the total land cost for 89,759sqm is 98 crores. The construction cost in Morbi is INR 15,000/sqm as discussed with local developers. The total construction cost becomes INR 403 crores. Hence, the total amount required to construct the labours' housing as per the need is only INR 501 crores, which is possible to be generated through various financial mechanisms.

Upgradation of existing units: It is possible to immediately improve the existing housing stock housing by improving the minimum requirement of infrastructure and standard of the unit. While improving the quality and standard of housing, reasonable and affordable rent can be charged for maintenance, as free quarters are taken for granted by the labours and the providers and quality of assets deteriorate.

Development Strategy: This development for labours' housing can be done by the Morbi Ceramics Associations as a group housing so that the maintenance can be improved, and infrastructure cost is reduced which will improve the supply and condition of labours' housing. If the labours' housing is constructed by the individual industries, sometimes for a smaller number of units, the construction cost increases. And thus, to reduce the construction cost, the industries adjust those labours in the available units which increases congestion. The funding can be from Corporate Social Responsibility (CSR) fund where according to the number of labour population, each industry can contribute the percentage amount to the Morbi Ceramics Associations or according to the individual industries share, the rooms for the labours can be provided in the group housing. The units those are constructed by the Morbi Ceramics Associations can have the rent-to-own housing model for the labours who want to own a house. The residential units can be on lease for a fixed number of years and the monthly rent can be deposited in the bank as the Equated Monthly Instalments (EMI). Once the payment becomes 100%, the property papers can be handed to the buyer. With rent-to-own housing, the labours will have a decent housing with affordable rents and have time to save fund to own the house.

Some of the public housing (AHP under the PMAY-U) for the economically weaker section can be constructed near the industrial area. For the permanent migrants, instead of paying rent for the whole life in the industrial quarters, they will prefer to invest one time and own a permanent house in reasonable price and thus can afford the public housing near the industrial area.

Hence, with the above interventions for improvement of housing stock and various options available to the labour, the quality and condition of the labour housing can be improved to the desirable level.

End Notes

This paper is part of the research supported by CEPT University under the directed research project (DRP) scheme. The authors are thankful to CEPT University for the support provided.

REFERENCES

Conference, I. L. (1960). Workers' housing. *Athens Center of Ekistics*, pp. 62–76 (15 pages).

Gujarat, G. O. (2019, September 4th). *Morbi District*. Retrieved from District Administration: https://morbi.nic.in/

(2018). *Indian Ceramics Industry*. Mumbai: Messe Muenchen India & EAC international consulting.

Kundu, D. A. (2011). *Report of the Technical Group on Urban Housing Shortage.*

(2019). *Labour Law Reporter.*

Nandan, A. (2019). *Rediscovering Affordability*. Mumbai: Knight Frank.

Neufert, E., & Neufert, P. (2002). *Architect's data.* Wiley-Blackwell.

Preece, J., Crawford, J., McKee, K., Flint, J., & Robinson, D. (2019). Understanding changing housing aspirations: a review of the evidence. *Housing Studies.*

Youth in India. (2017). *Youth in India.* New Delhi: Social Statistics Division.

How Social Infrastructure Influences Gender Discrimination in Intra-household Resource Allocation?: Case of Private Health-care Spending in India

Manik Kumar
Policy Analyst
Centre for Budget and Governance Accountability, New Delhi

Nilesh Kumar
Assistant Professor, Mahatma Gandhi Memorial College
M.J.P. Rohilkhand University, Bareilly

Abstract: The paper examines gender discrimination in household resource allocation with spatial reference to private health care expenditure; understand the role of factors underlying the discrimination. To estimate deference as well as discrimination this paper used Percentage Gap Ratio (PGR) and Bliender-Oaxaca (B-O) decomposition with help of two round (60th and 71th) national representative NSSO unit level data.

Results indicate that average health spending for female is not only; always lower than that of male regardless of type of social as well as economic group and survey rounds but this gap is also increase significantly over the period of time. The results indicate that there is clear gender bias in favor of man in rural and urban sector. This bias is also visible when we take into account the socio-economic indicators in India.

1. INTRODUCTION

The issue of gender discrimination in health sector has been highlighted by many scholars in India. There is a continuous rise in life expectancy of both sexes but better life expectancy of female in comparison to male is a new phenomenon in India. (Canudas et al., 2015, Saikia et al., 2011). Although better life expectancy for female is a great achievement, we cannot turn a blind eye on the reality of female feticide and excess mortality (Sudha et al 1999, Bongaarts et al., 2015). Gender bias in treatment-seeking behavior, immunization, nutrition and living arrangements are reality across the different age groups (Behrman 1998, Hill et al., 1995).

The issue of gender discrimination especially in healthcare utilization is explored by many researchers in India.

Most of researchers found that there is gender bias in favor of male in access to health care at successive phase of life and also found that female children less immunized than male children (Pandey 2003, Kurz et al., 1997). Asfaw et al., 2007 found that in case of hospital treatment and hospitalization before death male have better access (Asfaw et al., 2007). Sex composition of siblings also determines the outreach to health services (Pandey 2003). Due to less use of health care facilities at old aged women in India, they face issues like severe health complication and disabilities (Chaudhuri 2008, Bora et al., 2015). Even in the case of untreated morbidity rates women fall behind the man (Saikia et al., 2016).

One of the important study regarding health care expenditure strategies shows that the probability of hospitalization in case of emergency is lower among the girls than boys. It is also found that parents are more likely to get required amount of expenses any way possible for male child (Asfaw et al., 2010). A study shows that in the case of health expenditure on boys are greater in comparison to girls. There is clear bias in favor of male child is found in case of consulting doctors (Pandey et al., 2002). The mean health expenditure on neonatal period for boys was four times in comparison to girls in rural UP (Willis et al., 2009). It is also found that there is clear bias in favor of male newborn in selection of health care providers. The household with male newborn prefers private hospitals; on the other hand, household with female newborn prefers public hospitals which are considered cheaper (Willis et al., 2009).

A recent study found that the gap in health and food expenditure for male and female elderly is narrowing. The study also indicates that when the share of elderly in population increases expenditure on health also increases on the contrary if share of elderly female increases the expenditure on health decreases (Maharana and Ladusingh 2014).

Above studies document wide range of issues that deals with gender bias in use of or access to health care services. But studies fail to understand the role of factors underlying the discrimination. The above studies also do not shed light on the issue of gender discrimination in household resource allocation with spatial reference to private health care expenditure.

The current study with the help of recently available national level data examines whether gender disparity in private health care expenditure is still a phenomenon. This study also examines the factors determining the discrimination in household resource allocation for private health care expenditure in India, if so, at what extent. The present study deals with the issue of gender discrimination in household resource allocation with spatial reference to private health care expenditure in India.

2. DATA AND METHODS

This study uses two rounds of NSSO Data. The data is cross sectional and it is nationally representative. The survey is conducted by Ministry of Statistics and Programme Implementation (MoSPI). The NSSO 60th round (2004) collects detail information on health from 47,302 rural and 26,566 urban household. It covers 4,755 villages and 2,668 urban blocks from across India. The 71th round (2014) accumulates 36480 rural and 29452 urban household covering a total of 4577 villages and 3720 urban blocks from across India. Data for hospitalization for all members (current and former) were collected for last 365 days. Present study uses 365 day recall period of expenditure of hospitalization. Nominal health care expenditure was converted to 2014 price using index of private final consumption expenditure[1].

The response variable particular for the private health care expenditure model is the natural logarithm of expenditure for treatment (per-hospitalisation) during stay at hospital in Indian rupees (INR) during the last 365 days. Present study takes total medical expenditure occurred by household during the reference period which includes direct and indirect cost of treatment. In case of direct medical expenditure the study includes doctor's (Physician and surgeon's) fee, medicines cost, investigative tests, room charges and other medical expenses[2]. Other expenditure such as transportation of patient, cost of food of patient and attendant (paid or unpaid), lodging, escort etc treated as indirect health care expenditure incurred by the household (INR) during same reference period.

Independent variables related to demography are place of habitation (rural or urban sector), gender, belongs from a social specific groups (SC, ST, OBC and 'Other'), member of religious groups, and deferent region of India. All these are used as dummy variables.

In present study we grouped SC and ST together because SCs and STs both are traditionally underprivileged groups in India, like wise on the basis of similar characteristic of OBC and Other social group study club this social group together. To capture region specific variations Region dummies are also include.

The status of the family is identified through the education of household head, monthly per-capita consumption expenditure of household (MPEC) and family size of the household. Household head's education is classified into four classifications that are as follows; completed below primary level, primary, secondary and higher. We have taken natural logarithm of MPEC and number of person living together as size of household which is continuous variable[3].

2.1 Statistical Analysis

In this study, we have used two tools for analysis of the data. First is percentage relative gap (PGR) and second is Blinder-Oaxaca decomposition, for estimation of PGR present study use both 60th (2004) and 71th (2014) data and for B-O decomposition paper use only 71th (2014) data. The gender discrimination in education is measure through percentage gap ratio (PGR) in average annual educational expenses.

[1] EPWRF India Time Series.

[2] It's includes attendant charges, physiotherapy, personal medical appliances, blood, oxygen, etc.

[3] For detail description of Variables see Appendix A.

$$\text{PGR} = \frac{\textit{Average Annual Expenditure on Education for Male} - \textit{Average Annual Expenditure on Education for Female}}{\textit{Average Annual Expenditure on Education for Male}} * 100$$

An affirmative value of PGR shows gender bias in favor of male that means females are define at a disadvantage, whereas a negative assessment suggests the positive gender discrimination that means favoritism for female. However, percentage gap ratio is crude technique to measure gender discrimination in private health expenditure. So, there is need for econometric analysis, to find out whether this difference in health expenditure is caused by either difference in endowment (productive characteristic) or discrimination. There are basically two empirical methods for study gender discrimination in household resource allocation can be found in literature. The first is single equation model which includes gender as a predictor variable. Unluckily, this technique gives us biased result because it assumed health expenditure (household resource) structure is same for both male and female (Gunderson1989; Madheswaran & Attewell 2007). The second method employs a "decomposition technique" to partition the observed educational expenditure gap into two "endowment" and a "coefficient" components. The latter is derived as an unexplained residual and is termed the "discrimination coefficient". This method was developed by Blinder (1973) and Oaxaca (1973). We have employed Blinder-Oaxaca decomposition approach to identify gender difference in private health expenditure by household because of difference in individual characteristics and discrimination.

Subsequent the benchmark Oaxaca–Blinder (B-O), two distinct equations of the semi-log mathematical form for household health care expenses for both gender are anticipated based on ordinary least squares (OLS):

$$HE_m = \beta_m X_m + e_m \qquad \text{......................} (1)$$

$$HE_f = \beta_f X_f + e_f \qquad \text{......................} (2)$$

Where *HE* is the natural logarithm of private health care expenditure (365 day) in India, *X* is a vector of independent variables such as demographic and socio-economic factor and e is a random error term. The vector of independent variables controls for demographic, socio-economic and various other characteristics of patient. The OLS estimation of the above equations may be articulated as:

$$\overline{HE}_m = \beta_m \overline{X}_m \qquad \text{......................} (3)$$

$$\overline{HE}_f = \beta_f \overline{X}_f \qquad \text{......................} (4)$$

The bars indicate mean values of the independent variables and the caps symbolize OLS estimates. The divergence in per hospitalization private health care expenditure between the male and female can be articulated as:

$$\overline{HE}_m - \overline{HE}_f = \beta_m \overline{X}_m - \beta_f \overline{X}_f \qquad \text{......................} (5)$$

In absence of gender discrimination in per hospitalization private health care expenditure, that means average per-capita private health care expenditure (per hospitalization) is same in case of male (advantage group) and female (disadvantage group), then their average per-capita private health care expenditure would be given as:

$$\overline{HE}_f{}^* = \beta_m \overline{X}_f \qquad \text{......................} (6)$$

From equation (5) and (6), overall per-capita private health care expenditure gap between male and female can be expressed as:

$$\overline{HE}_m - \overline{HE}_f = \beta_f \overline{X}_m - \beta_f \overline{X}_f + \beta_m \overline{X}_f - \beta_f \overline{X}_m + \left(\beta_m \overline{X}_m - \beta_f \overline{X}_m - \beta_m \overline{X}_f + \beta_f \overline{X}_f\right) \qquad \text{......................} (7)$$

$$\beta_f\left(\overline{X}_m - \overline{X}_f\right) + \overline{X}_f\left(\beta_m - \beta_f\right) + \left(\overline{X}_m - \overline{X}_f\right)\left(\beta_m - \overline{X}_f\right) \qquad \text{......................} (8)$$

$$\beta_f \Delta\overline{X} + \overline{X}_f \Delta\beta + \Delta\overline{X}\Delta\beta \qquad \text{......................} (9)$$

$$\overline{HE}_m - \overline{HE}_f = E + C + EC \qquad \text{......................} (10)$$

Thus, the gap between male and female per-capita private health care expenditure can be explained on the basis of three dimensions. Where the first part (E) of the decomposition shows the element of the gap on the basis of gender in per-capita private health care expenditure due to differences in the personality of male and female members; it is called endowments effect (or due to the distribution of X_s), second one is 'C' is the element of the gender discrimination explained by gender differences in the plunder inward by male and female member with the same characteristics. Finally it is arising from interaction of endowment and coefficients (CE).

3. RESULT AND DISCUSSION

Results show that yearly household expenditure on health for different sex of family members are significantly different over the study period and on the other hand it become more vital during the last decade. Table one shows that in 2004 PRGs for rural area is 9.46 and 13.44 in urban areas. This indicates that in 2004 gender bias in household expenditure on health is very much visible in urban areas in comparison to rural area, but in 2014 PRG for rural area is 28.34 and 26.07, total opposite of 2004. It is evident that average yearly spending (AYS) is lowest for female patient in rural area. In case of male patient average yearly spending is highest.

In rural areas, average yearly spending per hospitalization for male and female in 2004 is 12359 and 11190 rupees respectively and 17261 and 14941 rupees respectively in urban area. But it became 19727 INR and 14136 INR in 2014 for male and female respectively in rural area.

Table 1 Average yearly spending per hospitalization (365 day) by gender and sector

Place of residence	2004			2014		
	Amount of spending (in INR)			Amount of spending (in INR)		
	Male	Female	PGR	Male	Female	PGR
Rural	12359	11190	9.46	19727	14136	28.34
Urban	17261	14941	13.44	30450	22511	26.07
All	13169	11747	10.80	23452	17103	27.07

Source: Authors estimation based on NSSO of 60th and 71th round unit level data.
PGR: Percentage Relative Gap.

Among the major type of household in India, self employed in agriculture in rural area female patient spends average 12370 rupees annually in 2004 and 15760 rupees annually in 2014, which is the highest for female patient in all other household categories. In case of male patient; self-employed non agriculture categories patient spends average 13286 rupees annually in 2004 and 23663 rupees annually in 2014 in rural areas; this is the highest Average yearly spending in all categories of household.

Table 2 Average yearly spending per hospitalization (365 day) by Household Type

Type of household	2004			2014		
	Amount of spending (AE (in INR)			Amount of spending (in INR)		
	Male	Female	PGR	Male	Female	PGR
Rural						
Self-employed in agriculture	13101	12370	5.58	22699	15760	30.57
Self-employed in non-agriculture	13286	8898	33.03	23663	13187	44.27
Casual labour in agriculture	7569	5715	24.50	13170	10036	23.79
Other	10123	11035	-9.01	17251	14552	15.64
Urban						
Self-employed	16357	13477	17.61	30912	24794	19.79
Regular wage/salary earning	19551	15747	19.46	32925	22649	31.21
Casual labour	6960	6668	4.19	16676	13993	16.09
Other	33102	28629	13.51	41660	26636	36.06

Source: Authors estimation based on NSSO of 60th and 71th round unit level data.

Social group is an important reality of India. To understand the gender discrimination in social group, percentage relative gap (PRG) in annual mean health care spending is computed and presented in Table 3. All the values of PRG in year 2004 and 2014 are positive, which indicate gender bias in favor of males.

Table 4 shows gender discrimination among deferent religious groups, namely Hindu, Muslim and others. Gender gap in health care expenditure is more significant for Hindu in 2004, but its gap is more vital in case of Muslim in 2014. Other social group which includes Christian, Sikh and other has negative gender deferential for health care spending.

Table 3 Average yearly spending per hospitalization (365 day) by Caste wise

Caste	2004			2014		
	Amount of spending (in INR)			Amount of spending (in INR)		
	Male	Female	PGR	Male	Female	PGR
ST	7778	6617	14.93	13835	13220	4.44
SC	9279	7830	15.61	15625	12131	22.36
OBC	11686	11371	2.70	23322	15792	32.29
Other	17313	14074	18.70	30300	23177	23.51

Source: Authors estimation based on NSSO of 60th and 71th round unit level data.

Table 4 Average yearly spending per hospitalization (365 day) by Religion wise

Religion	2004			2014		
	Amount of spending (in INR)			Amount of spending (in INR)		
	Male	Female	PGR	Male	Female	PGR
Hindu	13394	10912	18.53	23593	17502	25.82
Muslim	11517	10375	9.92	20234	14034	30.64
Other	11595	18446	-59.09	28431	18710	34.19

Source: Authors estimation based on NSSO of 60th and 71th round unit level data.

Table 6 shows that age group wise PRG of Average yearly spending per hospitalization. It is clear from the table that PGR is positive in all age group in 2004 and 2014 that indicates gender bias in favor of male child. But if we see the PRG of average annual expenditure per hospitalization in child categories we find that its value is very low in comparison to all other age group categories. It is also found that PGR value for child is 7.05 in 2004 which comes down to 2.15 in 2014.

Table 5 Average yearly spending per hospitalization (365 day) by Quintile wise

MPECQ	2004			2014		
	Amount of spending (in INR)			Amount of spending (in INR)		
	Male	Female	PGR	Male	Female	PGR
Poorest	6653	5991	9.96	14338	10261	28.44
Poor	9292	7753	16.57	14824	13486	9.03
Middle	12558	11005	12.37	17933	14101	21.37
Rich	14378	12843	10.68	23244	19090	17.87
Richest	24060	21508	10.61	50404	31791	36.93

Source: Authors estimation based on NSSO of 60th and 71th round unit level data.

On the basis of table 5 we can say that there is gender discrimination in average annual expenditure per hospitalization in favor of man in all the income categories and in both year 2004 and 2014.

Table 6 Average yearly spending per hospitalization (365 day) by age wise

Age Group	2004			2014		
	Amount of spending (in INR)			Amount of spending (in INR)		
	Male	Female	PGR	Male	Female	PGR
Child	7044	6547	7.05	12687	12414	2.15
Working	14936	12424	16.82	23576	17319	26.54
Aged	15961	14230	10.84	33135	19372	41.54
All	13169	11747	10.80	23452	17103	27.07

Source: Authors estimation based on NSSO of 60th and 71th round unit level data.

Table 7 Average yearly spending per hospitalization (365 day) by age wise

Level of education HH	2004			2014		
	Amount of spending (in INR)			Amount of spending (in INR)		
	Male	Female	PGR	Male	Female	PGR
Illiterate				16503	12824	22.29
Primary				20222	13622	32.64
Secondary				23901	17761	25.69
Higher				41447	30441	26.55
All	13169	11747	10.80	23452	17103	27.07

Source: Authors estimation based on NSSO of 60th and 71th round unit level data.

From table 7 we can say that Average yearly spending per hospitalization increases with the increase in parent education but gender discrimination in favor of male also increases with increase in education.

Gender discrimination based on PRGs in annual average household health care expenditure is greater in urban areas than rural areas in both year 2004 and 2014.

The simple observations are sufficient to go for an investigation into gender bias in household health care spending. To measure the discrimination in terms of quantity a well defined methodology is used.

It is important to use a well defined methodology to measure discrimination in quantifiable terms. The finding from table 4 indicates that all independent variables are significant except cast for both rural and urban household.

Table 8 Results from Oaxaca decomposition model: Contribution endowments and coefficients effects to gender difference in health care expenditure

Model Summary			Variables	Endowments			Coefficients		
	Coefficients	Standard error		Coefficient	Standard error	% of contribution	Coefficient	Standard error	% of contribution
Male	8.784***	0.008	MPCE	–0.0029***	0.0008	-5.9	0.038*	0.017	45.9
Female	8.654***	0.008	Type of household	0.0008	0.0005	1.7	–0.005	0.012	-6.6
Difference	0.131***	0.012	Place of residence	–0.0011**	0.0004	-2.1	–0.017	0.010	-20.5
Explained	0.049***	0.004	Caste	–0.0002	0.0011	-0.3	0.025	0.019	30.2
Unexplained	0.082***	0.015	Religion	0.0008*	0.0003	1.6	0.003	0.021	3.2
Explained (%)	37.8	-	Education	0.0547***	0.0028	110.8	0.051**	0.015	62.2

Unexplained (%)	62.2	-	Age	−0.0038**	0.0015	−7.8	−0.109***	0.020	−132.4
			Household size	0.0001	0.0007	0.3	0.045*	0.024	55.2
			Region	0.0009	0.0008	1.8	0.028*	0.015	33.7
			Constant	-	-	-	0.024	0.056	29.2
			Total	0.0494	-	100.0	0.082	-	100.0

*** $p<0.001$, ** $p<0.01$, * $p<0.05$

MPCE is positively significant at 5 percent level of significance. Variables like household size and educational status of the head are also positively significant. Age of the head of household is also important variable determining household spending on health on different member of the household. Religion is significant at 5 percent level of significant. So from the above analysis of the regression table we can say that MPCE, household size, educational status, age, religion type of household are significant determinants of spending on health of household members.

4. CONCLUSION

At first, it is clear from the data there is clear increase in average yearly spending per hospitalization in both male and female categories as well as urban and rural categories. The analysis also shows that there is significant increase in the gender discrimination in favor of male in household expenditure on health in India. This increase in gender discrimination is found both urban and rural areas of India. It is evident from the data that in case of Child, there is decrease gender discrimination in household expenditure on health over the time, but other age group does not follow this pattern. Increase in level of education is positively associated with increases in average annual household expenditure on health. It is also found that gender discrimination in favor of male also increases with increase in education. Mean health expenditure for female is not only; always lower than that of male irrespective of type of social as well as economic group and survey rounds but this gap is also increase significantly over the period of time. The result indicate that there visible differences in the nature of gender discrimination in favor of male in different socio economic indicators in India.

REFERENCES

Asfaw A, Klasen S, Lamanna F. (2007). Intra-household gender disparities in children's medical care before death in India. Institute for the Study of Labor (IZA) Discussion Paper.

Asfaw A, Lamanna F, Klasen S. (2010). Gender gap in parents' financing strategy for hospitalization of their children: evidence from India. *Health economics*. 19(3):265–79.

Behrman JR (1988). Intrahousehold allocation of nutrients in rural India: Are boys favored? Do parents exhibit inequality aversion? *Oxford Economic Papers*. 1:32–54.

Bongaarts J, Guilmoto CZ (2015). How many more missing women? Excess female mortality and prenatal sex selection, *Population and Development Review*. 41(2):241–69.

Bora JK, Saikia N. (2015). Gender Differentials in Self-Rated Health and Self-Reported Disability among Adults in India. *PloS one*. 10(11):e0141953.

Canudas-Romo V, Saikia N, Diamondsmith N. (2015). The contribution of age-specific mortality towards male and female life expectancy differentials in India and selected States, 1970–2013. *Asia-Pacific Population Journal* 30:(2).

Hill K, Upchurch DM (1995). Gender differences in child health: evidence from the demographic and health surveys. *Population and Development Review*.

Kurz K M, Johnson-Welch C. (1997). Gender differences among children 0–5 years: an opportunity for child survival interventions. A review paper prepared for the BASICS project. USAID/BASICS II, Arlington, VA.

Maharana, B., & Ladusingh, L. (2014). Gender disparity in health and food expenditure in India among elderly. *International Journal of Population Research, 2014*.

Pande RP (2003). Selective gender differences in childhood nutrition and immunization in rural India: the role of siblings. *Demography*. 40(3):395–418.

Pandey A, Sengupta PG, Mondal SK, Gupta DN, Manna B, Ghosh S, et al. (2002). Gender differences in healthcare-seeking during common illnesses in a rural community of West Bengal, India. *Journal of Health, Population and Nutrition*. 306–11.

Willis JR, Kumar V, Mohanty S, Singh P, Singh V, Baqui AH, et al. (2009). Gender differences in perception and care-seeking for illness of newborns in rural Uttar Pradesh, India. *Journal of health, population, and nutrition* 27(1):62.

Roy K, Chaudhuri A. (2008). Influence of socioeconomic status, wealth and financial empowerment on gender differences in health and healthcare utilization in later life: evidence from India. *Social science & medicine*. 66(9):1951–62.

Saikia N, Jasilionis D, Ram F, Shkolnikov VM (2011). Trends and geographic differentials in mortality under age 60 in India. *Population studies*. 65(1):73–89.

Saikia, N., & Bora, J. K. (2016). Gender difference in health-care expenditure: evidence from India human development survey. *PloS one, 11*(7), e0158332.

Sudha SS, Rajan SI (1999). Female demographic disadvantage in India 1981–1991: Sex selective abortions and female infanticide. *Development and change*. 30(3):585–618.

Appendix 1 Description of dichotomous and numeric variables included in the generalized linear regression and Oaxaca decomposition models

Categorical variables	Code	Description	Code	Description
Type of household	0	Self Employed[4]	1	Wage Employed
Place of residence	0	Rural	1	Urban
Caste	0	SC and ST	1	OBC and General
Religion	0	Hindu	1	Others
Region	0	Southern and North-eastern states	1	Northern States
Time dummy	0	2004	1	2014
Numeric variables	**Mean**	**SD**	**Minimum**	**Maximum**
MPCE	5.7	4.0	0	12.5
Education	2.8	1.9	1	7
Age	38.3	22.3	0	110
Household size	5.4	2.7	1	40

Note: SD: Standard deviation

[4] More than 50% income of the household's comes from self employment during the 365 days.

A Case Study on Agrovoltaic: Technology for Rural Infrastructure Development

VVG Sai Sreekar
Student
Veermata Jijabai Technological Institute, Mumbai

Nandini Ashish Gaikwad
Student
Veermata Jijabai Technological Institute, Mumbai

Tushar Sathe
Assistant Professor
Veermata Jijabai Technological Institute, Mumbai

Abstract: Electricity and water are two very essential factors every farmer across the globe is concerned about. The availability of electricity for various farming operations are still very limited in the developing country like India. Generation of electricity from conventional power plant requires huge infrastructure and sometimes it becomes very difficult to supply the generated electricity to the remote rural areas. The depth of ground water is also increasing year by year and it becomes very imperative to somehow increase the water level below the earth surface. Considering the necessity of electricity and water harvesting; agrovoltaic with rain water harvesting system is proposed in the present research work. Agrovoltaic stands for system that utilizes same arable land for the production of crops and generation of electricity from solar panels. Agrovoltaic with rain water harvesting system can generate electricity, produced conventional crops and deposit rain water from the same piece of land that used for farming. The theoretical case study is performed in the present research work for Indian conditions and it is observed that the proposed system can be a viable solution for the farmers issues related to basic water and energy requirements. The proposed system can also be employ for animal's shelter and other aligned applications. The possible challenges for the efficient utilization of proposed system like crop compatibility, effect of solar panels shadow and other issues are also enlightened in the current research work. The payback period of around 9-10yrs is observed from the present study with initial investment cost of around 8 million for Maize as a crop. The average annual income for farmers is also estimated to be around 0.8 million with additional benefits of rain water harvesting.

Keywords: **Agrovoltaic, water harvesting, rural infrastructure, Land equivalent ratio**

1. INTRODUCTION

According to the World Bank collection of development indicators, the total agricultural land in India was around 60.45% till 2016 and considering gross irrigated crop area, India stands first in the world (World Bank, 2021). India has a population of over 1.36 billion at present, which is rising progressively and with the increase of population, there is a steady increase for the land requirement to house these inhabitants. However, it is evident that the actual proportion of the land available in the country cannot be expanded physically. Hence, this calls for the flexible and versatile use of the available land for multiple purposes simultaneously. The importance of solar energy utilization for the generation of electricity using Photovoltaic (PV) power plant has also increased remarkably in recent times; however, the land requirement for installation of the PV power plant has been considered to be very serious issue (Sathe and Dhoble, 2017). Presently, many researchers around the world are working on utilization of available arable land for the multiple possible applications. One such method is termed as "Agrovoltaic" (AV) which can be broken down into two segments: Agro and Voltaic.

Fig. 1 Agrovoltaic system (Weselek *et al.*, 2019)

"Agro" refers to the science and technology of producing and using crops for agriculture, called Agronomy; "Voltaic" refers to photovoltaic which relates to the production of electric current at the junction of two substances that are exposed to light. Hence, Agrovoltaics is the usage of the same piece of land for producing solar power as well as for agriculture. Since it refers to the coexistence of both crops in the farmland and the photovoltaic solar panels, it implies that between these two types of production, there is a sharing of light received from the sun. The most assiduously researched types of agrovoltaics are the following three types: greenhouse solar array, solar arrays with space between for crops, and stilted solar arrays above crops. To maximize the amount of solar energy absorbed in the crops and panels, these types take into account several variables such as the tilt angle of the solar panels, location, height of panels, intensity of solar radiation, and climate of the location. Since the agrovoltaic technique is not suitable for a lot of crops, crop selection also plays a vital role in this system (Dinesh and Pearce, 2016).

Many researchers theoretically analyzed the importance of combined utilization of farm land and photovoltaic system and they concluded that agrovoltaic has high potential in today's world, even though it has its weaknesses and challenges. They also emphasized that to achieve clean energy goals, it is important to consider availability of land in energy planning (Amaducci, Yin and Colauzzi, 2018).

Moreover, there is a massive shortage of water in numerous parts of India. India being a country which pumps the maximum quantity of groundwater; out of all the nations, and has reached a severe groundwater depletion and contamination stage. India, the world's seventh largest economy and second largest country, has fallen prey to destabilization due to dirty aquifers and water paucity. It is plainly evident that this has motivated a fair number of farmers to use wastewater to raise their crops. Hence, it is imperative that there must be abundant harvesting of rain water, at least enough for the farmers to irrigate their acreage and for their daily use.

In India, renewable resources like solar, biomass, and wind are abundant and widely distributed, and there is significant potential for agriculture to be involved in their production and consumption. They have the potential to present solutions to the indelible energy problems faced by developing countries like India and their optimal use can minimize the impacts on the environment and produce minimum secondary waste. These renewable technologies are considered sustainable and clean and provide opportunities for extenuation of the emission of greenhouse gases and reduction of global warming by providing substitutes for nonrenewable energy resources. Hence, by the multiuse of a single piece of acreage for both agriculture and harnessing solar energy, not only can it be incorporated for cultivation of crops but also for using the solar energy for infrastructure development by production of electricity, internet, subsume rain water harvesting and so on (Amaducci, Yin and Colauzzi, 2018).

In the present research work, considering the need of maximum utilization of available land for the development of rural infrastructures in India; agrovoltaic with rain water harvesting system is proposed. Energy and water are the two basic requirements for the efficient farming; and the proposed system can be a more prominent solution to fulfill these basic demands from the farmers. A theoretical case study has also been carried out to understand the benefits of utilizing proposed AV system.

2. LITERATURE REVIEW

Agrovoltaic system is very new technology and considering its usefulness for overall development of nations infrastructure; recently, many researchers are performing several simulation and experimental studies for its efficient applicability to various region across the world with diverse relevant crops.

(Dupraz *et al.*, 2011) performed simulation study on utilization of same land for the combined PV panels and durum wheat crops. STICS crop model was used for the simulation. The term Land equivalent ratio were introduced to predict the land productivity with proposed agrovoltaic system. They observed 35-73% increase in global land productivity with the two different densities of PV arrays. It was also noted that the wheat crop yield were reduced by 19% with the 57% reduction in available radiations. (Barron-Gafford *et al.*, 2019) investigated the physical and biological impact of proposed agrovoltaic systems. Microclimatic conditions under PV arrays, PV panel temperature, soil moisture and water irrigation were monitored and analyzed during an experimentations. They observed reduction in PV surface temperature in agrovoltaic system compared to conventional system. The cumulative CO2 uptake were found to be greater in two of the three studied corps and water retention in soil were also slightly more in agrovoltaic system. (Marrou *et al.*, 2013) performed experimentally investigations on agrovoltaic systems. Three different food corps were selected for the analysis during three different weather seasons. Microclimatic conditions of corps were measured and analyzed to understand the effect of PV panels on the crop productivity. The results were observed for three system configurations includes: full PV density, half PV density and no PV density. It was concluded that the agrovoltaic needs little adaptations in cropping practices for its efficient utilization. (Agostini, Colauzzi and Amaducci, 2021) showed that AV performs similar to ground PVs, and are better than other energy resources except for wind energy. They observed that the AV system improves air quality and decreases greenhouse emission. They concluded that the AV systems has potential to increase or stabilize non irrigated crops in arid conditions by customizing specific conditions. The cost of AV is higher than ground PVs, but comparable, 14 /17 sustainable goals satisfied set by the UN.

(Proctor and Murthy, 2021) estimated the AV array cost at $1.12 trillion for a 35-year life project and $2.04 trillion revenue with a simple payback in 17 years, net difference between AV systems and traditional systems was $338.8 billion over 35 years project life. The US farmland occupancy requirement was observed to be 0.94%. AV systems for lithium storage would give a simple payback of 20 years. They found that the NPV of the system is most sensitive to changes in the electricity price, capacity factor, capital expenditures, and discount rate. The study to determine the impacts of agrovoltaic systems on the environment was conducted by (Ott *et al.*, 2020). The type of crop to be used and their water consumption was studied including the design of the PV systems. The result stated that hybrid agrovoltaic systems can reduce the water consumption by crops. (Andrew, 2020) conducted study to compare the pasture production and lamb growth in open pasture lands and under solar panels in spring of 2019 and 2020 in Oregon. The results showed that solar panels can increase the land productivity and create an environment which was more animal welfare friendly. (Malu, Sharma and Pearce, 2017) studied the Agrovoltaic potential on grape farms in India. First, the grape farm's economic and electricity potential benefits were analyzed, a sensitivity analysis was performed for geographical location, selection of modules, inverters, panel row spacing, selection of axis and azimuth angle. Results showed that the economic value of grape farm were increased 15 times than that of conventional farming with same production of grapes. (Poonia *et al.*, 2022) studied agrovoltaics with three experimental designs with three separate blocks. The crops which could tolerate a certain degree of shade and required less amount of water were chosen. The results showed that the agrovoltaics can be used not only for generating electricity but also for rain water harvesting during the rainy season.

(Hassanpour *et al.*, 2020) studied the remarkable agrovoltaic influence on soil moisture, micrometeorology, and water-use efficiency. Understood the microclimatology and other factors using AV arrays. After 2 years of installation, using neutron probe reading, 90% more biomass and, higher soil moisture were observed. Changes in relative humidity, temperature and 328% more water efficiency were also studied during the analysis. (Santra *et al.*, 2018) designed the 105 KW and 25 KW AV systems with the rain harvesting method. During experimentations 1.5 lakh liter water was harvested. Annual income generated was 7 lakhs per acre, and cost of installation was 55 lakhs. The payback period was calculated to be around 9 to 10 years. (Cho *et al.*, no date) examined the agrovoltaic farming impact on crops using energy information and communications technology. The grape cultivated land was divided in 6 sections and in 3 sections PV panels were installed. They recorded the electricity generated and concluded that agrovoltaic farming would not have a negative impact on grape farming.

Agrovoltaic can also be combined with animal farming or providing shelter to various farm animals. (Sharpe and Heins, 2021) studied the effects of PV systems on grazing cattle where they were provided shade under a 30 kW PV system. It was concluded that this could increase the wellbeing of cows by reducing the intensity of heat stress and also increase the land use efficiency. (Lytle *et al.*, 2020) analysed the pasture-raised and solar farming. They designed a rabbit based agrovoltaic system and performed economic analysis of PV and rabbit farming. They observed 1.4% to 7.9% reduction of operation and maintenance cost for rabbit inhabited solar farms. The economic gains were ranged from 1 to 17.1% considering solar revenue per acres of land. The PV structures were also found to be effective for cost saving as it was useful for fencing and shelter for the rabbits.

It is evident from the literature that the agrovoltaic systems have huge potential to fulfil ever increasing demand of food and energy of the mankind. In India, agrovoltaic systems combined with some other renewable and energy conservation techniques like rain water harvesting can certainly solved some of the very serious issues that farmers are facing like: land availability, scarcity of water and electricity. Agrovoltaic can also be used for the animal shelter and will be very helpful to increase the overall land utilization.

3. PROPOSED AV WITH RAIN WATER HARVESTING SYSTEM

Fig. 2 shows the proposed agrovoltaic system combined with rain water harvesting technology. It can be observed that the solar panels are tilted and thus using certain tube arrangements, rain water can be collected and deposited in the storage tanks.

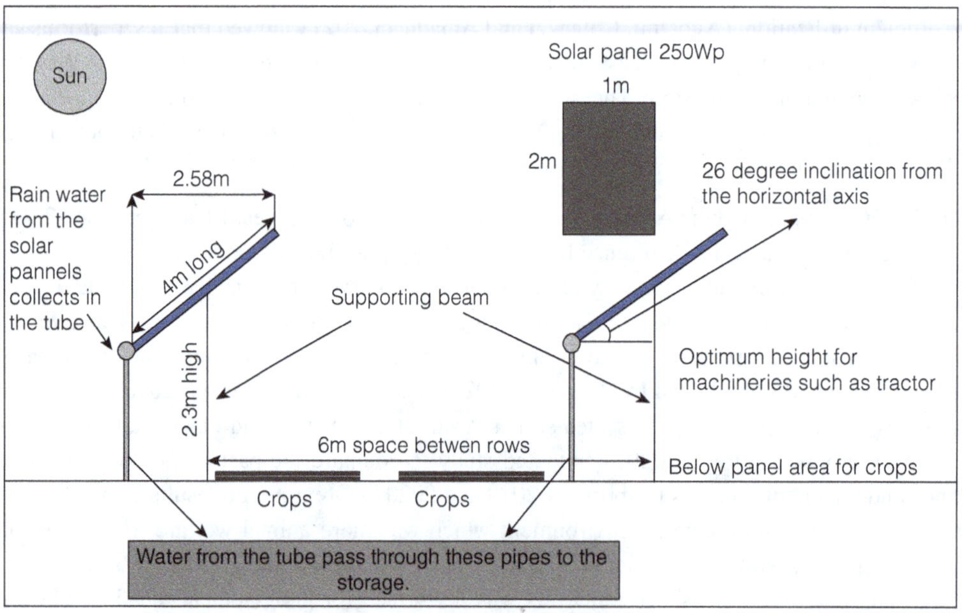

Fig. 2 Proposed Agrovoltaic with rain water harvesting system

The dimensions and system variables are selected based on the practical applicability. Solar panel inclination angle is fixed in the present study; however, tracking mechanism can also be implemented to get more PV panel effectiveness.

3.1 System configurations and methodology

The structure is assumed to be laid on 1 acre square land. The height of the supporting panel beam to ground is 7-8 feet, this is to prevent any hindrances during crop cultivation and make convenient use of modern machineries. Spacing between each solar panel is selected to be 0.6m, making 70 panels in a 63m long column. Each row is separated with a distance of 6m from the vertical supporting beam, so there will be 9 rows on a 63m long row. Optimum spacing is provided even between solar panels to have proportionate distribution of sunlight for the crops, and also having abundant land for crop growth. Taking advantage of the slope in PV panel's rain water harvesting system can be constructed, which will provide us with copious amount of water supply during scarcity. A total of 630 PV panels are structured with 26 degree tilt angle, having an average capacity of 250 Wp. The crop which can provide some shading tolerance such as Maize, Spinach, basil, sugar beetroot, lettuce, corn, swiss, chard, kale, pepper, broccoli, white asparagus, cranberry and so on can be used for performance analysis. Various agriculture practices can also be implemented in this system, such as hydroponics, polyculture, intercrop yielding, and more, which may bring a leap in profit, but in this scenario maize is selected as our major crop to calculate and analyze the income, investment, payback period, NPV, and other estimations. Price vary with crops, and in this structure maize is selected, which is the lowest income source. Maize is considered to calculate the maximum payback time, NPV, LER, and risk factors.

Diminutive investments such as providing electricity for agriculture practices, irrigation pumps, when summed can coalesce into a huge amount. These investments can be compensated by PV panels and rainwater harvesting systems. Extra income can also be collected with the remaining electricity according to the tariff rates. This way farmers will be self-sufficient having abundant electricity, water supply for their own use and as a source of their income. Solar panels have a life cycle period of 25 years, and the maximum payback time is 9-12 years, which leaves us 13-16 years of profit.

4. RESULT

AV system decreases evapotranspiration rates, which reduces the consumption of water for crops and increase moisture and micro culture of soil. More biomass productivity is obtained, Greenhouse gas emissions are decreased, and air quality is refined.

Approximately as estimated in the table 1, a part of 551.25 KW/day of the energy shall be sufficient to practice modern agriculture methods including machineries, and the remaining can be used to generate income using tariffs. Around 1.5 lakh liters of rainwater harvested will draw out water scarcity and can be used for irrigation and other essential purposes.

Table 1 AV with rain water harvesting system specifications and output

Components of AV with rain water harvesting	Specifications/values/output
Dimensions of solar PV panel having 250Wp average capacity	2m long and 1m wide
Inclination of solar panels.	26 degree from horizontal axis passing through supporting beam
Area of land including all other spaces	1 acre (assuming 63m long and 63m wide)
Maximum PV panels in each column (63m long) and spacing between each solar panel	70 panels and 0.6m $(0.6x + (Y/2) = 63, x = y + 1)$ Where, x = number of spaces between solar panels Y = number of solar panels.
Maximum number of rows (63m wide) and spacing between each row	9 rows and 6m $(6x + 2.58y = 63, x = y + 1)$ Where, x = number of spaces between solar panels. Y = number of solar panels.
PV panel efficiency and its life cycle period.	15-22% efficiency for 25 years
Annual Avg availability of solar radiation throughout India	4KWH/m^2/day
Maximum PV capacity on 1 acre land	70*9*250 = 157.5 KWp
Average effective availability of solar radiation in hours per day for electricity generation in India	3 - 5 hrs.
Average electricity generation per day per KWp for India	1KWp * 4hrs = 4KWh or 4units

Components of AV with rain water harvesting	Specifications/values/output
Average electricity generation for 1 acre land per day	157.5KWp * 4KWh/KW/day = 630 KWh/day
Average PV generated electricity tariff (according to 2020)	Rs.4/KWh
Average PV income generated for 300 days on 1 acre land according to the current price rate	7.56 lakhs annually
Cost of installment of PV panels (taking 49 Rs per Wp) including the installation, maintenance and other diminutive investments	49*157500 + 3 lakhs = 80 lakhs
Approximate rainwater harvested in 1 acre land from 157.5KWp AVS.	1.5 lakh liter
Income from Crop yield	0.5 - 0.6 lakhs annually (maize) Price vary with crops

Net present value (NPV) and Land Equivalent ratio (LER) is positive for this structure, making it feasible. Even taking cases into consideration with maximum investment and minimum income, this structure is viable. The maximum payback time of 15 years is estimated, with optimum income and minimal investments.

5. CHALLENGES AND OPPORTUNITIES

Initial investment is quite high as shown in the table 1. The income source is mainly dependent on the crops, so income becomes a variable feature, which cannot be determined with certain surety, as crop yield depends on climatic conditions, nature of the crop, yield time, etc. Only some particular crops have been identified for cultivation. Tariff values also varies, which makes it difficult task to calculate the payback time, IRR, NPV and LER. But, in every case AV system is practical.

Using versatile cultivation and cropping methods such as hydroponics, polyculture, greater income can be generated. PV panels with mirror backsides might also increase the light availability for the crops by multiple reflections of the incoming light not captured by the solar panels. AV systems could boost service industries in rural communities where new systems are installed and can also create employment in this sector.

6. CONCLUSION

In the present research work brief literature review on agrovoltaic systems are discussed. Considering need of electricity and water harvesting for the country like India, a case study on AV with rain water harvesting systems are proposed with Maize as a crop. The outcome from the case study shows very promising results in terms of farmers overall income, electricity generation and rain water harvesting. Rural infrastructure development is very challenging task; however, incorporation of proposed system on arable land can not only solved the farmer's basic requirement issues, but it can also beneficial for the overall development of the rural area. The development can be in the form of electricity availability, internet connectivity, support to animal farming and so on. It can be concluded that, the installation AV with rain water harvesting infrastructure on the farmers arable land can be very beneficial for not only individual farmers income; but also for nations overall development. The actual experimental work on the proposed system will be carried out in near future.

REFERENCES

Agostini, A., Colauzzi, M. and Amaducci, S. (2021) 'Innovative agrivoltaic systems to produce sustainable energy: An economic and environmental assessment', *Applied Energy*. Elsevier Ltd, 281 (June 2020), p. 116102. doi: 10.1016/j.apenergy.2020.116102.

Amaducci, S., Yin, X. and Colauzzi, M. (2018) 'Agrivoltaic systems to optimise land use for electric energy production', *Applied Energy*, 220, pp. 545–561. doi: https://doi.org/10.1016/j.apenergy.2018.03.081.

Andrew, A. (2020) *Lamb growth and pasture production in agrivoltaic production system*. Oregon State University.

Barron-Gafford, G. A. *et al.* (2019) 'Agrivoltaics provide mutual benefits across the food–energy–water nexus in drylands', *Nature Sustainability*, 2(9), pp. 848–855. doi: 10.1038/s41893-019-0364-5.

Cho, J. *et al.* (no date) 'Application of Photovoltaic Systems for Agriculture: A Study on the Relationship between Power Generation and Farming for the Improvement of Photovoltaic Applications in Agriculture', pp. 1–18.

Dinesh, H. and Pearce, J. M. (2016) 'The potential of agrivoltaic systems', *Renewable and Sustainable Energy Reviews*, 54, pp. 299–308. doi: https://doi.org/10.1016/j.rser.2015.10.024.

Dupraz, C. *et al.* (2011) 'Combining solar photovoltaic panels and food crops for optimising land use: Towards new agrivoltaic schemes', *Renewable Energy*, 36(10), pp. 2725–2732. doi: https://doi.org/10.1016/j.renene.2011.03.005.

Hassanpour, E. *et al.* (2020) 'Remarkable agrivoltaic influence on soil moisture, micrometeorology and water-use efficiency'. doi: 10.7267/N9W37T8D.Funding.

Lytle, W. *et al.* (2020) 'Conceptual design and rationale for a new agrivoltaics concept: Pastured-raised rabbits and solar farming', *Journal of Cleaner Production*. Elsevier Ltd, (xxxx), p. 124476. doi: 10.1016/j.jclepro.2020.124476.

Malu, P. R., Sharma, U. S. and Pearce, J. M. (2017) 'Agrivoltaic potential on grape farms in India', *Sustainable Energy Technologies and Assessments*, 23, pp. 104–110. doi: https://doi.org/10.1016/j.seta.2017.08.004.

Marrou, H. *et al.* (2013) 'Microclimate under agrivoltaic systems: Is crop growth rate affected in the partial shade of solar panels?', *Agricultural and Forest Meteorology*, 177, pp. 117–132. doi: https://doi.org/10.1016/j.agrformet.2013.04.012.

Ott, E. M. *et al.* (2020) 'Environmental Analysis of Agrivoltaic Systems', *Reference Module in Earth Systems and Environmental Sciences*, (January). doi: 10.1016/b978-0-12-819727-1.00012-1.

Poonia, S. *et al.* (2022) 'Popular Kheti', 3(3), pp. 128–133.

Proctor, K. W. and Murthy, G. S. (2021) 'Agrivoltaics Align with Green New Deal Goals While Supporting Investment in the US ' Rural Economy', pp. 1–11.

Santra, P. *et al.* (2018) 'Agri-voltaic system: crop production and photovoltaic-based electricity generation from a single land unit', *Indian Farming*, 68(01), pp. 20–23.

Sathe, T. M. and Dhoble, A. S. (2017) 'A review on recent advancements in photovoltaic thermal techniques', *Renewable and Sustainable Energy Reviews*. Elsevier Ltd, 76(October 2016), pp. 645–672. doi: 10.1016/j.rser.2017.03.075.

Sharpe, K. T. and Heins, B. J. (2021) 'Evaluation of solar photovoltaic systems to shade cows in a pasture-based dairy herd', *Journal of Dairy Science*. American Dairy Science Association. doi: 10.3168/jds.2020-18821.

World Bank (2021) Agricultural land (% of land area) - India, World Development Indicators. Available at: https://data.worldbank.org/indicator/AG.LND.AGRI.ZS?end=2016&locations=IN&start=1961&vi ew=chart.

Weselek, A. *et al.* (2019) 'Agrophotovoltaic systems: applications, challenges, and opportunities. A review', *Agronomy for Sustainable Development*. Agronomy for Sustainable Development, 39(4). doi: 10.1007/s13593-019-0581-3.

Reclaiming and Rejuvenating Urban Water Bodies: Case of Mullassery Canal, Kochi, Kerala

Akhila N Menon
Research Scholar
National Institute of Technology, Hamirpur

Puneet Sharma
Assistant Professor
National Institute of Technology, Hamirpur

Abstract: Water bodies play an important role in shaping the environmental, social and economic aspects of communities in an urban setting. Recent rapid urbanization and population growth has resulted in enormous degradation of such natural resources. Unchecked encroachment and pollution are continuously threatening the ecosystem services provided by these water bodies. Mullassery Canal, a tidal canal that flows through the city of Kochi in Kerala, India is one such example. This paper attempts to establish a framework for rejuvenation of urban water bodies for sustainable city development. First section of the paper explores various methods employed for improving deteriorated water bodies through various case examples. The second section lists out factors instrumental in restoration of the canal and prioritizes the first course of action through AHP. Subsequently, the evaluation and identification of the most vulnerable segment of the canal is performed through field study, interviews and visual analysis so as to begin the restoration process with that segment. The last section illustrates the reclamation and rejuvenation process through daylighting/de-culverting and the design interventions involving Low Impact Development (LID). The results indicate the suitability of employing daylighting process in addressing the most pressing concerns regarding the restoration of the canal. The proposed interventions are also instrumental in enhancing the environmental, social and economic qualities of the area.

Keywords: **Urban water bodies, Rejuvenation, Daylighting, Low Impact Development**

1. INTRODUCTION

The water bodies in the city of Kochi are indispensable to its environment, economy and tourism. The system comprising of canals, rivers and the backwaters have been the source of livelihood and used for transportation and recreation since antiquity. But, with the passage of time, many of these have fallen prey to deterioration due to unchecked developmental activities like encroachment and pollution stemming from improper waste management. One such water body is Mullassery Canal that flows through the heart of the Central Business District (CBD) in the city of Kochi (Mathew, 2005).

Mullassery Canal, a tidal canal, primarily served the purpose of directing the stormwater runoff from the central city into the Vembanad backwaters on its western end and the Thevara-Perandoor canal on its eastern end. The canal was also instrumental in navigation and fishing. In the present times, these purposes are not being fulfilled due to the anthropogenic interferences in its course. The dumping of solid waste and sewage, combined with culverting and construction of structures over it have impeded the flow of water in the canal, thus rendering it stagnant and anoxic, making it a breeding ground for diseases (Mathew, 2005). Adding to this is the insufficiency of the canal in carrying the stormwater runoff due to smaller cross-sections in particular areas, leading to floods in the core city even with an average amount of rainfall.

Water bodies, especially rivers, offer numerous ecosystem services to urban communities (Yang and Zhao, 2014). Thus, maintaining healthy water bodies is imperative to the sustainable development of their watershed area. The research article identifies the causes of deterioration of Mullassery canal and propose solutions for improving its current state.

2. LITERATURE REVIEW

A literature study was undertaken to examine the role of urban water bodies, the causes of their deterioration and methods of their eventual restoration. Often, water bodies in urban areas are a source of water supply, provide natural security and recreational features. They are rich in biodiversity, assist multiple ecological processes and advance urban development with its environmental, social and economic qualities (Yang and Zhao, 2014). It has been observed that urbanization, measures for prevention of flood damage, reclamation of land for agriculture and other interventions have caused degradation of the water bodies and associated ecosystems (Logar et al., 2019). Developing countries are more prone to urban flooding owing to the poor design and management of drainage systems. Dumping of solid waste clogs waterways and contaminates them, leading to floods during heavy rainfall. Adding to this is the increasing proportion of impervious surfaces that is associated with rapid urbanization which prevents percolation of water into the ground (Pervin *et al.*, 2020).

Out of the multiple procedures followed for restoration and rejuvenation of urban water bodies, daylighting or de-culverting was found to be more frequently used for the ones that are partially or fully buried underground. Stream daylighting refers to "the practice of removing streams from buried conditions and exposing them to the earth's surface in order to directly or indirectly enhance the ecological/economic and/or socio-cultural wellbeing of a region and its inhabitants" (Khirfan *et al.*, 2020). Urban stream daylighting has benefits encompassing ecological, economic and social aspects and are undertaken for a variety of reasons ranging from improvement of aquatic habitat to recreational purposes (Buchholz and Younos, 2007). These benefits include management of excess stormwater runoff, alleviation of urban heat island effect, enhancement of urban sustainability and creation of habitats and improved biodiversity that helps in climate change adaptation. Daylighting also helps in revitalizing neighborhoods and increasing property values that benefits nearby businesses which justifies the expenditure (Khirfan *et al.*, 2020).

The most well-known of such projects is the revitalization of Cheonggyecheon stream in Seoul, South Korea (Seoul Solution, 2014; Chung et al., 2012; Kee-yeon, 2006; Lee et al., 2020). Flowing through the dense downtown area, buried under an elevated highway, this stream underwent daylighting to create a waterfront space, improve the environment and restore the historical value. Laojie river in Taoyuan City, Taiwan is another such case where a channelized, piped river in a dense urban area was reshaped into an accessible green space through daylighting (Chou, 2016). Daylighting along with ecohydrology principles were used to create a framework for the evaluation of Ayamama river in Istanbul, Turkey which has endured extensive damages stemming from the growth of the city (Delibas and Tezer, 2017). Another similar scenario can be observed with the ancient Navigli canal system in Milan, Italy which was covered up in the course of urbanization. In the recent years, initiatives were taken to daylight this network of canals sensing the importance of urban waterways (Sibilla *et al.*, 2017). Low Impact Development (LID) techniques have also been found to be effective in controlling stormwater runoff and have been used in conjunction with stream daylighting methods (Palanisamy and Chui, 2015). The similarities between the contexts of these projects and the canal in question suggest the suitability of employing daylighting as a part of the procedure for its rejuvenation.

It was also noted that many such restoration works have taken into account the public opinion on the proposal by means of survey and the responses gauged on monetary or other basis. This has helped direct the project to be more beneficial to the largest group of stakeholders, the locals. Most of these have been carried out to provide the population with green open spaces, boosting the environmental and recreational aspects (Bae, 2011), which would have a significant positive impact on the residents. The preferred level of interaction of the public with the water body and their perception of its current condition can determine the decisions regarding the degree of restoration to a large extent (Brouwer et al., 2016; Chen et al. 2018). Locals assign a high value towards improving the ecological status of water bodies as they are aware of the ecosystem services derived from it (Kunwar et al., 2020). Provision for recreational activities was also found to be a strong reason for supporting revitalization of water bodies (Logar *et al.*, 2019).

From the literature it is quite evident that rejuvenation process is contextual; and along with the environmental and engineering inputs, one needs to consider the community participation for sustainable solutions. From literature various influential factors have also been extracted and analyzed on basis of appropriate tools.

3. METHODOLOGY

This paper employs a combination of primary and secondary data collected through visual survey, in-person interviews, literature study, official documents and survey drawings from the Corporation of Cochin along with newspaper reports to determine the issues associated with the canal. In the process more than twenty research articles and reports were reviewed to critically retrieve the actual site conditions and stakeholders. The entire stretch of the canal has been divided into segments based on character of the area imparted to them by the structures and activities nearby. This helps in focusing the proposed restoration process on the most vulnerable segment. The identification of vulnerability is based on the physical condition of the segment and its ability to serve the intended purpose. Factors influencing the restoration of the canal are compiled through the collected data and are sorted into seven broad categories (Table 1). The prioritization of these categories is done by Analytic Hierarchy Process (AHP) on the basis of expert opinions from urban designers, hydraulic engineers and hydrologists among others. Then, the design interventions are proposed according to the category of highest priority. The solutions recommended need to be executed in phases, starting with the identified segment.

Table 1 Factors influencing restoration of canal

Ensuring Smooth flow of water in the canal	Sewage/Solid Waste Management	Prevention of Encroachment	Aesthetics/ Recreation	Navigation	Protection of sensitive areas	Rehabilitation of displaced residents
Flood prevention	Water quality	Uniform canal width	Community interaction	Historical function	Water retention and percolation	Compensation by incentives
Consistent water flow in all seasons	Improvement of aquatic ecosystem	Buffer strip along the canal	Commercial benefits	Ensure vertical clearance	Maintain biodiversity	
Facilitate tidal action	Health benefits	Maintain canal edge treatment	Boost tourism			
Canal bed depth and gradient						

4. DESCRIPTION OF THE STUDY AREA AND CURRENT SCENARIO

Mullassery canal is located on the western side of the city, connecting the larger Thevara-Perandoor canal on the east with the Vembanad backwaters on the west. It is approximately 1500 m long with the width varying from 12 m on the western end to about 3 m on the eastern end. The canal, being in the CBD of the city, is intersected by multiple arterial roads and has many important landmarks in the vicinity, creating four segments with varying characters (Figure 1). These segments have been further divided into smaller parts for the ease of study.

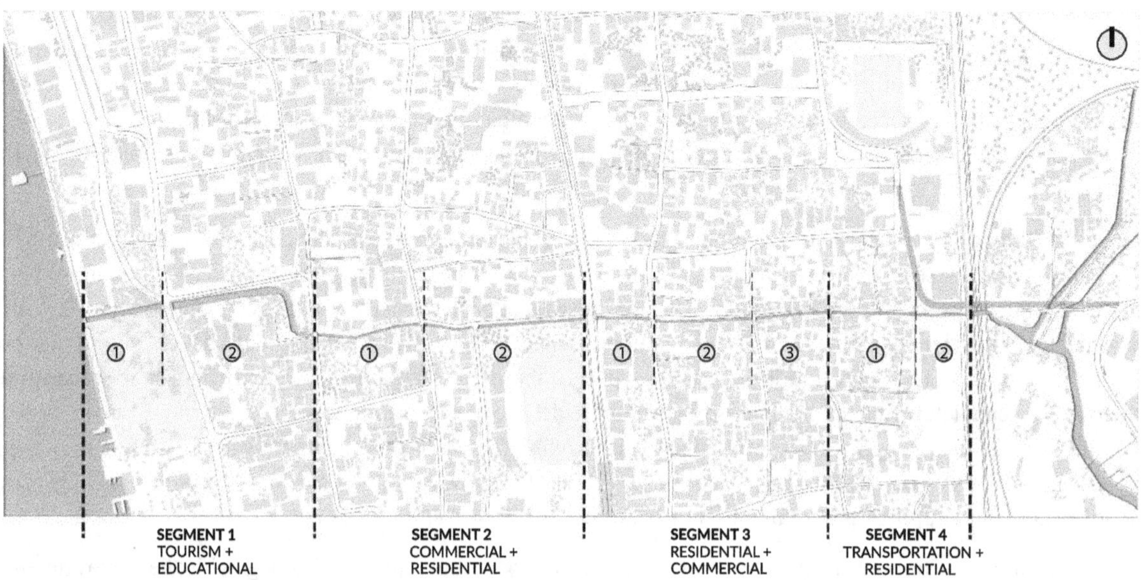

Fig. 1 Entire stretch of Mullassery canal divided into four segments based on character

The eastern end of the canal, where it joins the Thevara-Perandoor canal, is a low-lying area housing the Kerala State Road Transportation Corporation (KSRTC) bus stand and garage which gets flooded frequently. Approximately 400 m of the bed of this narrow eastern stretch has been concreted, turning it into a drain and making the gradient inconducive to smooth flow of water. Another major cause of the poor quality of water in the canal and the flooding are the physical obstructions in the course of the canal that includes debris, vegetation as well as buildings. Also, the entire eastern stretch along with almost half of the western stretch has been covered by concrete slabs with temporary structures and parking spaces above (Figure 2). The proposed expansion and renovation of KSRTC bus stand encompassing the plots on either side of the canal on the eastern end would add to the stormwater runoff due to the excessive hardscape. All these interventions prevent natural tidal flushing and the interaction between the canal and its surroundings, thus diminishing its ability to render ecosystem services and capacity in storm water management. This is evident from the online reports with keywords 'Mullassery canal' and 'flood' referred to from the year 2020 (Figure 3). These reports focus on the issues regularly faced by the residents of the area due to the flooding, its causes and impacts on their health and wellbeing.

Fig. 2 **a.** residential structures on the edge of the canal
b. concrete slabs over the canal used for parking
c. temporary structures and unwanted vegetation at the eastern end of the canal

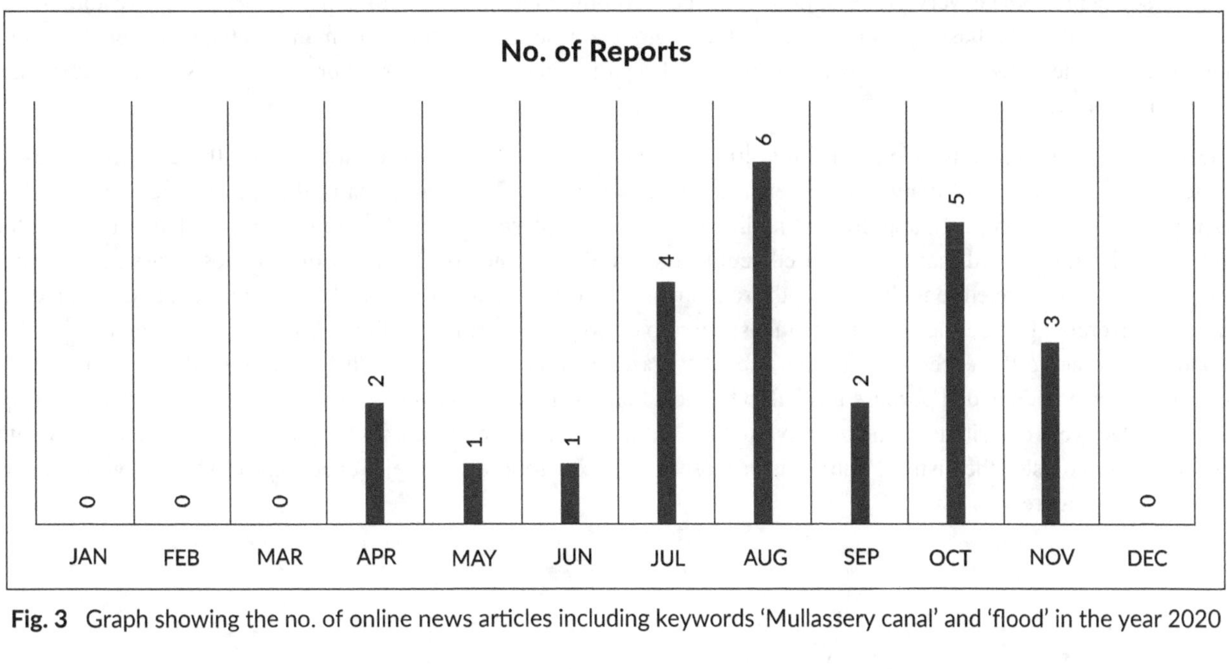

Fig. 3 Graph showing the no. of online news articles including keywords 'Mullassery canal' and 'flood' in the year 2020

5. ANALYSIS

AHP calculation is performed to identify the first course of action in the reclamation and rejuvenation of the canal, even though all the factors are to be considered at a later stage for a complete restoration. Upon pairwise comparisons of the broad categories given in Table 1, the weights obtained for each category have been indicated and ranked accordingly. The results obtained from the AHP analysis are shown in Table 2. The first category of 'Ensuring smooth flow of water in the canal' has been found to be the one having highest value among priority vector (45.0%) and thus requiring most immediate attention. It is followed by 'Prevention of Encroachment' (21.5%) and 'Sewage/ Solid Waste Management' (18.6%). This suggests that the proposed reclamation and rejuvenation process should start with removal of elements blocking the flow of water by daylighting (de-culverting) the underground sections of the canal. The increase in depth and width with appropriate gradient facilitates the periodic tidal flushing which would help improve the quality of water in the canal as well as its stormwater carrying capacity.

Table 2 Resulting weights of criteria based on pairwise comparisons of categories of factors

	Category	Priority Vector	Rank
1	Ensuring Smooth flow of water in the canal	45.0%	1
2	Sewage/ Solid Waste Management	18.6%	3
3	Prevention of Encroachment	21.5%	2
4	Aesthetics/ Recreation	4.1%	5
5	Navigation	2.8%	7
6	Protection of sensitive areas	5.2%	4
7	Rehabilitation of displaced residents	2.8%	6

5.1 Design Interventions

The Feasibility Report Kochi Smart City (Cochin Smart Mission Limited, 2019) takes note of the current condition of the western stretch of Mullassery canal falling under their Area Based Development Plan i.e., segments 1&2 (Figure 1). During the study, the hydraulic and hydrological studies which determine the factors affecting the surface runoff into the canal were carried out and adequacy in terms of carrying capacity for the set design criteria was determined. Flow simulation during design storm event and estimation of preliminary level cost were also performed. It established that the present water levels in the canal are hydraulically sufficient to carry stormwater as well as tidal flow, but the eastern stretch (segments 3&4) is very prone to flooding. The Corporation of Cochin is to undertake efforts for restoration the western segment of Mullassery canal to its former state, as close as possible. The main strategies adopted are Zero tolerance to waste water intrusion into the canal and to keep the canal merely a conveyor of both the surface water runoff and the tidal flow.

The study has also recommended transition arrangements for a smooth entry of water from the eastern to western stretch or the conversion of the western stretch into a cul-de-sac. As the elimination of the entire eastern stretch is not desirable, this paper proposes appropriate modifications to the eastern cross-section to be compatible with the western end. It has been observed that the culverted segment 4, barely two meters wide, has the smallest cross-section as its bed was heavily concreted reducing its depth from about 4 m to 1.5 m, affecting the gradient and reducing it to a drain. This has severely affected the function of this section to convey the stormwater flowing into it. This segment was also supposed to receive the excess water from the Thevara-Perandoor canal, to which it connects. The inability of this segment to meet its intended purpose has led to the area being waterlogged even with a small amount of rainfall. These factors collectively contribute to the negative impact on the area in spite of being a busy transportation hub frequented by people from outside the district. Thus, it is proposed that the restoration and rejuvenation process begin with segment 4 as shown in Figure 4.

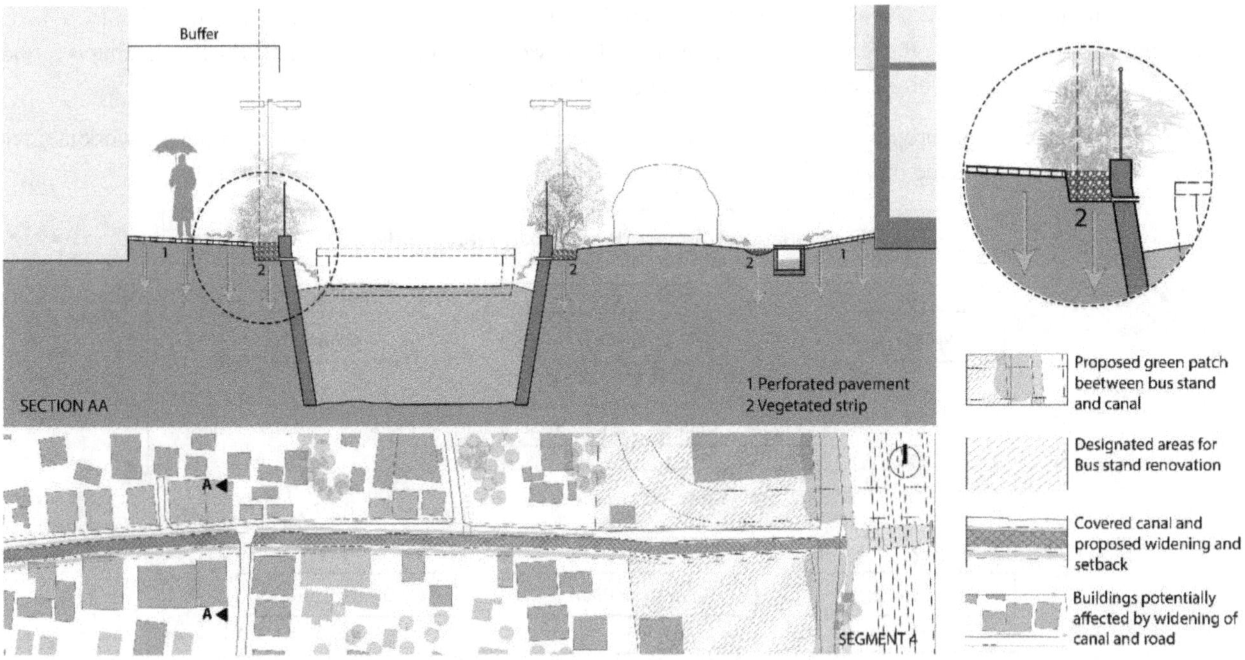

Fig. 4 Segment 4 at the eastern end of the canal and the proposed section

The restoration process would begin with daylighting, by removing the concrete slabs and structures over the canal. It would be followed by the widening of the segment to avoid a bottleneck where the eastern and western stretches meet; therefore, the width of the canal is determined to be at least 4 meters in accordance with the western stretch. The depth is to be maintained 0.5m below Mean Sea Level (MSL), on par with the western stretch, for smooth flow of excess water from Thevara-Perandoor canal into segment 4 and onward to the western stretch. This would also ensure presence of water in the canal at all times. The adjoining road is widened to maintain the current carriageway. These steps would comprise the first course of action required for reclamation and rejuvenation of the canal. It would be then followed by the addition of a setback on the southern edge to prevent structures from encroaching onto the canal; the process would entail partial or full demolition of structures abutting the canal edge. This buffer space would act as a pedestrian pathway and will have a perforated pavement. This type of paving would help percolate a substantial amount of stormwater runoff into the ground. The rest of the stormwater flowing into the canal from both banks would be filtered by a vegetation strip on the edge with a layer of gravel at the bottom. This strip on both edges of the canal would have openings on the side at regular intervals to let out the filtered water into the canal. A similar strip of gravel is also provided on the northern edge of the road without vegetation. The sewage drain running along the same edge is isolated to prevent the sewage from entering the canal. In addition to this, depressed patches of denser vegetation with gravel bed would also be introduced along the eastern edge of the KSRTC bus stand complex, which is to act as a buffer and to collect and eventually percolate excess runoff, preventing the frequent flooding in the area. These patches would also add to the recreational value of the space which is anticipating a surge in footfall. These Low Impact Development (LID) techniques help replenishment of ground water by infiltration at the source by reducing surface runoff.

6. RESULTS AND DISCUSSION

The AHP calculations indicated that ensuring smooth flow of water in the canal is the issue that requires immediate attention, to prevent the frequent flooding. It was observed that this issue is most exacerbated in the eastern stretch of the canal which is buried underground and thus neglected. By remedying this issue, the concern regarding the water quality can also be alleviated to an extent as the constant flow of water will flush out pollutants discharged due to waste disposal. This requires widening and deepening of the canal section by removing the unwanted structures on the conduit and correcting the gradient of the canal bed. The redressal of encroachment on the canal can thus be performed through this, which is the issue ranking third in terms of priority. Thus, the daylighting of segment 4 is the most appropriate action to be taken whereby the top three concerns related to the restoration of Mullassery canal would be addressed. The daylighting is further augmented by the introduction of green buffer strips on either side of the canal.

From the research, the authors propose the framework that will help researchers to carry out the rejuvenation work in urban water bodies. Figure 5 shows the framework in a systematic pattern for better understanding and usage.

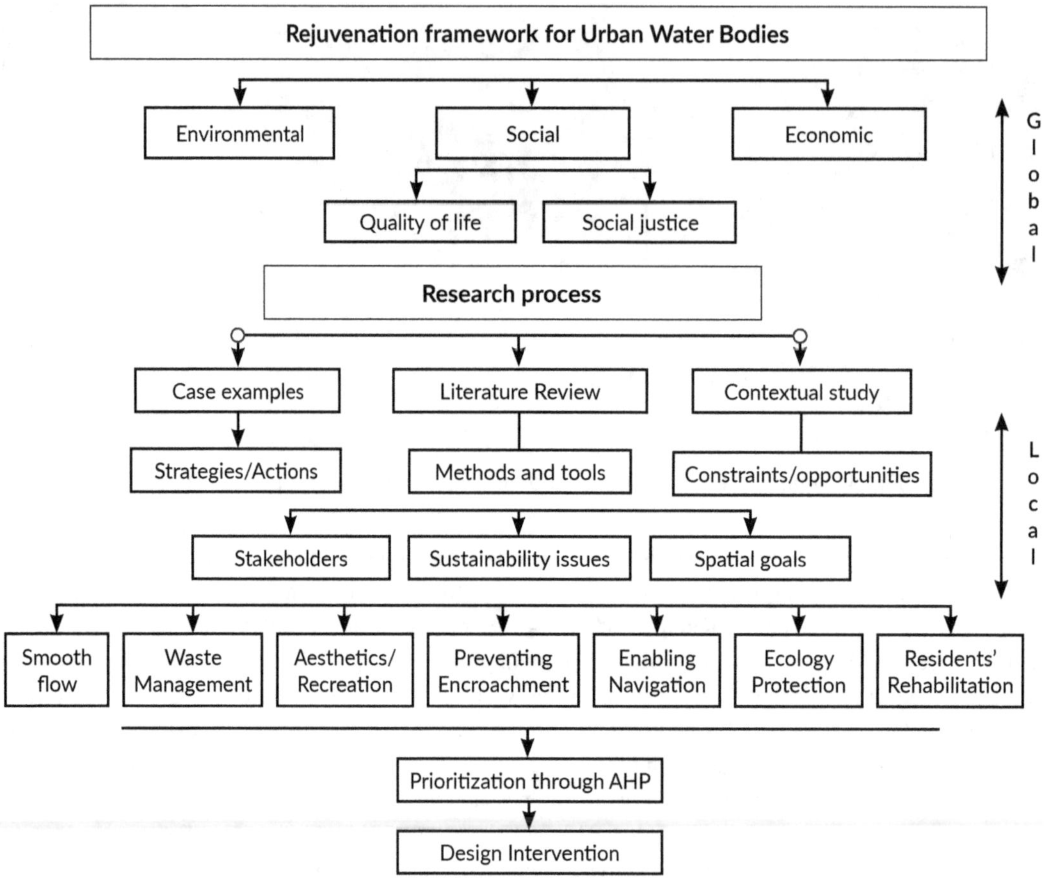

Fig. 5 Framework for Rejuvenation of Urban Water Bodies

These measures under the proposed framework will boost the aesthetics and recreation aspects in addition to having ecological benefits like improvement of biodiversity and reduction of urban heat island effect. This design intervention would ensure the engagement of public with the water body and its surroundings, providing an incentive for its upkeep. Additionally, the environmental and social benefits are advantageous to the economy by providing more opportunities for setting up commercial establishments in a predominantly residential area.

7. CONCLUSION

Water bodies in densely populated urban areas are often neglected in the course of urbanization. They are polluted and encroached upon incessantly, affecting the biodiversity and natural processes associated with them. Mullassery canal flowing through the city of Kochi, Kerala is one such water body impacted by human interventions. Many water bodies around the world which faced similar predicaments were restored fully or partially to their natural state by various means. One such method is daylighting where the parts of the channel previously underground are exposed to open air for ecological, economic and social benefits. The same approach is adopted for the proposal of rejuvenation of Mullassery canal in phases starting with its most vulnerable section. This section is identified as the one at the eastern end of the canal. Further, factors influencing the restoration are identified and grouped into categories after which AHP calculations are used to determine the category requiring immediate attention. Keeping in mind the present conditions, attaining smooth flow of water in the canal takes precedence and removal of obstructions on the channel is recommended as the first course of action. Through the research, a framework has been established to assist with the rejuvenation of such deteriorated urban water bodies.

REFERENCES

Mathew, A. P. (2005). Salinity Intrusion and Seasonal Water Quality Variations in the Tidal Canals of Cochin. Cochin University of Science and Technology.

Bae, H. (2011). Urban stream restoration in Korea: Design considerations and residents' willingness to pay. *Urban Forestry and Urban Greening*, 10(2), 119–126. https://doi.org/10.1016/j.ufug.2011.02.001

Brouwer, R., Bliem, M., Getzner, M., Kerekes, S., Milton, S., Palarie, T., Szerényi, Z., Vadineanu, A., & Wagtendonk, A. (2016). Valuation and transferability of the non-market benefits of river restoration in the Danube river basin using a choice experiment. *Ecological Engineering*, 87, 20–29. https://doi.org/10.1016/j.ecoleng.2015.11.018

Chen, W. Y., Hua, J., Liekens, I., & Broekx, S. (2018). Preference heterogeneity and scale heterogeneity in urban river restoration: A comparative study between Brussels and Guangzhou using discrete choice experiments. *Landscape and Urban Planning*, 173 (November 2017), 9–22. https://doi.org/10.1016/j.landurbplan.2018.01.010

Chou, R. J. (2016). Achieving successful river restoration in dense urban areas: Lessons from Taiwan. *Sustainability* (Switzerland), 8(11). https://doi.org/10.3390/su8111159

Chung, J. H., Yeon Hwang, K., & Kyung Bae, Y. (2012). The loss of road capacity and self-compliance: Lessons from the Cheonggyecheon stream restoration. *Transport Policy*, 21, 165–178. https://doi.org/10.1016/j.tranpol.2012.01.009

Cochin Smart Mission Limited. (2019). Feasibility Report - Restoration of Canals, Kochi: Part B-Mullassery Canal (Issue February).

Delibas, M., & Tezer, A. (2017). 'Stream Daylighting' as an approach for the renaturalization of riverine systems in urban areas: Istanbul-Ayamama Stream case. *Ecohydrology and Hydrobiology*, 17(1), 18–32. https://doi.org/10.1016/j.ecohyd.2016.12.007

Kee-yeon, H. (2006). Cheonggyecheon Restoration and Downtown Revitalization. When Creative Industries Crossover with Cities.

Khirfan, L., Mohtat, N., & Peck, M. (2020). A systematic literature review and content analysis combination to "shed some light" on stream daylighting (Deculverting). *Water Security* (Vol. 10). https://doi.org/10.1016/j.wasec.2020.100067

Buchholz, T., Younos, T. (2007). Urban Stream Daylighting Case Study Evaluations. Virginia Polytechnic Institute and State University.

Kunwar, S. B., Bohara, A. K., & Thacher, J. (2020). Public preference for river restoration in the Danda Basin, Nepal: A choice experiment study. *Ecological Economics*, 175(May), 106690. https://doi.org/10.1016/j.ecolecon.2020.106690

Lee, C. S., Lee, H., Kim, A. R., Pi, J. H., Bae, Y. J., Choi, J. K., Lee, W. S., & Moon, J. S. (2020). Ecological effects of daylighting and plant reintroduction to the Cheonggye Stream in Seoul, Korea. *Ecological Engineering*, 152(May), 105879. https://doi.org/10.1016/j.ecoleng.2020.105879

Logar, I., Brouwer, R., & Paillex, A. (2019). Do the societal benefits of river restoration outweigh their costs? A cost-benefit analysis. *Journal of Environmental Management*, 232(August 2018), 1075–1085. https://doi.org/10.1016/j.jenvman.2018.11.098

Palanisamy, B., & Chui, T. F. M. (2015). Rehabilitation of concrete canals in urban catchments using low impact development techniques. *Journal of Hydrology*, 523, 309–319. https://doi.org/10.1016/j.jhydrol.2015.01.034

Pervin, I. A., Rahman, S. M. M., Nepal, M., Haque, A. K. E., Karim, H., & Dhakal, G. (2020). Adapting to urban flooding: A case of two cities in South Asia. *Water Policy*, 22, 162–188. https://doi.org/10.2166/wp.2019.174

Seoul Solution (2014). Seoul Urban Regeneration: Cheonggyecheon restoration and Downtown Revitalization. Urban Planning. https://www.seoulsolution.kr

Sibilla, S., Sciandra, M. C., Rosso, R., & Lamera, C. (2017). Hydraulic approach to Navigli canal daylighting in Milan, Italy. *Sustainable Cities and Society*, 32, 247–262. https://doi.org/10.1016/j.scs.2017.03.017

Yang, Z. F., & Zhao, Y. W. (2014). Theoretical framework of the urban river restoration planning. *6th International Conference on Environmental Informatics*, ISEIS 2007, 5, 241–247.

SECTION II

Process to Achieve the Desired Outcomes (How)

India as a Global Hub at the Intersection of Technology and Sustainable Infrastructure

Arun Kumar Sharma
Group Head for Sustainability & Climate Change and Advisor to the Chairman, Adani Group
Distinguished Professor Emeritus, Queensland University of Technology, Australia

The Indian economy must grow at a significant pace to improve the quality of life for its people. Infrastructure linked to the affordable provision of energy, transportation, and urbanisation is the key to this growth. According to a report from the India Brand Equity Foundation (IBEF, 2021), the country requires an infrastructural investment of USD 777.73 billion by 2022. The report also notes that the construction development and infrastructure activity sectors received foreign direct investment inflows of USD 25.93 billion and USD 23.99 billion, respectively, between April 2000 and December 2020. Thus, Indian infrastructure is due to see an investment of several trillions of dollars over the next decade.

At the same time, the world faces a host of systemic risks as a result of climate change. Every country has a role to play in mitigating this risk, regardless of how significant or insignificant a part it played in contributing to the problem. It should also be noted that the effects of climate change are likely to be most severe for the countries in the Global South.

Given that India's infrastructural growth will likely be driven by an unprecedented spike in urbanisation—perhaps on a scale comparable only to that of China—it is critical that this expansion is as environmentally sustainable as possible. According to the World Economic Forum's Net-Zero Carbon Cities report (World Economic Forum, 2021), cities account for less than three percent of the world's land mass, but more than seventy percent of its emissions. Unlike the developed world, and regions of Asia that have undergone urbanisation in recent decades, India's infrastructural growth will occur amid increasing concerns about climate change.

However, the size and scale of the investment also presents an opportunity for India to lead globally in terms of innovation, standards, and technology in the sustainable infrastructure sector. An example of such a platform could be a trust architecture that assists sustainable infrastructure projects with overcoming the challenge of attracting investment, especially in relation to the perceived cost premium associated with low carbon footprint.

1. A TECHNOLOGY PLATFORM FOR THE FINANCE CHALLENGE

A question that proponents of sustainable infrastructure projects often face is one of who will pay the sustainability premium. They point to the fact that low-emission design and construction often requires a larger outlay of funds, at least in the initial stages, even if the total life cycle cost may be lower. There is some justification to these assertions, especially in the absence of a credible price on carbon or a strong regulatory signal.

At the same time, there is significant global capital currently chasing green projects. Investors are rewarding renewable energy companies with higher valuation, and the recent superior performance of ESG-aligned funds further supports this trend (ISI, 2020).

So, how does one bridge the gap between the vast pool of funds chasing environmentally-sustainable opportunities and the difficulty that proponents of these projects face in attracting investment? How does one give confidence to investors that the material used in these projects has a low carbon footprint, that the energy is renewable, and that all sustainability claims made about the project can be validated?

One way to address these issues is to put the building blocks of a trust architecture in place for sustainable infrastructure projects. If such an independent and credible platform were available, then promoters of sustainable infrastructure projects and ESG-aligned investors could readily find one another.

Fortunately, the significant progress made over the past decade in blockchain technology—the foundation of cryptocurrencies—forms the groundwork for such a trust architecture. Much has been written about blockchain's various use cases – for example, its potential to do away with a trusted intermediary (as in financial transactions), and its use as a secure registry of value (say, as in an immutable record of land titles information) (Tapscott & Tapscott, 2016; Werbach, 2018).

Blockchain can also be used to trace proof of origin – a use case that is now being explored in the context of sustainability. ClearTrace[1] is a start-up that uses this technology to validate whether a customer is receiving renewable power as part of its contract with its energy supplier. Energy Web Foundation[2] is a consortium building an open-source, enterprise blockchain platform tailored to the energy sector.

Blockchain is also being deployed as a guarantee of origin verification system for different shades of hydrogen (National Grid, 2021) as the market develops in preparation for this promising storage and carrier of energy. Hydrogen can be produced via the electrolysis of water using renewable electricity – referred to as green hydrogen. Hydrogen produced from reformation of natural gas (also known as grey hydrogen) and from coal or lignite (black or brown hydrogen) is associated with significant Greenhouse Gas (GHG) emissions. If the GHG emissions from the production of grey, black, or brown hydrogen are captured and stored (CCS), then the hydrogen produced is referred to as blue hydrogen. Green and blue hydrogen are collectively referred to as renewable or clean hydrogen. As the world transitions to a low carbon economy, the demand for green and blue hydrogen will increase as it is one of the few potential solutions for hard-to-abate sectors and for the long-term storage of energy needed to compensate for the intermittency of renewables. But how to be certain that the hydrogen one is purchasing is indeed green or blue? This is where a blockchain layer on the industrial process and logistics supply chain helps establish a proof of origin. Examples of this approach include the European Union project, CertifHy[3], and an initiative from the Spanish multinational, Acciona (Jones, 2021).

While the above use cases provide guarantee of origin verifiability for some aspects of the infrastructure puzzle, what is needed is a broader trust platform that encompasses the entire ecosystem—both the suppliers and customers—of infrastructure projects.

It is useful to look at how a business aiming to attract green finance may be able to demonstrate its low-emission credentials. According to the GHG protocol[4], Scope 1 emissions refer to emissions from owned or controlled assets; Scope 2 emissions are indirect emissions from the generation of purchased electricity, heating, or cooling. Scopes 1 and 2 are together referred to as the operational emissions of a business. Scope 3 emissions include all other indirect emissions that occur in the value chain—upstream and downstream—of the business. While a business may be able to demonstrate its low-emission credentials for Scopes 1 and 2, as per its independently audited submissions to various ESG ratings agencies, Scope 3 poses a unique difficulty as these emissions depend on the operational emissions—the Scope 1 and 2—of suppliers and customers who may not always be transparent or are otherwise reluctant to share information in case it disadvantages them in future contract negotiations. However, the same suppliers and customers may be prepared to selectively share their emissions information if the incentive of a premium price (for a supplier) and a discounted offer (for a customer) were to exist.

Such a scenario presents another use case of blockchain, which can be viewed as a linked database suitable for situations where:

- data belongs to multiple stakeholders who are prepared to share under certain conditions,
- an immutable history of updates is desired, and
- while the various stakeholders may not always trust one another, they see a benefit in sharing their data selectively

[1] https://cleartrace.io/

[2] https://www.energyweb.org/

[3] https://www.certifhy.eu/

[4] https://ghgprotocol.org/

A business looking to demonstrate its green credentials can implement a trust architecture of this kind to share detailed information about its carbon footprint with potential investors, insurers, suppliers, customers, and other stakeholders. Cooperation among members of the ecosystem can be assured by the inherent incentives, such as: lower cost of capital, favourable insurance rates, premium prices for suppliers, and discounted prices for customers.

So, who should take the lead in developing a trust architecture of this kind? While a number of entrepreneurial solutions have been discussed above, a comprehensive trust platform should be a joint initiative involving multiple business sectors that constitute the entire value chain of infrastructure development. Such an initiative could also be supported and seeded by public funds in its initial stages.

2. INDIA AS AN INNOVATION HUB FOR A TECHNOLOGY-ENABLED SUSTAINABLE INFRASTRUCTURE

Technology will play an important role in the productivity improvement needed to create sustainable infrastructure. Low-emission targets, coupled with a price on carbon, will enable new products, services, and business models at the intersection of infrastructure domain knowledge and Information and Communication Technology (ICT) to be developed. Relevant technologies that will play an important role at the intersection include: the Internet of Things, cloud and edge computing, AI and machine learning, augmented reality and virtual reality, and, as previously discussed, blockchain.

The scale of future infrastructure investment in India, combined with a competitive culture of technology entrepreneurship, is the crucible from which numerous innovative start-ups can emerge. With careful nurturing, some of these ventures may even flourish on a global scale.

There is a depth of literature concerned with how entrepreneurial ecosystems successfully evolve, such as Josh Lerner's landmark book, *Boulevard of Broken Dreams* (Lerner, 2009). The MIT Regional Entrepreneurship Acceleration Program (REAP)[5], pioneered by Scott Stern, Fiona Murray, and Phil Budden (Murray & Budden, 2017; Delgado *et.al.*, 2014), combines Michael Porter's work on competitive strategy (Porter, 1980) and clusters (Porter, 1988) with Lerner's insights in order to provide a useful data-driven framework for a successful innovation-driven entrepreneurial ecosystem.

According to the REAP framework, there are five stakeholders that are essential to a thriving ecosystem: entrepreneurs, risk capital, corporates, government, and universities. At the heart of the ecosystem are the entrepreneurs. Their level of interaction with the other four stakeholders (together with interactions among the stakeholders) is central to the ecosystem's success. Entrepreneurs need corporates to whom they can sell, access to risk capital in order to grow, partnerships with universities and research organisations to access innovation, and supportive government policies that encourage these interactions.

All these ingredients exist in India. What is needed are more opportunities and policy settings in order to increase the linkages required to accelerate the ecosystem. Some suggestions include:

- Creating more opportunities for university-industry collaboration on focussed industry-specific problems[6];
- Encouraging universities to not only spin-out start-ups from their intellectual property (IP), but to also actively engage with start-ups that may have originated elsewhere, beyond the university. This could be done by making their technical facilities available to outside users at subsidised rates (such subsidies could be provided by public funds);
- Enlisting the aid of the government via preferential procurement policies to support home-grown start-ups, which will help these young businesses demonstrate their capacity and credentials (World Economic Forum, 2019);
- Increasing the availability of risk capital by co-investing public funds[7].

Another approach that may accelerate an entrepreneurial ecosystem is the adoption of open architectures and standards. This environment allows competing start-ups to acquire scale as they can access a larger market for their products. In the

[5] https://reap.mit.edu

[6] Australia's Cooperative Research Centres program
https://www.industry.gov.au/funding-and-incentives/cooperative-research-centres

[7] Activity of the Israel Innovation Authority's Divisions (Seed Program)
https://innovationisrael.org.il/en/reportchapter/activity-israel-innovation-authoritys-divisions

absence of standards and open architecture, this effort can be fragmented. This is because solutions must be customized for individual customers, or else there is a tendency towards vertical integration. This results in multiple closed platforms, leading to a suboptimal ecosystem. AnnaLee Saxenian (Saxenian, 1996) provides a compelling case for open architecture ecosystems – she compares the evolution of Silicon Valley and Route 128 in Boston in the 1980s, and discusses how Silicon Valley's open architecture was eventually more successful in creating an entrepreneurial ecosystem.

3. CONCLUSION

The sheer scale of investment expected in the forthcoming decades allows India a chance to redefine sustainable infrastructure practices, to set new standards, and to leverage its formidable entrepreneurial capacity and make the country a global innovation hub at the intersection of infrastructure domain knowledge and technology. After all, clusters of entrepreneurial activity often combine deep sectoral expertise with technological prowess, as in the case of London emerging as a hub for FinTech, or Israel for dry land agriculture and security.

4. ACKNOWLEDGEMENT

This piece is based on remarks made at the inaugural panel of the International Conference on Infrastructure Development (ICID-2021). Assistance of Dr Sandhya Sreekumar, Vivek Panda and Mindy Gill is gratefully acknowledged.

REFERENCES

Delgado, M., Porter, M. E., & Stern, S. (2014). Clusters, convergence, and economic performance. *Research policy, 43*(10), 1785–1799.

IBEF (2021). *Indian Road Industry Report.* India Brand Equity Foundation. https://www.ibef.org/industry/roads-presentation

ISI (2020). *Sustainable Funds Outperform Peers in 2020 during Coronavirus.* Morgan Stanley Institute for Sustainable Investing. https://www.morganstanley.com/ideas/esg-funds-outperform-peers-coronavirus

Jones, J. (2021). First blockchain platform for green hydrogen tracking developed. Smart Energy International. https://www.smart-energy.com/industry-sectors/new-technology/first-blockchain-platform-for-green-hydrogen-tracking-developed/

Lerner, J. (2009). *Boulevard of broken dreams.* Princeton University Press.

Murray, F., & Budden, P. (2017). *A systematic MIT approach for assessing 'innovation-driven entrepreneurship' in ecosystems (iEcosystems).* Working Paper. MIT Lab for Innovation Science and Policy, MIT Innovation Initiative.

National Grid (2021). Energy explained. Accessed on 05 May 2021. https://www.nationalgrid.com/stories/energy-explained/hydrogen-colour-spectrum

Porter, M. E. (1980). *Competitive strategy: Techniques for analyzing industries and competitors.* New York. Free Press.

Porter, M. E. (1998). Clusters and the new economics of competition. *Harvard Business Review.* 76 (6). pp. 77–90.

Saxenian, A. (1996). *Regional Advantage: Culture and Competition in Silicon Valley and Route 128.* Harvard University Press.

Tapscott, D., & Tapscott, A. (2016). *Blockchain revolution: how the technology behind bitcoin is changing money, business, and the world.* Penguin.

Werbach, K. (2018). *The blockchain and the new architecture of trust.* MIT Press.

World Economic Forum (2019). *Accelerating the Emergence and Development of Innovation Ecosystems through Procurement: A Toolkit.* White Paper. World Economic Publication.

World Economic Forum (2021). *Net Zero Carbon Cities: An Integrated Approach.* World Economic Publication.

Skilling for Sustainability

Veni Mathur
Vice-chairperson
Chartered Institute of Logistics & Transport, New Delhi

The growth in technology will slowly replace manpower is more of an exaggeration! What is more relevant is that manpower needs major efforts on Skilling to keep pace with and better utilize the advantages of the growing technological advancements. Therefore Skilling for Sustainable Growth is the key!

The current Pandemic has brought to the forefront the importance of Logistics and Transport. All the concepts like - efficiency of the modes of transportation, optimal modal mix, Logistics Performance Index, warehousing, freight forwarding, 3PL and 4PL service providers can be understood and made use of with modern technological solutions for achieving Global competitiveness. At the base of all this build up is a pool of skilled manpower! Skilling or up-skilling of the human resource is an integral part of sustainable growth for any nation. Economic growth will create a sizeable number of jobs most of which will be skill based. It is estimated that only 2-4% of the Indian workforce has received some form of formal skill training. Thus, the Skill Gap is to be filled up by partnering with institutes of repute for imparting quality training. SKILL is an art. It is not only a key …

"Even if you're on right track, you'll get run over if you sit there!" – **Will Rogers**.

Skilling should have a long term perspective towards sustainability and must focus on anticipating and adapting to change in both the present and future. It is to be remembered that **climate change, income inequality, and social injustice** are the biggest threats to building strong, sustainable economies and hence these challenges must be addressed in the training programs.

Skilling for Sustainability must ensure Ecological Integrity and Economic Security aspects/goals such as –

- Clean air and water and nutritious food
- Conservation of non-renewable resources through reduction, recovery, reuse and recycling of waste
- Use of appropriate technology to minimize pollution
- Use of renewable resources at a pace no faster than their rate of renewal
- Growth of local economies through generation of employment opportunities and financial viability
- Providing for OJT (on job training) and education to upgrade/equip the workforce to meet future needs.
- Adaptability to changing circumstances and conditions

The economies today must have specific Sustainable Development Goals (SDGs) which are very complex; therefore, Skilling up is essential for all to achieve these ambitious targets. Targets such as better utilization of energy, transportation, water or urban development along with the use of digital technology require substantial re-skilling and up-skilling and capacity building support at all levels - ranging from top policy makers to ordinary citizens, from elected representatives to service delivery providers, from civil society organizations to the general public and youth. It is also observed that traditional learning and capacity building methods of live classroom and online courses merely focus at transferring and retaining knowledge. But in the case of Logistics and Transport practical application of the knowledge in terms of On-The-Job training is a must.

According to the World Economic Forum, 2018:

"54% of the workforce will require significant up-skilling and re-skilling within the next five years."

Therefore, having the skills to apply the knowledge to address complex problems is the solution. However, in India we face a severe skill shortage in many areas of our work, and this stunts innovation, hurts quality, and limits the ability to achieve development outcomes.

This fact was clearly highlighted in the Harvard Business Publishing report on "How the Workforce Learns 2019" that the current format of training is not working for most employees and creates a skill gap! The report also brings out three strategic shifts in learning -

1. To devise an integrated skilling program that goes beyond formal learning (via classes, courses, and structured programs), and connects people with the right resources at the right time to get things done.
2. Learning to become empowering and inclusive, giving employees the autonomy to pursue the skills they need on their own time on a continuous basis.
3. **Make the shift from learning to skilling**.

The report further states -

"Workforces thrive when managers give learning recommendations, open up development opportunities, and agree on relevant goals for up skilling."

"India's youthful manpower, a result of the demographic dividend, need to be provided with skills and ability to tackle global challenges. The more we give importance to skill development the more competent youth will be. It is important to predict the possibilities of the future, and prepare for them today itself. We have to make India the skill capital of the world."

– Shri Narendra Modi, Prime Minister of India.

To make this vision possible, India has been working towards a common goal called 'Skill India'. The main aim of this program has been to develop the skills of the youth within the country in order to produce a more skilled workforce for a more efficient future. A number of establishments such as NSDC, MSDE, Skill councils, Central & State missions and more than 250 partners and well over 3,200 training centres are engaged in training of youth in India.

Another attempt in this direction is the flagship scheme of the Ministry of Skill Development & Entrepreneurship's (MSDE), the Pradhan Mantri Kaushal Vikas Yojana (PMKVY) that trains young people in industry-relevant skills to secure a better livelihood and quality of life for both them and their families.

Traditionally most of the vocational trainings focus on technical skills rather than 'soft' or 'green' skills, which contribute to preserving or restoring environmental quality for sustainable future, aimed at creating jobs that protect ecosystems and biodiversity, reduce energy consumption, cost of transportation and minimize waste and pollution. Developing training modules for Logistics and Transport could also be counted as Green Skills aimed at reducing wastes, time and costs in transportation of goods from production to consumption centres.

A positive step in this direction is the mapping of Skill Gaps in the Logistics sector by the Ministry of Commerce & Industry with the assistance of an academic think tank and developing courses at Basic, Advanced and Specialization levels. Besides, the Logistics Skill Council, representing the MSDE along-with many stakeholders and knowledge partners including the Chartered Institute of Logistics & Transport (CILT) India is successfully running training programs in different areas of Logistics and Transport at various ITIs and similar institutes. As training is designed to meet industry needs, placement is more or less assured.

The Skill India mission is growing in strength but more can still be done to improve. Although over ten million youth have been trained already, a greater effort needs to be made if the target of training 400 million by 2022 is to be achieved. The points that should be looked into are –

- **Focus on Aspirational goals rather than Targets:** as most schemes are target oriented, it results in candidates/beneficiaries dropping out of the skill courses; instead skilling should be done keeping individual's aspiration in mind. Awareness programs about certain job roles will encourage Youth to choose skill courses based on their aspiration.

- **Industry Connect by way of Apprenticeship Scheme:** it should be introduced to the Youth (both boys & girls) at school level which will enable knowledge and choice for right skills and right job. All corporates and companies should mandatorily run apprenticeship programs.
- **Leverage Technology:** Skilling programs must include Video based tutorials, Mobile labs and other innovative technologies.
- **Need for Focus on Non-Cognitive and Behavioral skills:** the biggest factor of attrition and unemployment is attitude and behavior of the Youth. Focus on Non-Cognitive skills/soft skills such as Customer engagement, Verbal & Body language; Other skills such as Personal finance management, Yoga & health skills must be imparted during training.
- **Skilling must pave the way for Career Growth:** through the PMKVY students/beneficiaries are not seeing any advantage in terms of career advancement or wages.

Overall, the introduction of PMKVY and its relative success proves the government's faith in the system and support for young people. Most Logistics companies are certainly starting to see the benefit of training at a younger age and willing to induct and impart on the job Hands on training but there is still a lot of hard work to be done for the goals to be reached. We need a synergistic alignment between stakeholders such as Government, Ministries, Skill Councils, Training Partners and most importantly participation of the Youth.

We are definitely on the right path that will lead to a **Better India**.

"Success is no Accident. It is hard work, perseverance, learning, studying, sacrifice and most of all, love of what you are doing." – **Pele**

Sustainable Accounting Practices

Amit Shrivastava
Associate Professor, Finance & Accounting
Adani Institute of Infrastructure Management, Ahmedabad

M. Chandra Shekar
Assistant Professor, Finance
Institute of Public Enterprise, Hyderabad

K. Sreshta Rebecca
Housing Development Finance Corporation Limited, Hyderabad

Abstract: Sustainable Development has always been the focus area ever since we have noticed climatic changes. The last 20 years have seen the companies start focusing on this crucial segment and laying emphasis on reporting these practices, and thus has paved the way to the concept of Sustainability Reporting, which has gradually started to gain prominence. However, it is still in a very nascent stage in most countries. Still, the respective authorities are taking measures to mandate Sustainability Reporting and making the companies and the individuals trace a way out, most importantly in times of unprecedented changes like a pandemic. This paper provides an overview of sustainable reporting and its subsets and its impact on investor sentiment and company valuations. The best practices followed by certain countries are also discussed. However, the main focus of this paper is to provide an overview of Sustainable reporting's influence in the post-pandemic era.

Keywords: Sustainable Accounting, Carbon Accounting, ESG Practices, Sustainability, New era Accounting

1. INTRODUCTION

With an increasing emphasis being laid on protecting the environment and the corporates are beginning to realize the worth of sustainability, the twenty-year-old concept of Sustainable Accounting has started to gain prominence in recent times. Adding to it is the novel coronavirus, which has directed the various institutions worldwide to redefine their vision and redesign their roadmap without letting them derail from their set goals and objectives during their inception. The key highlights of the trends that are noticed in sustainable reporting as well as its subsets include:

- 80% of the companies all over the world have started to report on feasibility and sustainability
- An increase in unified information and reporting has been observed in countries like India, France, Japan and Malaysia since the year 2017
- Approximately 40% of the industries admit the economic threat caused due to climate change in the information passed
- Most of the industries all across the globe have currently set goals to decrease the release of carbon and other greenhouse gases
- The Sustainable Development Goals of most companies are attached to financial broadening, climatic changes and careful utilization and there has been an increase in sustainable reporting (KPMG, 2020).

The last two decades have seen a drastic increase in sustainable reporting by most retail and institutional investors, realizing how a small tweak in ESG factors can minimize risks and upside opportunities. In this regard, the Sustainability Accounting

Standards Board (SASB) has adopted an industry-based approach by taking into consideration 79 different industries that belong to 10 different sectors and has thus classified the various issues that are more likely to pop up for each of these industries and has also identified the vital/ appropriate KPIs to capture then rightly and report them effectively. Thus, at this very moment when there is an urgent need to develop accounting standards for material ESG issues, the SASB comes into playing a very crucial role and would be of great help to the companies. While reading along, we get to understand what is sustainable accounting, why is it the need of the hour, the various factors that affect sustainable accounting, sustainability accounting practices in India, its role and impact on company evaluation and investor sentiment, and most importantly about its impact during the pandemic and several good practices that are being followed by countries as a way out in these stressed times.

2. WHAT IS SUSTAINABLE ACCOUNTING?

The motto of sustainability accounting is 3P - People, Planet, and Profits (Ozili, 2021). This says it all about the concept of Sustainable accounting, which is a sub-category of financial accounting with a focus on disclosing externally to stakeholders the non-financial information about the firm's performance in terms of ecological and social effects arising from the manufacture of products, and also the management of ecological and social funds required to form social capital to create sustainable value. The five endurability dimensions accounting to the Sustainability Accounting Standards Board (SASB) are ecological, social funds, Human funds, Business model and Evaluation, and guidance & Governance. As per the definition of Sustainable accounting, the three critical dimensions of sustainability are:

- Environment
- Social
- Governance

Various shareholders have different and diverse interests. One such area of interest is about the carbon emission by a company so that their neighboring regions are neat and out of danger. Thus, the shareholder's interest in the current day situation is a company's financial position, which also includes ESG (CFI, n.d.).

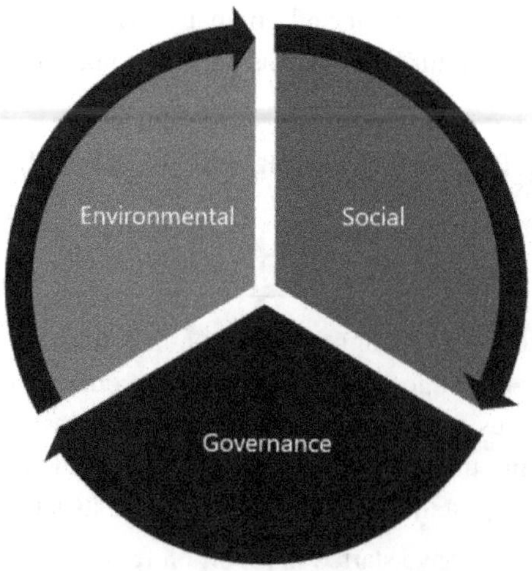

Fig. 1 Three broad categories of socially responsible investors

ESG refers to the environmental, social, and governance information of an institute. It has been observed that the companies that take their ecological and social resolutions seriously tend to do better economically too. Also, Sustainable Responsible Investing (SRI) or ESG investing utilizes this company's data to inform investment resolutions. It has been known that certain ESG investors pressurize the company to do a better job at their ESG performance, or they might also strip them off that company on this basis (KPMG, 2020).

Table 1 The key focus areas from a reporting perspective

Environment	Social	Governance
Focus on emission moderation measures by adopting work from a home culture where applicable	Redesigning health and safety systems	Long term considerations in governance mechanisms like policing and strategic planning
Minimize the use of non-biodegradable material being used at the workplace	Work on employee retention mechanisms, especially in case of contract and migration workers	Review Business Continuity Plan (BCP) and setting recovering time objectives
Adequate use of natural resources	Revise need assessment and the focus areas for CSR	Ensure alignment by changing the regulatory requirements
Take initiatives to reduce emissions, water, and electricity consumption and work towards meeting environmental goals	Self-assessment and upgrading the fitness and security systems to encompass fitness and security risk assessment.	Manage change strategy based on the time-to-time learning
Contribute towards global climate and formulating ways to reduce the emission of greenhouse gases	Augment stakeholder relationship management	Communicate governance insights in unprecedented situations
Preventive maintenance of critical operational facilities	Initialize workforce infrastructure up-gradation to support the innovative and agile work environment	Establish new synergies and governance mechanisms for recovery in times of unprecedented situations

3. WHY SUSTAINABLE ACCOUNTING?

Sustainable considering helps identify, evaluate, and manage communal and ecological threats by recognizing resource productivity and savings and linking improvements in social and environmental matters with economic chances. It also helps compare and set a standard for the firm's performance and identify the most efficient practices. Without sustainable considering standards, we will not have the capital markets required to create a sustainable society for the coming generations.

Sustainable accounting facilitates:

- Competitive advantage: Through creative and proper linking of sustainability practices to business goals, competitive advantage can be achieved and also creates awareness.
- Company image and reputation: Company that uses renewable energy sources is likely to have a good company image than the one that relentlessly used up fossil fuels.
- Access to capital: Producing sustainability reports open doors to new and less expensive sources of funds.

4. FACTORS THAT INFLUENCE SUSTAINABLE ACCOUNTING

- Corporate Governance Index: Enhanced corporate governance structures provide a high level of corporate disclosures, and a weak governance structure hinders the company from providing adequate information to the stakeholders.
- Sustainability Committee: It enables to address the sustainability risks and opportunities, thus enhancing the integrity of sustainability.
- Industry: As different industries have different characteristics, the nature of disclosing also changes. One of the reports has observed a strong association between the sustainability report and industry type.
- Firm size: The most frequently used factor to understand the behavior of a company. Most of the studies have observed that there is a strong association between firm size and ESG reporting.

- Profitability: Several arguments have reported that there is a positive association between sustainability reporting and profitability. A profitable company is subject to higher scrutiny, thus engaging more in activities contributing to sustainable development.
- Leverage: A high leverage company tends to disclose more of its information in addition to sustainable reporting to prove its ability to pay its obligations (Lawrence, 2017).

The other factors that influence sustainable accounting include growth opportunity, ownership structure, free cash flow, return on equity (ROE), and a company's liquidity position.

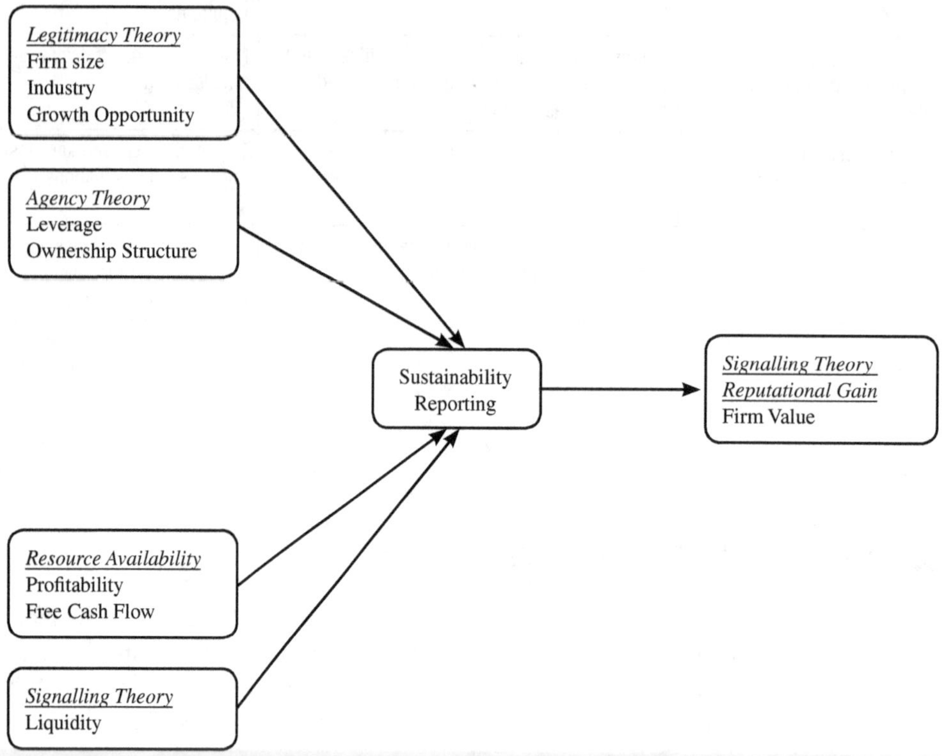

Fig. 2 Determinants of sustainability reporting

5. SUSTAINABLE ACCOUNTING PRACTICES IN INDIA

As per the recent update, dated May 10th, 2021, a circular has been issued by SEBI notifying about the new disclosure norms on sustainability reporting. As a result, the top 1000 companies by market capital will need to provide an overview of their environmental, social, and governance risks and opportunities and the approaches to mitigate the risks involved and the financial implications. However, the Business Responsibility and Sustainability Reporting (BRSR), which is an initiative towards ensuring that the investors have access to disclosures on ESG parameters, has said that the reporting of BRSR would be voluntary for FY 2022 and will be made mandate from FY 2023, and this would just be like a forefront for Sustainability reporting.

In India, as sustainability reporting is optional, most companies don't opt for it. However, certain sectors like Oil & Gas, Metals & Mining, and Construction related companies have adopted separate sustainability reports as it is mandated for these sectors to conduct Environment Impact Assessment. Considering the importance of sustainability reporting, the Ministry of Corporate Affairs, GOI, had issued CSR voluntary guidelines in 2009. It also includes guidelines for the environment and activities for social and inclusive departments. For Indian companies to become globally competitive, they must adopt the GRI-based sustainability reporting framework (Ozili, 2021).

The Cement industry is another classic example that has recognized the importance of sustainable practices but has lacked commitment towards disclosing the financial information related to the practices adopted in these activities. It is thus essential to build awareness about sustainability reporting to achieve a company's long-term strategic goals.

6. SUSTAINABLE ACCOUNTING PRACTICES AND INVESTOR SENTIMENT

It is seen that in the current day, a large portion of the investors requests Environmental, Social, and Governance Exposures. From the ramifications of Professional Accountants who are ready to go, it is deciphered that Environmental, Social and Governance (ESG) data is utilized by shareholders (investors) to comprehend a company's main ESG factors and to know what they mean for generally speaking execution throughout a more extended time skyline. Proof of this shift can be found in the number of financial backers marking the UN's Standards for Mindful Speculation, the growing number of investor propositions containing ESG goals; studies of financial backers that show an expanding number accept that ESG reconciliation into the venture cycle augments recipients' drawn-out revenue, and that great administration and manageability rehearses add to the production of long haul investor esteem. Such shareholders are taking regard in what is underlying the presentation of firms.

These shareholders look for a better understanding of the organisation's business model, plan of action, governance key dependencies, and the main risk factors. Proof additionally proves that organizations can draw in various types of stockholders through their sustainability disclosure strategies. Examination demonstrates that incorporating sustainable reporting in a company's annual report can positively affect the sort of financial backers an organization draws in, particularly those who are explicitly searching for reasonable value creation. Organizations with an incorporated and outward-looking methodology can profit by clearly conveying critical issues identified with strategy, governance, presentation, and prospects. That throws light on its money-oriented, societal, and ecological setting (IFAC, 2015).

7. SUSTAINABLE ACCOUNTING AND ITS IMPACT ON COMPANY VALUATIONS

Sustainability reporting doesn't only disclose information about the company's practices that contribute to social good. It also emphasizes how they add value to the company, thus providing better returns to the investors. In addition, specific studies on sustainable reporting have suggested that it has positive relations with the firm's market value. The table below depicts how the various theories come into play to understand the impact of sustainable reporting on a company's valuation.

Table 2 Contribution of theories to understand sustainable reporting impact on a company's valuation

Theory	Inference
Agency Theory	It says that the voluntary disclosure of the firm's social and environmental aspects reduces the agency cost. This will, in turn, impact the risk profile and profitability of the markets, subsequently affecting the peddle value.
Signal Theory	It says that the company's voluntary disclosure of environmental issues sends out signals of them proactively being involved in environmental strategies, which will make the company more attractive to shareholders in the stock market.
Legitimacy Theory	It suggests corporate social reporting of a company determines the legitimized behavior of a company and, in turn, aims to attract stakeholders from the society's perspective, thus resulting in a higher firm value.

In addition to reporting on sustainability, the quality of the report also makes quite a difference as it, in turn, contributes to improving the firm's value (Lawrence, 2017).

8. SUSTAINABLE ACCOUNTING & CARBON ACCOUNTING

As mentioned in the beginning, most companies worldwide have already set targets to work on carbon emission levels, thus making carbon accounting a topic of reasonable interest in the present-day situation. On a formal note, carbon accounting can be defined as the processes used to measure the quantity of carbon dioxide and its equivalents an organization emits into the atmosphere. Carbon accounting does more than just merely identifying the places of harmful gas emissions. It enables the quantification of emissions of various gases harming the environment and helps figure out ways to curb the unforeseen global emergency. The most common users of Carbon accounting are the State governments, companies, and individuals to create credit commodities and, in turn, sell them in the "Carbon Markets."

Carbon accounting is a subset of sustainability accounting and is an accounting tool that companies use to respond to climate change issues. The two primary approaches of carbon accounting are:

- Accounts that facilitate un-sustainability
- Carbon accounts that enable sustainability practice betterment

Two of these perspectives play a vital part in corporate duties such as manufacturing, dispensation, extraction/procurement, supply chain management, alteration, reporting, and advertising. Carbon management accounting supports all degrees of control in an organization in taking the decisions, irrespective of whether a sector is distinctly questioned to follow and cooperate with the orders to better carry out and execute energy and material flows for substantial reduction effects, or is motivated to increase eco-efficiency, alteration of the product, or genuinity (Stefan, 2012).

It is also observed that certain companies in India have already recognized the importance of Carbon Accounting and have begun to report it in specific public forums like "Carbon Disclosure Project (CDP)" and "Sustainability reporting".

9. SUSTAINABLE ACCOUNTING IN PANDEMIC

One evident change that the crisis has brought in is the importance of transparency and sustainability in business development. Experts say that sustainability reporting is the primary way to reach global aims after the pandemic. United Nations Conference on Trade and Development's Secretary-General noted that at these difficult times, advertising best quality communication on financial and non-financial presentations of firms has become crucial and necessary. By formulating a set of equivalent and compatible standards, the International Financial Reporting Standards Foundation will allow firms to gain trust from the public through higher legitimacy of their sustainability initiatives, enabling the investors to make more informed decisions (UNCTD, 2020).

In case of the worldwide spread of 2019, Covid-19 has set the member states of the United Nations unparalleled hurdles to meet their objectives under the 17 Sustainable Development Goals (SDGs), including subjects from decreasing worldwide scarcity, aiming to reach gender equality and institutional legitimacy to reducing climate change. On the other hand, the pandemic has made all member states grasp the significance of longevity for the global economy, society, and ecology. Moreover, the scarcity has certainly caused measuring and rate the organizational productivity, accountability, and genuine to shift, permitting accountants and auditors to play significant roles. Importantly, accountants and auditors can create a world of transparency in the process of implementing the SDGs in the post-Covid-19 era (IFAC, 2015, & Hörisch, Jacob, 2021).

Table 3 Impact of covid-19 on the Operating profits in Q3 of 2020 industry-wise

Industry	Q3 Change in % YOY
Automobile	8.5%
Chemicals	-89.3%
Consumer Goods	-11.5%
Engineering & Construction	-23.2%
Life Science	-253.1%
Mining/Commodities	9.6%
Real Estate	4.9%
Services	-56.6%
Telecommunication	0.7%
Transport & Logistics	38.6%
Travel & Leisure	-41.3%
Energy	2.4%
Grand Total	**-65.5%**

Source: Perspectives: How COVID-19 continues to infect financial reporting Survey Q3 2020

The above table shows that the Y-O-Y progressions were very varied and unstable from firm to firm and business to business. With this large amount of insecurity and questions for the coming days, it is essential to address clearly and genuinely with stockholders to provide them the needful insights apt for their investment decisions. Furthermore, it has become necessary for all business owners to remember that the primary purpose behind sustainability reporting is to ensure to stakeholders that their business is functioning efficiently, legally, and sustainably (ShineWing TY TEOH., 2020).

10. PRACTICES ADOPTED IN MALAYSIA TO CONTROL COVID-19

Some companies are struggling to find modern technologies to generate effective sustainability reports. Here we see some sustainability reporting trends. They include the trends of certain countries that are doing well in enhancing their economy by striving to come back to normal from the adverse effects of covid-19. The case of Malaysia and other countries are taken into consideration.

1. The coronavirus pandemic caught companies by surprise. In terms of financial or accounting purposes, nobody would have even thought of such a period on earth, and thus no company is prepared for this vast crisis. As a result, many organizations have started to review the report issued in December 2019 and to which they have added some statements about the coronavirus. Web pages and other similar platforms are also being updated.
2. All stakeholders and experts have begun to give their attention to the following consecutive sustainability report. Many financial transactions rely heavily on these reports because investors are not comfortable making large-scale investments during uncertain times and these reports help investors make sound decisions.
3. The sustainability reports depict social impact and have now become very important than ever before. These reports also report on the treatment of their employees. Thus, these reports are widely used by investors and stakeholders about employee management in unprecedented times like these to make informed decisions.
4. Sustainability reports are a part of financial reports. However, the importance of it has increased in the present times because of the pandemic. These reports are now of great help to the accounting and auditing companies in Malaysia to provide transparent financial reports and depict the losses suffered during pandemics and make it possible to develop forecasts based on the data collected.
5. Because of the severe monetary downturn, investors requested organization records to be straightforward, dependable, and predictable. Dealing with the effect of COVID-19 on the business stays the first concern for entrepreneurs, and its significance can't be underestimated. Investors anticipate that companies should make extensive reports and distribute records, regardless of a slight delay.

As a part of concluding thoughts, I would say that one could argue that sustainability reporting is more critical than ever before because every business expert, owner and investor needs to fully know the impact of COVID-19 on the sustainability of a company and make strategies to move on from this adverse crisis.

REFERENCES

CFI. (n.d.). What is ESG (Environmental, Social, and Governance)?. https://corporatefinanceinstitute.com/resources/knowledge/other/esg-environmental-social-governance

Deloitte. (2020). How COVID-19 continues to infect financial reporting. https://www2.deloitte.com/ch/en/pages/audit/articles/financial-reporting-survey-q3-2020.html

Graybeal, Patty., Franklin, Mitchell., & Cooper, Dixon. (2019). Describe Sustainability and the Way It Creates Business Value. Principles of Accounting, Volume 2: Managerial Accounting. https://opentextbc.ca/principlesofaccountingv2openstax/chapter/describe-sustainability-and-the-way-it-creates-business-value/

Hörisch, Jacob. (2021). The relation of COVID-19 to the UN sustainable development goals: implications for sustainability accounting, management and policy research. Sustainability Accounting, Management and Policy Journal. https://www.emerald.com/insight/content/doi/10.1108/SAMPJ-08-2020-0277/full/html

IFAC. (2015, July). Accounting for Sustainability - from Sustainability to Business Resilience, 2014-2015 report. Retrieved May 24, 2021, from https://www.ifac.org/knowledge-gateway/preparing-future-ready-professionals/publications/accounting-sustainability-sustainability-business-resilience

KPMG. (2020). Sustainability reporting during COVID-19 pandemic. https://assets.kpmg/content/dam/kpmg/in/pdf/2020/05/sustainability-reporting-during-covid-19-pandemic.pdf

KPMG. (2020). Time has come. https://home.kpmg/xx/en/home/insights/2020/11/the-time-has-come-survey-of-sustainability-reporting.html

Lawrence, Loh., Thomas, Thomas,. and Yu, Wang. (2017, November). Sustainability Reporting and Firm Value: Evidence from Singapore-Listed Companies.

Ozili, Peterson K. (2021, May). Sustainability Accounting.

ShineWing TY TEOH. (2020). The Effects of Covid-19 on Sustainable Reporting. https://www.shinewingtyteoh.com/covid-19-on-sustainable-reporting/

Stefan, Schalteggera., Maria, Csutora. (2012, November). Carbon accounting for sustainability and management. Status quo and challenges. https://www.sciencedirect.com/science/article/abs/pii/S0959652612003186

UNCTD. (2020, November). Sustainability reporting central to achieving global goals post pandemic. https://unctad.org/news/sustainability-reporting-central-achieving-global-goals-post-pandemic

Hybrid Infrastructure for Effective Sustainable Growth: Theory, Practice and Policy (ICID-2021)

Abhishek Singh
Doctoral Research Scholar
Indian Institute of Technology Guwahati

Pratul Chandra Kalita
Associate Professor
Indian Institute of Technology Guwahati

Abstract: The rapid urbanization around the globe is exploiting the natural resources exponentially, may it be water, air, land or minerals. In last couple of decades, the awareness for sustainable growth has attained significant pace and the same can be observed in the global policies also.

Innovation and smart integration can be a very efficient tool to improve the efficacy of the output of technologies with sustainable goals. In this paper we have considered a case study of Guwahati, where a metro rail network is in planning stage and parallelly we have also conducted field surveys to identify the issues pertaining to the people of the city which can be solved through proper infrastructure planning. The motive was to design a user centred infrastructure model. After listing out all major issues, brain storming sessions were organized between a group of researchers and consultants. The literature pertaining to these issues and sustainable goals were also analysed to develop a hybrid model of infrastructure.

To understand the space constraints of the project, 3D modelling of the city was done with hybrid infrastructure. For understanding the financial implication of the project, Break Even Analysis was conducted. The outcome of this paper is that smart infrastructures can give multi fold benefits with some additional cwost and this cost can be recovered from the earning of the infrastructure within 15 years in this particular case. Hence instead of conventional infrastructure practices, smart and innovative infrastructure should be promoted for a more efficient and sustainable growth.

Keywords: Hybrid Infrastructure, Smart infrastructure, Integrated infrastructure design

1. INTRODUCTION

The development of any infrastructure is a land intensive project. Rapid urbanization has formed huge sprawls all around the globe (Gillham, 2002). The term sprawl with respect to urbanization was first used in 1937 Earle Draper, he was a the very first town planner of south eastern United States (Black,1996). The new cities are built with exhaustive planning for the coming 50 years but the cities which develop over time without any planning are facing difficulties in adopting to new infrastructure due to space constraints. All the old cities are having single or double lane roads, they are not sufficient to cater to the existing population requirement. Then how can it cater to the future population? In spite of rapid expansion of the sprawl (Nechyba & Walsh, 2004), the cities are not in a position to cater the need of existing population. This has forced the city to move in the Z axis of this 3D world. All the duplex buildings are converted into high raise buildings with multiple basements. roads are being converted in to flyovers and tunnels, since the surface of earth is not sufficient for the rapidly growing population.

Apart from expanding along the Z axis, each and every service are also having their own network to further complicate the landscape of the city. The road networks are intersecting with the water supply network, sewerage network, transmission line network (High Tension, low tension, low voltage, fibre optic, etc.), LPG pipeline network, drainage network and many more. Each of these networks cover a large amount of space and also face multiple issues related to repair and maintenance.

On the other hand, in case of any repair or shut down the services of other network are also hampered. Sine all these networks move along road but are either underground or hanging on the road sides.

The transportation networks like roads, highways, metros, trains, trams, flights all require large stretches of lands for implementation. The existing pressure on transportation system have already forced them to be a multi-layered system and are spreading in the Z axis like the other infrastructures. The main concern is that all these infrastructures requires huge patches of land for them and all are necessary for the growth. Apart from these services and infrastructure the race for green energy and sustainable growth are also on priority (Acharya & Bennett, 2001). Since the fossil fuels are reaching saturation, hence alternative sources of renewable energy are the new point of focus.

All the transport system is converting into electric based services. By the next 50 years majority of countries will be fossil fuel free, since there won't be any fossil fuel left to use. For acquiring such an ambitious goal, huge investments are being done on wind and solar energy. These two forms of renewable energy also require very huge land areas for generating energy.

Hence the overall scarcity in the near future will be of land. Remaining all the resources will be recyclable. In order to be future ready with sustainable growth (Jabareen, 2006), the infrastructure design should be planned for at least next 100 years. Smart features are to be embedded in the infrastructure to make it more efficient. While designing any infrastructure, apart from the primary purpose of the infrastructure other issues pertaining to the locality should also be addressed for giving a more comprehensive solution. Instead of planning single infrastructure, always plan for multi-functional infrastructure.

2. THE PROBLEM

In this project we have taken a case study of Guwahati metro project. It is under planning stage. We have also analysed other prominent issues pertaining to the infrastructure and requirement of citizens of the city. The list of issues with respect to the citizens of Guwahati city, as identified during the personal interviews, group discussions, news articles and papers published are as under:

1. Flash Floods: The geographical position of Guwahati is very beautiful, on three sides it is surrounded by hills and on one side it is intersected by Brahmaputra. This gives Guwahati a very beautiful environment but at the same time also causes a lot of issues during the monsoon season. The water level of Brahmaputra increases during heavy rains and the quick runoff of hilly terrain is also not able to escape from low laying areas of Guwahati easily. This results in frequent flash floods in many low laying areas of Guwahati. These flash floods last for couple of hours after the rain, during this period every year numerous lives are lost due to electrocution, loss of movable and fixed assets in the submerged area. The loss of life is mainly due to electrocution of people while they accidently touch the electric pole or the earthing wire hanging from the pole in the submerged areas.
2. Poor sewerage network: In many parts of Guwahati, the sewerage network is not functional and all the waste is being dumped in the tributary of Brahmaputra passing through the city. The tributary originates from the neighbouring hills of Guwahati and the water of the river while entering the city limit is very clean. When the river enters Guwahati, it is converted into choked drain, even the movement of water cannot be seen. The river water is converted in to thick black viscous fluid which is the breeding ground for several diseases. During monsoon season, the choked river is flushed out along with flash floods. So, for a healthy city it is very important to isolate the sewerage network, surface drain and the river to maintain its sanctity.

3. Traffic Congestion: The population density of Guwahati is increasing very fast. Guwahati being the gateway to North Eastern India, is also the business hub of North East. Which attracts a lot of companies to open their centres in Guwahati to explore the market of North East. The residents of North Eastern states of India are moving to Guwahati for better employment and growth opportunities. Hence more and more people are coming and settling in Guwahati. The famous traditional Assam type houses are being transformed to multi storey flats to accommodate the population burst in Guwahati. The city is expanding in all possible directions. The policy makers have already started to merge the neighbouring rural areas in the city limits. The increasing city limits are also inducing higher vehicle demands in the city. At current stage itself the city is facing heavy traffic congestion throughout the day (Das, 2008). Multiple flyovers are constructed to ease the pressure on traffic movement but by the time flyovers are ready the number vehicles in the city also increases. With increasing numbers of vehicles on road and restricted road widths the situation is going to further deteriorate in terms of traffic congestion. The rapidly increasing population needs mass transit system to cater the needs of the citizens. The construction of metro rail network is already in the planning stage but it will further narrow down the width of the road. By the time metro network will be ready for use, the number of vehicle in Guwahati will increase multi folds and the issue of traffic congestion will still persist.
4. Water scarcity: In the heart of the city the near Christian Basti area, with the increase in number of flats and increase in number of very deep boreholes, the water table in this particular area has gone down drastically and is not able to recharge since the water demand in the area is very high and slowly this water scarcity in the city is spreading. In spite of the majestic Brahmaputra passing by a couple of kms away, the water table is not able to recharge. People are buying water in this area even for taking bath and other purposes. Since the entire area is converted into concrete, hence the rain water is also not able to percolate to recharge the ground water level.
5. Electricity shortage: As per the data published by "Load Generation Balance Report 2017-18, Central Electricity Authority, Govt. of India" it was found that Assam is having shortage of 452 MW capacity to cater its current population requirement and this demand will further increase with increasing population. So power shortage is another issue to be faced in the near future.

These were some of the major issues related to infrastructure identified in Guwahati city.

3. CONCEPTUAL FRAMEWORK

After identification of all the issues, they were listed for brainstorming session between research scholars and consultants. All the possible solutions for each and every issue identified during field survey was listed out. The most voted ideas were taken up for final conceptualization of the model. Then all the solutions were merged to form hybrid infrastructure. Various solutions were discussed during the brainstorming session. A general consensus was established for the following:

1. The infrastructure will not only cater to metro network but also act as a multi layered road.
2. The infrastructure space will be used as renewable power generation facility.
    a. Solar Power
    b. Piezoelectric power
    c. Wind power

The arrangement of all these three units will be positioned in such a way that they will compliment each other and increase the efficiency of each other.

3. The infrastructure will also have inbuilt transmission line networks.
4. The infrastructure will also have water supply, surface drain and sewerage network isolated lines.

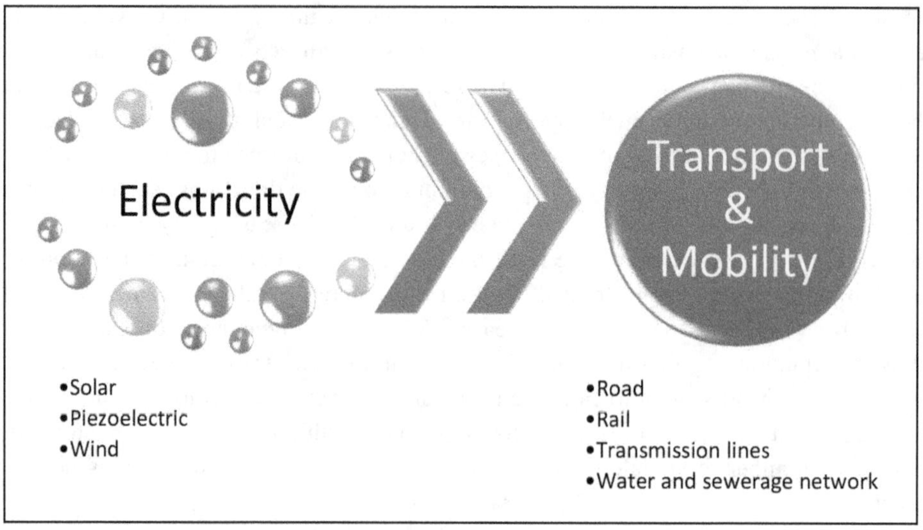

Fig. 1 Integration of multiple services to make it smart infrastructure

Multiple combinations were worked out. The combination of services to be imbedded in the infrastructure is shown in the Figure 2. In this section the existing road with reduced road width due to construction of pillars of Hybrid infrastructure will also remain functional. At the same time a second layer of road will be constructed for reducing the pressure of heavy traffic on the existing road.

The sewerage and drinking water network will be installed below the ground level and on either sides of the pillars of the infrastructure. The first platform will be used for the metro rail networks and the second platform as a road for traffic movement. The road will be covered with Photovoltaic cells. And the side walls of road and metro rail will have vertical shaft wind turbines. The floor of the road will have piezoelectric materials embedder for power generation.

The base of the metro rail platform will be used as the transmission line network (including all the High tension, low tension, low voltage and FO cables passing through proper cable trays). This will help in maintaining the aesthetics of the city, which is hampered due to unorganized way of handling of cables and other lines. This also leads to many accidents during monsoon season.

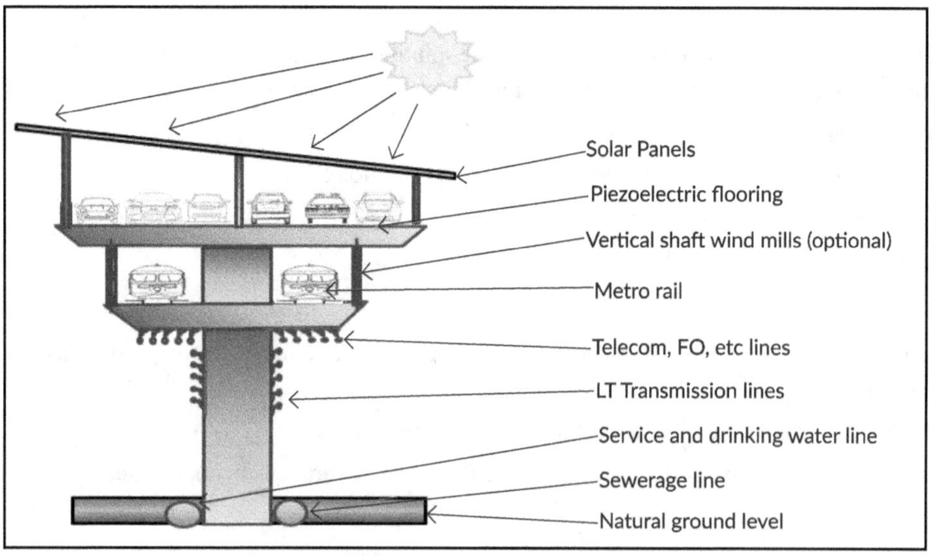

Fig. 2 Proposed Hybrid metro rail project

The combination of three technologies photovoltaic cells, piezoelectric floors and vertical shaft wind turbine in roads, railways and metros can produce electricity with higher efficiency as compared to the three working individually.

The photovoltaic cells will be mounted as the roofs of the road/railway/metro. It will prevent the damage of road due to rain and harsh weather condition. At the same time will cast shadow on road/railway/metro keeping it cooler. The cooler area will cause pressure difference from the area exposed to sun, causing flow of wind. The sides of the road/railway/metro will be mounted with vertical shaft wind turbine. It will rotate with the wind flow and by the wind caused by moving vehicles/ trains/metros and generate electricity. Hence, the solar roof will complement the vertical shaft wind turbine. The floor of the road/railway/metro will be embedded with piezoelectric transducers to generate electricity. It will generate renewable energy from road/railways/metro. We need not wait for the vehicles all the time, since the pressure difference will ensure that the vertical shaft wind turbines are rotating.

Solar roof roads are better than PV embedded in the roads because, each time there will be shadow on road due to vehicle the voltage will drop. For maintenance of photovoltaic embedded roads traffic have to be diverted in case it is embedded in roads. Whereas solar roof road can have temporary suspended platforms to do the work without disturbing the traffic. Solar roof will also prevent accidents due to rain, over heating of vehicles and tire bursting accidents due to hot road and direct exposure to sun. Photovoltaic embedded in roads are also costly to make since transparent concrete is required and in case the panel is damaged then the road have to be recast after repair. Whereas in solar roof the panels can be easily maintained with service bay and provision of suspended platform.

4. WORKING AND METHODOLOGY

To understand the space feasibility of the planned infrastructure, we have done 3D modelling of the busiest road of Guwahati city. The road width and open space available was modelled to the scale, where as the buildings and other facilities were made with approximate dimensions. The financial implication was studied by doing break even analysis of the construction cost of the hybrid infrastructure to the conventional infrastructure cost.

4.1 3D Modelling

Site survey was conducted and more than 600 photographs were taken to understand the formation of Guwahati city at human eye level. To understand the layout of the city trough bird eye view, google maps and google earth were used. Guwahati station and the Paltan Bazar area was observed to have the highest level of traffic congestion, that's why this area kept as focus of the study. Initially the city was replicated into a 3D model in Google sketchup software. The width of the road and pathways are taken as per scale, where as building and other facilities were built in reference to the width of the road as found in the photographs taken while site survey.

The typical section in 3D model for Paltan bazar metro station is shown in Figure – 3. As per the available space, a 2lane road will be available at the existing ground level for visiting the local places, where as a bypass road for people travelling farther distance is built at the top level of the infrastructure. The road is covered with photovoltaic cells on the top and the floor of the road are made up of piezoelectric ceramics. On the sides of the roads vertical shaft wind turbine are installed to generate electricity while vehicles/ metro is moving next to it.

Fig. 3 Proposed multilevel hybrid transport network in Paltan bazar

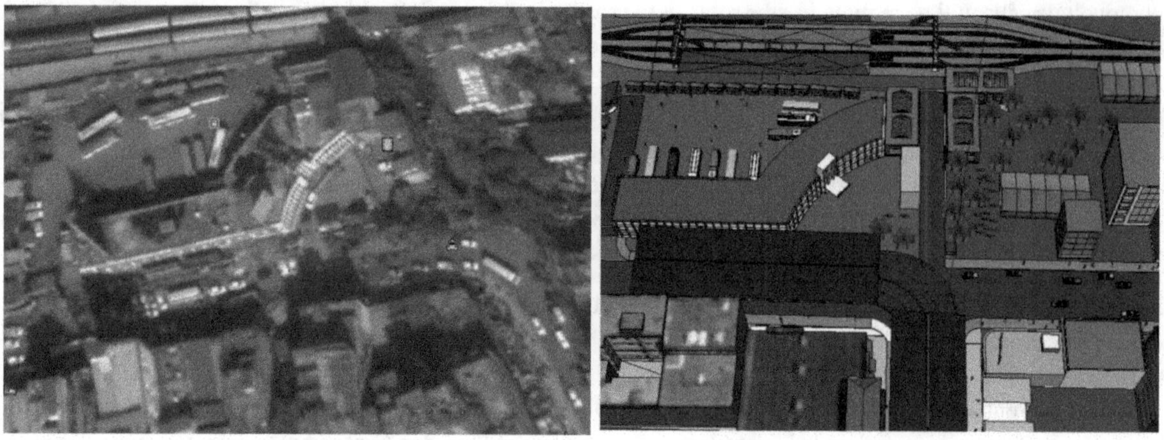

Fig. 4 Satellite view and 3D view of Bus stop at Paltan Bazar

In Figure 4 the Assam state Transport corporation bus stop is shown, this is the area with highest traffic density in Guwahati inspite of being a one way road.

Fig. 5 Guwahati railway station

In Figure 5, Guwahati railway station is shown and since it is next to the ASTC bus stop, hence very heavy traffic due to continuous movement of passengers in auto and taxi increases the congestion in the area.

After framing the structures in 3D model, it was observed that hybrid metro rail infrastructure can be built in the area. There is sufficient space in the area for the infrastructure. Since the road width of the existing road is reduce due to pillars of metro rails hence additional layer for road network is to be provided to cater the heavy traffic needs and requirement of road in the near future.

5. BREAK EVEN POINT ANALYSIS

Metro rail Proposal for Guwahati - There were two route proposals for Guwahati metro project. One was of 81.5 Kms and the other network was of 62Kms. The route map of Proposal A is shown in Figure 6.

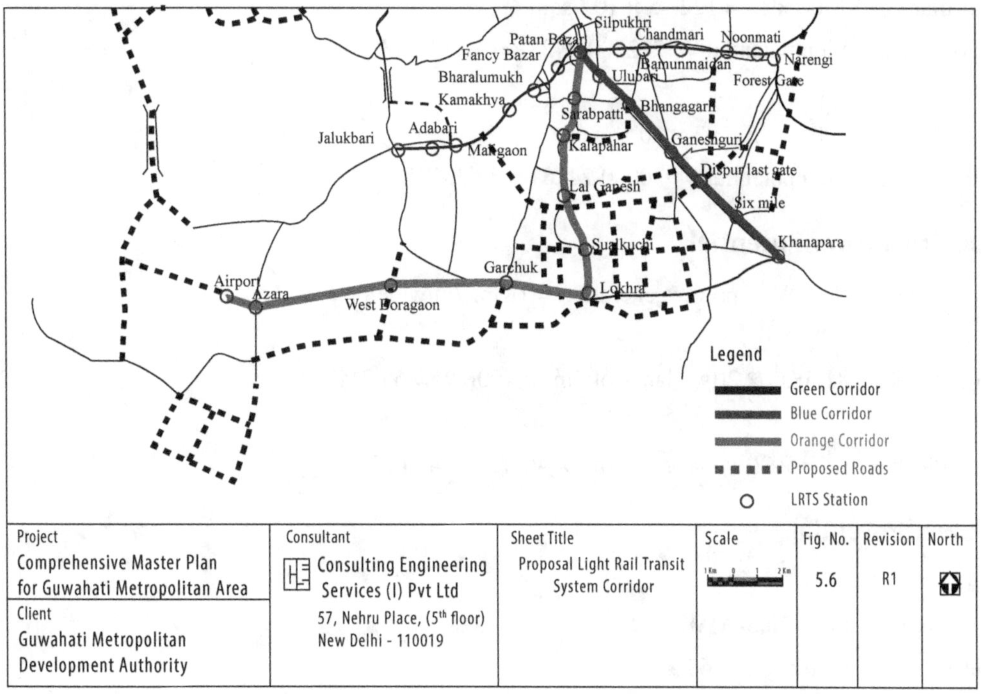

Fig. 6 Proposed route maps of Metro line

(This image appears in colour at the end of the compendium).

The corridors of both the proposals are as under:

- Proposal A
  - Corridor 1 : Dharapur to Narangi to airport = 35Km
  - Corridor 2 : MG Road to Khanapara = 11.5Km (underground)
  - Corridor 3 : Jalukbari to Khanapara = 25Km
  - Corridor 4 : ISBT to Paltan Bazar = 10Km

  Total = 81.5Km

- Proposal B
  - Corridor 1 : Narengi to Jalukbari = 22.7 Km
  - Corridor 2 : Paltan Bazar to Lokhra to Airport = 30km
  - Corridor 3 : Paltan Bazar to Khanapara = 9.3Km

  Total = 62Km

5.1 Cost of Metro Rail Project

- Cost for 1 km of elevated Metro line * = Rs 250 crores
- Cost of 1Km of underground Metro line * = Rs 400 crores
- Proposal A cost = 70 × 250 + 11.5 × 400 = Rs. 22,100 crores
- Proposal B Cost = 62 × 250 = Rs 15,500 crores

5.2 Solar Power Potential

- Area requirement for 1MW of power generation = 24,281 sqm (6 acres*)
- Proposal A
  - Area available = 81500 × 15 = 122.25 × 10^4 sqm
  - Peak Power generation potential = 1222500/24281 = 50.34MW
- Proposal B
  - Area available = 62000 × 15 = 93 × 10^4 sqm
  - Peak Power generation potential = 930000/24281 = 38.3MW

5.3 Piezoelectric Power Potential

- Area requirement for 400KW of power generation = 1Km, 7m wide lane.
- Proposal A
  - Power potential = 81.5Km × 2(two lanes of 7m) × 400KW = 65.2MW
- Proposal B
  - Area available = 62Km × 2(two lanes of 7m) × 400KW = 49.6MW

5.4 Total Power Potential

- Proposal A
  - Solar Power potential = **50.34MW**
  - Piezoelectric Power potential = **65.2MW**
  - Approx unit generations
    - by solar power/year = 50.34MW × 4 hrs × 365 days = **73.5 MU**
    - by piezoelectric power/year = 65.2MW × 16 hrs × 365 days = **380.76 MU**
    - **Total units produced per year = 454.26 MU**
- Proposal B
  - Solar Power potential = **38.3MW**
  - Piezoelectric Power potential = **49.6MW**
  - Approx unit generations
    - by solar power/year = 38.3MW × 4 hrs × 365 days = **55.9 MU**
    - by piezoelectric power/year = 49.6MW × 16 hrs × 365 days = **289.66 MU**
    - Total units produced per year = **345.56 MU**

5.5 Comparison of Power Generation

- Thermal power plant of 50 MW produces
  = 50MW × 24 hrs × 365 days
  = 438 MU/year
- Proposal A produces = 454.26 MU/Year
- Proposal B produces = 345.56 MU/Year

5.6 Cost of Thermal Power Plant

- Fixed Cost
  - 1000MW power plant installation cost * = Rs 6000 crores
  - Land requirement for imported coal based powerplant** = 1Acre/MW

- Cost of land per Acre = 8 – 10 Lakhs/Acre
- Cost of 1MW Thermal Power Plant = Rs. 6.1 crores
- Cost of **50MW** Thermal power plant = **Rs. 305 crores**

- Variable Cost
  - Cost of Coal for 1MW plant per hour*** = $ 35/hr = Rs. 2380/hr
  - Cost of coal per year per MW = 2380 × 24 × 365 = Rs. 2.08 crores/yr/MW
  - Cost of coal per year for **50MW** = **Rs. 104.25 crores/yr**
  - Plus service and maintenance cost

5.7 Cost of Solar Power Project

- Area requirement for 1MW of power generation = 24,281 sqm (6 acres*)
- Cost for installing 1MW power plant ** = Rs 4.50 crores
- Prefabricated factory shed cost per sqm = Rs 2690/-
- Cost of fabrication per MW = 2690 × 24281 = Rs 6.5 crores
- Cost Of Solar Power setup per MW = 4.5 + 6.5 = Rs. 11 crores

5.8 Cost of Piezoelectric Power Project

- 1Km of piezoelectric installation in road (14m wide) cost * = Rs 4,42,000 × 400
  = 17,68,00,000/-
  = Rs. 17.68 crores

- Cost of Piezoelectric installation in praposal A
  = Rs 17.68 crore × 81.5 Km
  = Rs 1440.92 crores

- Cost of Piezoelectric installation in praposal B
  = Rs 17.68 crore × 62 Km
  = Rs 1096.16 crores

Table 1 Comparison sheet

Sl NO	Description	Thermal Power Plant (50MW)	Proposal A			Proposal B		
			Solar Power	Piezoelectric power	Total	Solar Power	Piezoelectric power	Total
1	Electricity generated per year (Million Units)	438 MU	73.5 MU	380.76MU	454.26 MU	55.9 MU	289.66 MU	345.56 MU
2	Construction cost	Rs.305 Cr.	Rs. 553.74 Cr.	Rs. 1440.92 Cr.	Rs. 1994.66 cr.	Rs. 421.3 cr.	Rs.1096.16 cr.	RS. 1517.5 cr.
3	Variable cost/Fuel cost	Rs. 104.25 Cr./Yr.	nil	nil	nil	nil	nil	nil
4	Service and maintenance	High	Low	Low	Low	Low	Low	Low

Calculation:

Cost of HYBRID-Metro Rail project

- Cost for 1Km of elevated Metro line = Rs 250 crores
- Cost of 1Km of underground Metro line = Rs 400 crores
- Approx. Cost for 1Km multilayer metro rail and road line
  = Rs 250*1.7 = Rs 400 crores

- Total cost for solar, piezoelectric and multilayer transport system:
  - Proposal A = 81.5 × (6.8 + 17.68 + 400)
    = Rs. 34595.12 crores
  - Proposal B = 62 × (6.8 + 17.68 + 400)
    = Rs. 26317.76 crores

It was found that the net cost implication for converting the infrastructure into smart infrastructure will be recovered within 15 years and after that the same infrastructure will generate continuous income with very nominal maintenance cost.

6. CONCLUSION

The land required for multiple services like road, metro network, solar power plant and other services are very huge and it can be saved by smart and Hybrid infrastructure.

The cost of hybrid infrastructure is very less as compared to the conventional infrastructure build individually even if the cost implication due to land is not considered.

The renewable energy embedded in it will earn carbon credits for the project.

By the time conventional infrastructures are constructed and commissioned the demand of the locality increases, making the infrastructure obsolete within few years of commissioning. Hence the policy makers should have futuristic vision, because without their will and level of understanding, it is not possible to have smart and Hybrid infrastructure.

Huge solar farms and other power generation facilities can be built in the heart of the city, reducing the cost of transmission since the source of generation will be very close to the point of consumption.

REFERENCES

Gillham, O. (2002). *The limitless city: a primer on the urban sprawl debate.* Island Press.

Black, J. T. (1996). The economics of sprawl. *Urban Land, 55* (3), 6–52.

Nechyba, T. J., & Walsh, R. P. (2004). Urban sprawl. *Journal of economic perspectives, 18*(4), 177–200.

Acharya, G., & Bennett, L. L. (2001). Valuing open space and land-use patterns in urban watersheds. *The Journal of Real Estate Finance and Economics, 22*(2), 221–237.

Brueckner, J. K. (2000). Urban sprawl: diagnosis and remedies. *International regional science review, 23*(2), 160–171.

Adams, C. F., Fleeter, H. B., Kim, Y., Freeman, M., & Cho, I. (1996). Flight from blight and metropolitan suburbanization revisited. *Urban Affairs Review, 31*(4), 529–543.

Das, D. (2008). Urban quality of life: A case study of Guwahati. *Social Indicators Research, 88*(2), 297–310.

Jabareen, Y. R. (2006). Sustainable urban forms: Their typologies, models, and concepts. *Journal of planning education and research, 26*(1), 38–52.

Daniels, T. L., Keller, J. W., Lapping, M., Daniels, K., & Segedy, J. (2007). The small town planning handbook. *Washington (DC).*

Anton, S. R., & Sodano, H. A. (2007). A review of power harvesting using piezoelectric materials (2003–2006). *Smart materials and Structures, 16*(3), R1.

Wang, S., Wang, C., Yu, G., & Gao, Z. (2020). Development and performance of a piezoelectric energy conversion structure applied in pavement. *Energy Conversion and Management, 207*, 112571.

Yang, H., Wang, L., Zhou, B., Wei, Y., & Zhao, Q. (2018). A preliminary study on the highway piezoelectric power supply system. *International Journal of Pavement Research and Technology, 11*(2), 168–175.

Goldfarb, M., & Jones, L. D. (1999). On the efficiency of electric power generation with piezoelectric ceramic.

Martin, R. M. (1972). Piezoelectricity. *Physical Review B, 5*(4), 1607.

Sharma, A. (2011). A comprehensive study of solar power in India and World. *Renewable and Sustainable Energy Reviews, 15*(4), 1767–1776.

Bhutta, M. M. A., Hayat, N., Farooq, A. U., Ali, Z., Jamil, S. R., & Hussain, Z. (2012). Vertical axis wind turbine–A review of various configurations and design techniques. *Renewable and Sustainable Energy Reviews, 16*(4), 1926–1939.

Spera, D. A. (1994). Wind turbine technology.

Dursun, E., & Kilic, O. (2012). Comparative evaluation of different power management strategies of a stand-alone PV/Wind/PEMFC hybrid power system. *International Journal of Electrical Power & Energy Systems, 34*(1), 81–89.

https://www.hindustantimes.com/india-news/make-metro-a-complete-make-in-india-project-e-sreedharan-to-narendra-modi/story-DoFTRSDvMcjPkl1qAVcONO.html, cited on 19/06/2018

https://gas2.org/2009/01/05/piezoelectric-road-produces-electricity-from-traffic/, cited on 19/08/18)

Load Generation Balance Report 2017-18, Central Electricity Authority, Govt. of India

http://www.indiaspend.com/cover-story/indias-renewables-investment-in-2016-cost-of-11-coal-fired-power-plants-60251 (cited on 19/08/18)

http://www.cea.nic.in/reports/others/thermal/tpm1/land_requirement.pdf cited on 19/08/18)

https://www.brighthubengineering.com/power-plants/52544-basic-calculations-for-a-power-plant-calculating-the-coal-quantity/cited on 19/08/18)

https://www.renewableenergyworld.com/articles/2013/08/calculating-solar-energys-land-use-footprint.html cited on 19/08/18)

https://solarenergypanels.in/solar-power-plants/mw-solar-power-grid, cited on 19/08/18)

https://www.indiamart.com/proddetail/prefabricated-factory-shed-5769250097.html, cited on 19/08/18)

Potential of Blockchain Based Tokenized Securities for Green Real Estate Bonds

Ravi Shankar
Doctoral Research Scholar
National University of Singapore

Abstract: Green financing in the real estate sector has been rising recently because of trend towards ESG (environmental, social, and corporate governance) investing and increased consensus towards a need for carbon neutral construction in the real estate sector. The popular instruments of green financing include, green bonds, green loans, equity-based instruments, sustainability-linked loans etc. However, the green investment vehicles face several bottlenecks such as high transaction costs for managing the principal agent relationship, higher minimum sum to be invested, and opportunity costs. The recent popularity of green bonds also leads to high incidences of green washing. Blockchain based tokenized securities can improve transaction efficiency, liquidity, and transparency through better management of intermediaries in the real estate sector. However, they face certain risks such as the regulatory risk, technology risk, and acceptability of the asset class. The objective of this research is to determine whether the blockchain technology has the potential to solve the existing problems of paper-based transactions, high transaction costs, lack of transparency, high costs of property valuation, slow and opaque process, fraudulent transactions, and green washing related to green real estate bonds. The benefits and barriers of tokenizing real estate green bond issuance were also explored. The data sources include in-depth interviews with diverse stakeholders such as developers, subject matter experts including practitioners and academicians, and industry analysts as well as other secondary sources of data. It is found that the blockchain based tokenized securities for green real estate bonds can help in improving liquidity and efficiency of real estate transactions. The transparency is also improved due to disintermediation. The study regarding potential of tokenization is still in its infancy. The interviewed experts also opined that the potential of tokenization has not yet been fully realized because of paucity of technical infrastructures, weak state capacity for regulation, immature asset class, volatilities in the token market, and missing out of an entrepreneurial public sector.

1. INTRODUCTION

Real estate transactions historically been based on paperwork (Malloy & Smith, 2013). The common Problems associated with real estate transactions include opaqueness, illiquidity, high costs and time (Baum, Hartzell, & Wiley, 2011; Kitajima, 2017; Krupa & Akhil, 2019; Latifi, Zhang, & Cheng). The transaction costs range between 5-6% of the total price (Global Property Guide 2016). Instances of Fraudulent practices in real estate market lead to the loss of 5% of revenue (ACFE 2017). Currently, several types of bonds such as green, blue, and transition bonds exist in the market for tackling the issue of climate change. They are faced with several challenges which are discussed in next section. The scope of this research is limited to the conveyance of properties in India.

This research is organized in five sections. First section defines the research problem, justification, scope, objectives, and Organization of the study. Second section provides literature review and develops the framework. Third section provides the research methodology that consists of research design and methods. Research design comprises of case study, survey, and in-depth interview. Fourth section presents the data analysis. The key research findings are summarized in the final section.

2. LITERATURE REVIEW

2.1 What is blockchain technology?

Blockchain technology allows participants to keep maintain a distributed ledger without any control of a central authority. (Ahmad, Alqarni, Almazroi, & Alam, 2021; Nofer, Gomber, Hinz, & Schiereck, 2017; Quiniou, 2019; Swan, 2015; Zheng, Xie, Dai, Chen, & Wang). It helps in achieving decentralization to eliminate the issues such as manipulation, fraud, and corruption due to control of a centralized entity. (Bhanushali, Koul, Sharma, & Shaikh; Zheng et al.). Blockchain can be deployed to create a digital scarce asset. It allows peer to peer trading without involvement of a centralized entity with minimal risk of duplication or counterfeiting.

Blockchains can be public and private. The public blockchains are generally immutable as it is open to all the participants, without any censorship, no third-party entity involvement, and it is neutral. The private blockchain on the other hand are open to only authorized participants with governance involving a control of third party. The public blockchain provides decentralization however it is usually slow and inefficient as compared to private blockchains. The private blockchain for most cases do not need a blockchain technology to achieve its goals.

The blockchain technology depends on five critical components including: peer to peer infrastructure, cryptography, consensus mechanism, incentives and penalties, and market adoption (Connors, 2018; Quiniou, 2019). The peer-to-peer network comprises of a network of computers known as nodes which are open to all the participants for remote communication. Cryptography is used in hostile situations for a secure communication. This becomes crucial as the network can be accessed by scrupulous elements. The new blocks of information are added to the existing blockchain using consensus algorithm. The consensus rules can be based on proof of stake, proof of work, proof of activity and so on. To reach consensus, the participant needs to deploy computational power to solve complex math problems. This process involves lots of energy and hence the participant is rewarded. The market adoption of the system is most crucial element to reach decentralization, as without a critical mass, the system can never be truly decentralized.

Another interesting feature supported by blockchain is what is called a smart contract which essentially allows trust minimizing contracts based on conditionalities. Blockchain is a protocol which allows one to build applications using its infrastructure. The idea of smart contract was invented first by Nick Szabo who discussed vending machine as a smart contract. Efficient smart contracts can be used to codify provincial, local, and national rules on a digitally distributed ledger. Smart contracts can be utilized to codify and streamline deeds, contracts, mortgages, tax procedures, and so on.

The blockchain technology has been deployed to solve numerous issues faced in various sectors of economics such as the financial sector, insurance megacity logistics, healthcare, energy, food safety, equity crowdfunding, smart city, supply chain, network media, IOT, digital certificates, pharma, stocks, governance, government agencies, data security, banking, aviation and so on. The following table demonstrates how the blockchain technology finds application into various industries for eliminating the involvement of third-party intermediaries and better record keeping in terms of an immutable and a secured ledger.

Table 1 Application of blockchain technology across various industries

Field	Application	Problem targeted
Financial Sector	High throughput, reliability, security/privacy, and strict regulatory enforcement (Connors, 2018)	Fraud
Insurance	Faster claim processing, frauds identification, identity verification, pay per use, P2P insurance (Connors, 2018; Gayvoronskaya & Meinel, 2021); Escrow service (for goods) (Crosman, 2018).	Fraud
Logistics	To combat information asymmetry by creating a peer-to-peer audit system for price rationalization (Connors, 2018)	Fraud Transaction cost
Healthcare	Interoperability and data security (Gayvoronskaya & Meinel, 2021)	Fraud Transaction time
Energy	P2P energy transactions through microgrids (Gayvoronskaya & Meinel, 2021).	Transaction cost
Smart City	Secure communication platform in a smart city (Gayvoronskaya & Meinel, 2021; Lehavi & Levine-Schnur, 2020; Morena et al., 2020; Pankratov, Grigoryev, & Pankratov, 2020).	Transaction cost Fraud
Supply Chain	Solution to Double Marginalization and Information Asymmetry (Connors, 2018)	Fraud

IOT	Permissioned BT in Securing User Identity and Transactions (Connors, 2018) Preventing objective information fraud for online businesses (Gayvoronskaya & Meinel, 2021)	Transaction time Fraud
Pharma	Payment of medical bills (Gayvoronskaya & Meinel, 2021).	Transaction time
Banking	Expedited Settlements and International Payments (Gayvoronskaya & Meinel, 2021) Faster payment clearing and credit information systems (Connors, 2018)	Transaction cost

2.2 Issues faced by green real estate bonds

The green real estate bonds are still in their infancy and hence faced with several challenges. Firstly, the market size of the existing green bond market is very small so there is the problem of liquidity. Secondly, there are issues with conventional bonds regarding their payment schedule, settlements, or any corporate actions due to absence of digitization. This is crucial as upfront digitization allows downstream traceability. Thirdly, there are issues with regards to reporting and credentials of the asset itself. There are instances of so-called green washing where the money pooled from investors are allocated to the projects which are pseudo green. Fourth, there is lack of a harmonized standards for green practices. Fifth, there needs to be a benchmark for how an investor understands and access this particular asset class.

2.3 Application of Blockchain Technology to solve Issues faced by green real estate bonds

The blockchain can be utilized to solve plethora of problems faced by real estate sector such as: inconvenient title transfer, issue of price discovery, opaqueness in due diligence due to not unlisted market space, poor data integrity as there is no consolidation and data is all over the place, high transaction cost due to middlemen, proprietary based software which begs the issue of interoperability, poor legal standards and variance even at province level, fraud and corruption deed, mortgage fraud different payment systems and so on.

The blockchain technology can be used for lowering the cost of intermediation for the issuance of green real estate bonds. It can also be used for structuring and capturing these asset classes at the issuance point by listing the investment profile of the bond digitally to start with. The payment schedule, settlements, or any corporate actions can be fully digitized as well. It can help in better data analytics for the investors through trusted, traceable, and transparent data with high level of standards and openness. Such better quality of information can help in attracting lots of capital and global investors.

The digitization has potential in identity management thereby reducing the possibility of frauds and counterfeiting. The blockchain also fixes the issue of provenance through a cryptographically secured digital identity. The assets can also be better secured through hashing of geo coordinates along with description. The hash can be tied to issuer's id and the result is hashed and added to the blockchain. The issuers stand to benefit through: listing marketing & syndication, price auction, the scoring methodology, tokenized issuance and so on.

2.4 Research framework

Each of the steps of real estate bond issuance is explored for its suitability of facilitating it through a blockchain enabled platform. The following diagram shows the process flow for the issuance of a real estate green bond and the issues that can be solved using blockchain:

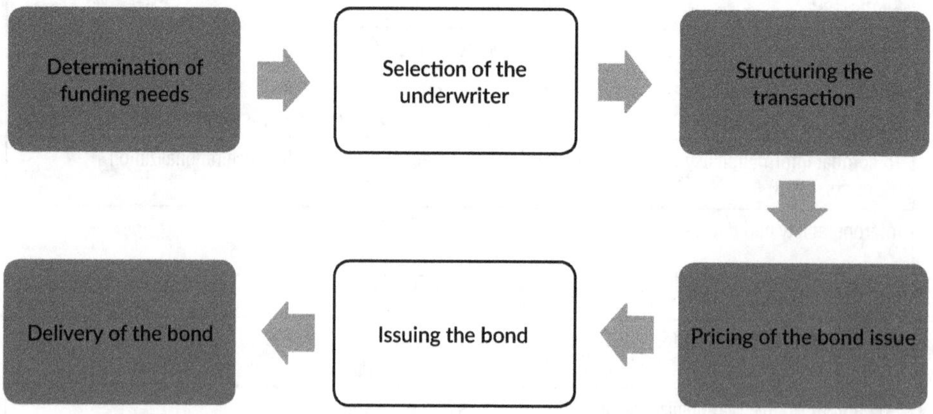

Fig. 1 Process flow for the issuance of a real estate green bond (*Source:* Author)

3. RESEARCH METHODOLOGY

The research methodology section is divided into three sections. Section 3.1 provides the general research design to pursue the objectives of the study. Section 3.2 describes sampling techniques including sampling methods, target population and sampling size are presented. Section 3.3 describes the detail method of data collection for the research.

3.1 Research design

Research methods such as surveys and in-depth interviews were adopted to achieve the research objectives. This research was carried out in two stages. A survey analysis was conducted in the first stage to investigate the acceptance of the blockchain enabled platform for real estate green bond issuance in India. The influencing factors identified in the previous stage could guide the survey activities as well as structuring the questionnaire. The questionnaire consists of different types of questions including close-end questions, open-ended questions, and Likert-scaling questions to obtain both issuer and investor's particulars, perceptions, and preferences for the blockchain enabled platform. The major challenges were also highlighted in the survey result. Thereafter, the subsequent stage will put more efforts on the key challenges highlighted.

In the second stage, regarding to the feasibilities of implementation of the blockchain enabled platform for real estate green bond issuance process in India as well as the challenges highlighted in the second stage, a further deep analysis based on in-depth interviews with real estate experts in India was executed. Thus, the perceptions and visions of real estate experts on the blockchain enabled platform for real estate green bonds issuance process were revealed. Consequently, the difference between real estate experts and potential users was pointed out which gives room for recommendations in the later chapter.

3.2 Sampling

The target population of the survey is current issuer s and investors in India. The survey data was selected based on the convenience sampling and the snowball sampling. In the convenience sampling, the potential issuers and investors who may have some knowledge of blockchain were selected. In particular, the on-site survey was conducted against the issuers and investors who had shown up at the broker's office after obtaining the preceding permit. In the online survey, the questionnaires were distributed in accordance with the snowball sampling in which respondents were asked to forward the link to others who might have interests in the same topic. The sample size for categorical data is determined based on three factors:

- The estimated proportion of an attribute that is present in the population (p)
- The desired level of confidence
- The acceptable margin of error (m)

Thus, the sample size n is calculated according to this following formula by Cochran (1977):

$$n = \frac{z^2 \times p(1-p)}{m^2}$$

Assuming the level of confidence of 95% is chosen, the value of z is 1.96 by using the z-score table, while the margin of error is determined at 5%. The population proportion p is estimated at 0.2. As a result, the proposed sample size for this study is 245.8. The actual number of responses is 251; however, four surveys are illegible due to missing information. Therefore, the final sample size is 247 in which 150 responses were collected from the on-site survey and 97 were obtained online.

The sampling for in depth interview involved a purposive sampling method. A diverse set of stakeholders with divergent demography and credentials were interviewed to ensure complete and in depth understanding of the phenomenon. These stakeholders include industry experts, analysts, consultants, and academicians. These respondents have demonstrated experience in the real estate sector with good knowledge of blockchain. In total, six experts from both the industry and academia were identified and interviewed.

3.3 Methods of data collection

Review of Documents

Data was collected from published documents such as released reports, research papers, newspapers, websites and so on. Accuracy of the data is most important, so the original or official source that often contains the actual data was recommended to use.

Questionnaires

Quantitative evidence gathered from the questionnaire would be used to identify overall trends and challenges involved in the blockchain enabled platform for real estate green bond issuance process. The questionnaire comprises of three main parts.

The first part is with regards to demography of participants where they were enquired about their age, gender, occupation, marital status, and monthly income. Second part is about the issuer's perspective and the final part is about investors perspective.

Semi-structured Interviews

The interview questions were drafted based on an in-depth literature review. These questions were used to guide the interviews. The interviewees were required to provide open ended answers to the questions. Some of the questions were added in subsequent interviews based on the emergent findings.

The aim of the interview is to identify the crux of the problem and understand in depth probe on the key challenges highlighted by the survey results. Interviews also allow for the participants to tell the researchers more than what could be uncovered by surveys, if the researcher is able to establish a rapport with the interviewees and gain their trust. The data collection method employed in this study is in depth interviews. Each interview will last at least for an hour and will be held in the offices of the interviewees. Holding the interview at a location convenient for the interviewee will allow for a more relaxed environment, which will enable the interviewee to be more upfront and candid with their answers.

4. DATA ANALYSIS

4.1 Quantitative data analysis

The data will be analyzed to provide an insight on the major problems which the blockchain enabled online platform can solve for the issuer and investor, as well as understanding the factors that could potentially deter the adoption of the blockchain technology for property green bond issuance.

Analysis encompasses two major parts, namely, descriptive statistics and the use of ANOVA (Analysis of variance) to examine the relationship between variables. Descriptive statistics were used in the tabulation of the frequency data and mean scores of all the variables. ANOVA using f-test to examine whether there is relationship between role of respondent and the priority of problems they believe can be solved better. As chief objective of the research is to explore what problems are more likely to be solved, means ratings (sum of ratings divided by the number of stimuli) were used to compare the degree of easiness of problems that can be solved. To run data, the level of effectiveness was allocated the value. "Totally ineffective" choice was with value of 1, till "Totally effective" was with value of 5. The mean ratings considered of all values of ratings and help compare the level of importance of easiness of problems that can be solved.

4.2 Respondents' profile

Most respondents belong to the age group from 24 to 34 years old. Those in (35 – 44) age range take the second largest pie by 23.4%, followed by those in (15-23) range with 17%. The older groups account for smaller parts with only 5.3% in (45 – 54) age group and 1.7% from 55 years old and above. The age distribution of this survey is in line with the "young population" in India.

4.3 Type of responders (issuer /investor)

Table 2 The survey response based on the respondents' type

S/N	Respondent type	Response Rate
1	Investor	98%
2	Issuer	96%

4.4 Descriptive statistics

The mean rating for the problems that the investors believe can be solved best using blockchain enabled platform is ease of property search with a mean score of 2.86. Similarly, the mean rating for the problems that the issuer s believe can be solved best using blockchain enabled platform is automated payment through smart contract with a mean score of 2.64. The exhaustive table with the mean and standard deviations of scores corresponding to the benefits by the blockchain is given as below:

Table 3 Mean and standard deviations of scores corresponding to the benefits by the blockchain

Benefits by using blockchain	Mean	Std. Deviation	Types of Respondent
No limit for capital required for investing due to tokenized securities	1.56	.735	investor
Better due diligence due to digitization	1.72	.731	investor
Better quality of information	1.92	.777	investor
Better due diligence due to known benchmarks	2.86	.970	Investor
Better accountability through reporting true credentials of the asset	1.57	.761	investor
Transaction efficiency	2.08	.864	investor
Transparency	1.98	.738	investor
Improved liquidity	1.77	.845	investor
Better data analytics for the investors through trusted, traceable, and transparent data	1.95	.861	investor
Data security of investor's credential	1.56	.735	investor
Less adversarial relation due to less chance of financial friction	1.72	.731	investor
Lowering the cost of intermediation	1.62	.711	issuer
Establishment of market standards and benchmarks	1.91	.815	issuer
Structuring and capturing asset information through digitization	2.51	.840	issuer
Better quality of information	2.36	.843	issuer
Establishment of market standards and benchmarks	2.58	.851	issuer
Better accountability through reporting true credentials of the asset	2.64	.778	issuer
Transaction efficiency	2.32	.796	issuer
Less adversarial relation due to less chance of financial friction	1.85	.875	issuer

Table 4 Explanation of total variance by two extracted factors defining benefits for investors

Components	Initial Eigenvalues			Extraction Sums of Squared Loadings			Rotation Sums of Squared Loadings		
	Total	% of Variance	Cumulative %	Total	% of Variance	Cumulative %	Total	% of Variance	Cumulative %
1	7.826	47.741	47.741	7.826	47.741	47.741	5.842	38.294	38.294
2	3.984	24.211	61.952	3.984	24.211	61.952	3.893	23.658	61.952
3	.901	4.290	64.992						
4	.787	3.750	68.742						
5	.760	3.621	72.362						
6	.698	3.326	75.688						
7	.682	3.248	78.937						
8	.610	7.670	86.086						
9	.483	5.364	90.450						
10	.399	4.436	94.886						
11	.309	3.438	100						

Table 5 Explanation of total variance by two extracted factors defining benefits for issuers

Components	Initial Eigenvalues			Extraction Sums of Squared Loadings			Rotation Sums of Squared Loadings		
	Total	% of Variance	Cumulative %	Total	% of Variance	Cumulative %	Total	% of Variance	Cumulative %
1	4.119	45.767	45.767	4.119	45.767	45.767	3.150	35.004	35.004
2	1.196	13.287	59.054	1.196	13.287	59.054	2.165	24.051	59.054
3	.973	10.808	69.862						
4	.770	8.554	78.416						
5	.610	7.670	86.086						
6	.483	5.364	90.450						
7	.399	4.436	94.886						
8	.309	3.438	100						

4.5 Factor analysis for investor attributes

The following table provides the KMO's measure of sampling adequacy along with the Barlett's test for sphericity about 11 attributes explaining benefits for investors in the factor analysis. The factor analysis is deemed appropriate as the result of KMO test yields the value of 0.820. Furthermore, Barlett's measure tests intra variable relationships included in the analysis. For our data, the test is highly significant ($p < 0.001$) and hence the factor analysis is valid.

Table 6 KMO and Barlett's Test for investor attributes

Kaiser-Meyer-Olkin Measure of Sampling Adequacy		.820
Bartlett's Test of Sphericity	Approx. Chi-Square	874.392
	df	36
	Sig.	.000

Given the preliminary results of these two tests, SPSS continued to extract two factors with eigenvalues greater than 1. In this analysis, the two extracted factors account for 59% of total variance. Factor 1 helps explain 45.767% of total variance, and factor 2 accounts for 13.28%. After rotation, factor 1 and 2 account for smaller percentage of variance (35% and 24% respectively).

The commonalities after extraction are estimates of the variance in each variable accounted for by the factors in the factor solutions. In Tables 7-9, over 50% of the variance in all nine variables is accounted for by the two extracted factors.

Table 7 Factor extraction for investor attributes

	Initial	Extraction
No limit for capital required for investing due to tokenized securities	1.000	.589
Better due diligence due to digitization	1.000	.536
Better quality of information	1.000	.566
Better due diligence due to known benchmarks	1.000	.631
Better accountability through reporting true credentials of the asset	1.000	.680
Transaction efficiency	1.000	.557
Transparency	1.000	.551
Improved liquidity	1.000	.622
Better data analytics for the investors through trusted, traceable, and transparent data	1.000	.584
Data security of investor's credential	1.000	.589
Less adversarial relation due to less chance of financial friction	1.000	.536

We then rely on the Rotated Component Matrix to identify variables that are highly correlated with each factor. In Table below, variables with loadings less than 0.4 are hidden and only the factors with higher absolute value of factor loadings are shown.

Based on the factor loading results, we identify two main segments of problem to be solved for the issuer. We can see factors such as "cost saving" resulting from the efficient process and Ability for investor to take advantage of digitization highly in the first factor. Another factor has been weighted heavily is "time saving".

Table 8 Factor extraction for issuer attributes

	Component	
	1	2
Lowering the cost of intermediation	.776	
Establishment of market standards and benchmarks	.767	
Structuring and capturing asset information through digitization	.733	
Better quality of information	.700	
Establishment of market standards and benchmarks	.593	.463
Better accountability through reporting true credentials of the asset		.778
Transaction efficiency		.679
Less adversarial relation due to less chance of financial friction		.633

These two factors reflect the general ease with which problems in green bond issuance market for investors can be solved. In the first factor, it shows the high loading of cost saving due to efficient process. Hence, it's evident that "Cost Saving", illustrated by the highest loading of "cost saving due to efficient process" variable in the factor 1. Therefore, the first factor can be tentatively named as "Cost Saving".

On the other hand, the second factor suggests the highest loading of hassles process, online process. Hence, the second factor in investor's attributes should be labelled "Time Saving" factor.

4.6 Factor analysis for issuer attributes

We apply the same method to extract factors from the data of issuer attributes. The values of the KMO (.846) and Barlett's Test for sphericity (.000) indicate that the data of 8 variables are appropriate for factor analysis.

Table 9 KMO and Barlett's Test for issuer attributes

Kaiser-Meyer-Olkin Measure of Sampling Adequacy		.846
Bartlett's Test of Sphericity	Approx. Chi-Square	1.965E3
	df	210
	Sig.	.000

Factor analysis using varimax rotation yielded two issuer factors with eigenvalues greater than 1. These two extracted factors amount for 60.7% of the variance. The factor loading analysis like investor's case was done. The factor loading suggests that the constructs can be grouped into two broad factors which reflect the general ease with which problems in real estate green bond market for issuer s can be solved.

5. CONCLUSION

This research helps in coming up with the potential of blockchain to solve some of the existing problems for the issuer and investor in green real estate bond market. It was found that the blockchain based tokenized securities can improve transaction efficiency, liquidity, and transparency through better management of intermediaries in the real estate sector. However, they face certain risks such as the regulatory risk, technology risk, and acceptability of the asset class. paper-based transactions, high transaction costs, lack of transparency, high costs of property valuation, slow and opaque process, fraudulent transactions, and green washing related to green real estate bonds. It was also found that the blockchain based tokenized securities for green real estate bonds can help in improving liquidity and efficiency of real estate transactions. The transparency is also improved due to disintermediation. However, the study regarding potential of tokenization is still in its infancy and the interviewed experts also opined that the potential of tokenization has not yet been fully realized because of paucity of technical infrastructures, weak state capacity for regulation, immature asset class, volatilities in the token market, and missing out of an entrepreneurial public sector.

REFERENCES

Ahmad, I., Alqarni, M. A., Almazroi, A. A., & Alam, L. (2021). Real Estate Management via a Decentralized Blockchain Platform. *Computers, materials & continua, 66*(2), 1813. doi:10.32604/cmc.2020.013048

Baum, A., Hartzell, D., & Wiley, I. (2011). *Global property investment: strategies, structures, decisions*. Hoboken, NJ; Chichester, West Sussex; Wiley-Blackwell.

Bhanushali, D., Koul, A., Sharma, S., & Shaikh, B. (2020). *BlockChain to Prevent Fraudulent Activities: Buying and Selling Property Using BlockChain.*

Connors, K. (2018). *Blockchain: how Bitcoin and Blockchain are reshaping the world of finance*: Createspace Independent.

Crosman, P. (2018). Could Blockchains Replace Banks In Real Estate Lending? Startups that have developed blockchains for real estate finance are starting to conduct a broader array of transactions, including property sales. *National mortgage news, 42*(7), 10.

Gayvoronskaya, T., & Meinel, C. (2021). *Blockchain: Hype or Innovation* (1st 2021. ed.). Cham: Springer International Publishing.

Grover, P., Kar, A. K., & Janssen, M. (2019). Diffusion of blockchain technology. *Journal of enterprise information management, 32*(5), 735–757. doi:10.1108/JEIM-06-2018-0132

Gupta, A., Rathod, J., Patel, D., Bothra, J., Shanbhag, S., & Bhalerao, T. (2020). Tokenization of Real Estate Using Blockchain Technology. In (pp. 77–90). Cham: Springer International Publishing.

Hoksbergen, M., Chan, J., Peko, G., & Sundaram, D. (2019). Asymmetric Information in High-Value Low-Frequency Transactions: Mitigation in Real Estate Using Blockchain. In (pp. 225–239). Cham: Springer International Publishing.

Hoxha, V., & Sadiku, S. (2019). Study of factors influencing the decision to adopt the blockchain technology in real estate transactions in Kosovo. *Property management, 37*(5), 684–700. doi:10.1108/PM-01-2019-0002

Huh, J.-H., & Kim, S.-K. (2020). Verification Plan Using Neural Algorithm Blockchain Smart Contract for Secure P2P Real Estate Transactions. *Electronics (Basel), 9*(6), 1052. doi:10.3390/electronics9061052

Kalyuzhnova, N. (2018). Transformation of the real estate market on the basis of use of the blockchain technologies: opportunities and problems. *MATEC web of conferences, 212*, 6004. doi:10.1051/matecconf/201821206004

Kitajima, T. (2017). Possibility of new real estate registration system by using blockchain. *The Japanese Journal of Real Estate Sciences, 31*(1), 72–77. doi:10.5736/jares.31.1_72

Krupa, K. S., & Akhil, M. S. (2019). Reshaping the Real Estate Industry Using Blockchain. In (pp. 255–263). Singapore: Springer Singapore.

Latifi, S., Zhang, Y., & Cheng, L.-C. (2019). *Blockchain-Based Real Estate Market: One Method for Applying Blockchain Technology in Commercial Real Estate Market.*

Lehavi, A., & Levine-Schnur, R. (2020). *Disruptive Technology, Legal Innovation, and the Future of Real Estate* (1st 2020. ed.). Cham: Springer International Publishing.

Malloy, R. P., & Smith, J. C. (2013). *Real estate transactions: problems, cases, and materials* (Fourth ed.). New York: Wolters Kluwer Law & Business.

Morena, M., Truppi, T., Pavesi, A. S., Cia, G., Giannelli, J., & Tavoni, M. (2020). Blockchain and real estate: Dopo di Noi project. *Property management, 38*(2), 273–295. doi:10.1108/PM-01-2019-0005

Nofer, M., Gomber, P., Hinz, O., & Schiereck, D. (2017). Blockchain. *Business & information systems engineering, 59*(3), 183–187. doi:10.1007/s12599-017-0467-3

Pankratov, E., Grigoryev, V., & Pankratov, O. (2020). The blockchain technology in real estate sector: Experience and prospects. *IOP conference series. Materials Science and Engineering, 869*(6), 62010. doi:10.1088/1757-899X/869/6/062010

Quiniou, M. (2019). *Blockchain: the advent of disintermediation* (1 ed.). London: ISTE Ltd.

Swan, M. (2015). *Blockchain: Blueprint for a new economy*: " O'Reilly Media, Inc.".

Tilbury, J. L., de la Rey, E., & van der Schyff, K. (2019). *Business Process Models of Blockchain and South African Real Estate Transactions.*

Ullah, F., & Al-Turjman, F. (2021). A conceptual framework for blockchain smart contract adoption to manage real estate deals in smart cities. *Neural computing & applications*. doi:10.1007/s00521-021-05800-6

Verheye, B. (2017). Real estate publicity in a blockchain world: a critical assessment. *European property law journal, 6*(3), 441–476. doi:10.1515/eplj-2017-0020

Zheng, Z., Xie, S., Dai, H., Chen, X., & Wang, H. (2017). *An Overview of Blockchain Technology: Architecture, Consensus, and Future Trends*.

APPENDIX A

Survey questionnaire

Dear respondents,

I am Ravi Shankar, a fourth-year student of Department of Building, National University of Singapore. I am currently pursuing a research on "*potential of blockchain based tokenized securities for green real estate bonds*". Therefore, I conduct this survey. Your response is extremely valuable to my research. It will take you no more than 10 minutes. Your details and information will be kept confidential and used strictly for academic purposes only.

Thank you!

Section A: Respondents' profile

Please tick your answer

Q1. What is your age?

☐ 20-30 ☐ 31-40

☐ 41-50 ☐ >51

Q2. What is your Monthly earning?

☐ <4000 ☐ 4000-8000

☐ 8001-12000 ☐ >12000

Q3. Which of the following category you belong to?

☐ issuer ☐ investor

Section B: Perception towards ability of blockchain based leasing platforms to solve green bond issuance problems

Please rate the following on the scale provided below

Not effective Highly effective

☐ 1 ☐ 2 ☐ 3 ☐ 4 ☐ 5

Q4. Perception towards ability of blockchain based leasing platforms to solve investor's problems

Q5. Perception towards ability of blockchain based leasing platforms to solve issuer 's problems

Q6. Which feature of block chain enabled leasing system do you feel appreciable? (Chose 1 or more)

☐ Information security ☐ Reduction in time for leasing process

☐ User friendly interface ☐ Reduction in cost for leasing process

☐ Safe transaction ☐ Others (please specify)

THANK YOU

APPENDIX B

Interviews

Six participants are chosen and interviewed:

A) Mr. Sonam Udasi, Head of research in TATA Asset Management Ltd

Mr. Sonam is the head of research of TATA Asset Management Ltd. He has great knowledge about investing in new technologies such as blockchain and about the industry.

B) Sanjeev Bikhchandani, Founder of 99Acres.com

Sanjeev is passionate about new technologies and has worked closely to help various organizations derive benefit from the digital transformation throughout his career.

C) U.P.S. Madan, Metropolitan Commissioner MMRDA

MMRDA is a government organization under the government of Maharashtra and is responsible for the infrastructure development of Mumbai. Mr. Madan's insights are crucial to understand the viewpoint of government with regards to implementation of modern age technologies for provision of key infrastructures.

D) Akansha Bakshi,Analyst, Deloitte India.

Akansha Bakshi has deep interest in modern age technologies in fintech and digital transformations. She is a part of the blockchain and cryptocurrency team at Deloitte which provides blockchain strategies and solutions to diverse set of clients.

E) Abhishek Lodha, Managing Director, Lodha group.

As the Managing Director of Lodha Group, Abhishek is well known in the media and industry for his deep insights on the subject. He appears regularly on major print media including newspapers, television, and internet.

F) Prof Deng Yong Heng, National University of Singapore (NUS).

Prof Deng is works at the NUS Business School. His main research interest lies in evaluation of conditions in China's housing markets. He is also keenly involved in publishing on latest innovations in capital markets and 4 IR technologies and its application in real estate industry.

The interviews were all carried through phone calls due to Covid-19. Due to the different knowledge of the participants, different questions have been asked. The questions are based on the theoretical framework and how blockchain might affect specific markets within real estate, targeting mostly for real estate rental in India.

Interview questions

1. What are the issues faced by bond issuers in conventional bond issuance?
2. What are the issues in conventional bond issuance that the blockchain technology can potentially solve?
3. What are the expected challenges for market adoption of blockchain based tokenized securities for green real estate bonds?

Coding

The raw data of interviews require some processing before the actual data analysis. The aim for coding is to identify the key points or concepts in the conversation for further analysis. Open coding would be performed using transcriptions.

Categories

After the preliminary processing the raw data of interviews, a sample summary of the different participants' opinions regarding the discussed subject in the interviews are summarized in the below table.

Interview Summary	Governmental authority	Companies				Academic world
	MMRDA	TATA	99Acres	Deloitte	Lodha	Prof Deng
General attitude towards digitalization	Positive	Positive	Positive	Positive	Positive	Positive
Develops blockchain based platforms	Yes, in cooperation	No	Yes	No	No	No
Biggest obstacles towards Blockchain	Building a unhackable and reliable system	Development and implementation costs	Regulations in the financial sector	The real estate industry lags several years behind other markets	Secure reliable information	People's preference to a brokers contact
Attitude towards transparency	It is utterly important for a governmental institution to have transparent systems	Bigger arbitrage opportunities lie in a less transparent market	Transparency benefits everyone in the market	Increased transparency will create more competition in the market	A transparent market is a contradiction, but efficient in some matters	Transparency is just positive
Most interesting benefit from blockchain	"Trust-machine"	Improved know-your-customer process	Transparent to its customers	More secure and faster transaction processes	Help in market efficiency	Transparency on the rental market

SECTION III

Measuring the Outcomes - Focusing on the 'How' to Ensure 'Why'

Infrastructure Development: Ensuring Environmentally Sustainable Outcomes

G. Raghuram[1]
Principal Academic Advisor
National Rail and Transportation Institute, Vadodara

Rachna Gangwar
Associate Professor, Transport and Public Policy
Adani Institute of Infrastructure Management, Ahmedabad

Infrastructure projects are key drivers of economic and social development; however, poor planning, design and implementation can pose serious threat to the environment. As per a World Bank study, approximately 70% of global greenhouse-gas emissions emanate from infrastructure construction and operations such as power plants, buildings, and transportation systems (The World Bank, 2018). Efforts are being intensified from governments across the globe and multilateral agencies to achieve the set emission targets, as per the Paris Agreement and various other international treaties. Developing economies face greater challenge as the financial support from governments for promoting low carbon infrastructure and relevant research is not able to keep pace with the scale at which the infrastructure development is taking place.

As infrastructure projects are vulnerable to environmental hazards at all stages, due diligence in identifying the potential risks throughout the life cycle of a project is essential. We view development, construction and operations as the three important stages. In addition, research and development is an important support input. While sustainable outcomes include social, economic and environmental sustainability, we focus on environmentally sustainable outcomes.

1. DEVELOPMENT

Most infrastructure projects require huge land parcels either at one location (power plants, ports, airports, buildings, social economic zones, etc) or along a corridor (roads, railway lines, power transmission lines, metro lines, etc). The site selection and thereof the impact assessment on inhabitants, environment, ecology, and natural habitat is critical to ensure sustainability. To minimize/mitigate the risks, Environmental Impact Assessment and Social Impact Assessment have been made mandatory in India for all infrastructure projects, beyond a threshold. However, the robustness of these studies and the implementation of environmental management measures is often questioned, resulting in undesired outcomes. For example, urban flooding is a consequence of poor planning and development of urban infrastructure. The frequency and the intensity of such events is increasing in India, putting Indian cities at much greater risk. These flooding events lead to outbreaks of many diseases that lasts for a much longer time than the rainfall season. Effective policies and regulatory instruments must be designed and implemented for sustainable growth of cities. This stage is the most critical since wrong decisions taken at this stage can result into costly mistakes later. A study based on the review of six infrastructure projects in UK identifies that not enough attention by decision makers at early stages as one of the reasons for projects turning into white elephants (Atkins et al., 2017).

This stage is also crucial for decision making on key aspects of the project i.e. the use of the materials, technology, equipment, etc that will have implications on sustainability. For example, the policy decision of government to promote

[1] Former Director, Indian Institute of Management Bangalore

railways vis-s-vis airways for regional connectivity has consequences on the environment. Carbon emissions from short haul flights (less than 1000 kms) are approximately 250 gm CO_2 equivalent per passenger kms which is nearly 5-6 times of rail (Statista, 2021). While China has invested heavily in high-speed railway network in the past decades, India has been a slow starter. The first high speed rail corridor is being constructed in India and few more are being planned. The policy thrust also been towards promoting regional air connectivity under UDAAN[1] scheme in India. With an expected growth of 8% per annum in air passenger traffic, the challenges are inevitable for India.

In the case of high-speed railway projects, the decision on whether to select the Indian broad gauge (1676 mm) or the standard gauge (1435 mm) is an important strategic decision that have long term implications for the sector. The standard gauge selection requires the entire infrastructure (track, stations, depots) to be built dedicatedly for high speed which may not get optimally utilized if the realized traffic volumes are less than projected. Dedicated stations and depots also pose additional land requirements. The uniform gauge on the other hand provides better integration with existing infrastructure, thus increasing the sustainability. However, the design/technology for broad gauge coaches is not readily available. Policy research in these directions will help long term sustainability.

2. CONSTRUCTION

The next stage in the project life cycle is the construction stage. The use of environmentally friendly, local building materials, provision for rainwater harvesting, green cover, energy efficiency, etc are some of the measures that minimize resource consumption, thus making built environment more sustainable. The rating systems in India - Leadership in Energy and Environmental Design (LEED), Indian Green Building Council (IGBC), and Green Rating for Integrated Habitat Assessment (GRIHA) certify the green rating of buildings. Similarly, there are rating systems for other infrastructure domains as well such as Greenroads rating systems for roads. Research is underway for new technologies and materials that can be used as substitutes in road construction, making them more environmental friendly.

Other than the 'green' aspect, the basic 'quality' is another major problem resulting in substandard and unsustainable infrastructure at construction stage. As an example, the newly constructed Byappanahalli railway terminal in March 2021 in Bangaluru city suffered water leakage and flooding after first rainfall. This has happened before the terminal was officially inaugurated. There are many such examples where the quality is greatly compromised. People engaged in designing/constructing this infrastructure do not understand what it is required to put in appropriate infrastructure that delivers what it's expected to do. Firstly, this highlights the need for more professionalism and bringing in organizations whose reputation is at stake for quality. This is where the PPP logic in India has come in where the best organizations are selected through an open and competitive bidding. Second important aspect is training to bring in the sense of quality until the last level in the organizational hierarchy. The third aspect is defining the scope of the project considering all possible dimensions of sustainability rather than just 'green'. For example, having a tree based green cover using social forestry on the side or on the median of expressway hinders visibility of the driver and poses a safety risk. Safety over green may be more significant in this context.

3. OPERATIONS

Low carbon infrastructure would entail less energy consumption during the life of the operating phase. In the case of road transport, this would mean use of vehicles which are environmental friendly such as electric vehicles, bio-fuel vehicles, etc. Electric vehicle policy is gaining momentum across the globe. Since the transport industry accounts for almost 23% of energy related global green-house gas emissions of the world (Sims R et al., 2014) and the road transport contributes the highest, electric vehicles could be a significant step towards environmental sustainability. The Government of India has targeted 30% electric vehicle penetration by 2030 (GIZ, 2021). However, the lack of charging infrastructure, poor battery life, and higher costs are some of the reasons hindering the growth of this industry.

While there is a policy thrust on electric vehicles, the demand for energy is going to increase many folds as the market for electric vehicles matures. It is important that the increased energy demands are met from renewable sources otherwise it will only shift the pollution from urban areas to power plant locations instead of abating it. The growth in renewable

[1] UDDAN (Ude Desh ka Aam Naagrik) is a regional air connectivity scheme of Ministry of Civil Aviation, Government of India.

sources of energy, particularly solar, has been impressive in India. Technological innovations and government support has helped the industry grow.

Research on cleaner fuels such as bio diesel for road vehicles, airlines, and shipping lines is underway for its viability for mass production. The pollution from aircraft operations is very high and a large share is at the time of take-off and landing. France and some countries in Europe have stopped short haul flight operations due to limits set by European Commission for each country.

The waste that gets generated at the end of the life cycle of the products used in provisioning of infrastructure services such as vehicles, equipment, machinery, etc pose a serious risk to the environment. Disposal of rubber tyres of vehicles, other material that cannot be recycled is a major challenge faced by the governments. As per an estimate, approximately one billion waste tyres are generated globally every year (WBCSD, 2008). With 6-7% share, India's challenges include collection of waste tyres, curbing illegal dumping, banning of waste import, stricter regulatory oversight, etc (Aggarwal, 2021).

4. RESEARCH AND DEVELOPMENT (R&D)

Underlying all these challenges is the R&D that will provide long-term solutions. It cannot be more emphasised that India is highly under leveraged in terms of R&D. We depend on other countries for technology. In-spite of the fact that there is no dearth of talent in India, the R&D support is lacking. It must come from (i) government and (ii) business. We definitely need government policies, international cooperation and, businesses to support the R&D.

The assessment of sustainability holistically is a complex process. The research is focused largely on assessing the environmental impact. Giving equal attention to all the three pillars of sustainability – economic, social, and environmental - is a challenge, particularly for assessments in longer terms. There are several approaches for evaluating the impact on all three pillars of sustainability. The most common and well-established ones have been the life cycle approaches such as Environmental Life Cycle Assessment, Life Cycle Costing, and Social Life Cycle Assessment that have been addressing individually the three sustainability pillars. Life Cycle Sustainability Assessment, which integrates all three approaches, is gaining significance for making integrated assessment across all three pillars (UNEP, 2011).

However, choices that lead to positive environmental outcomes may not come naturally to manufacturers, project developers, end consumers, and other stakeholders due to lack of information, higher costs, difficulty in sourcing, availability of trained human resource. Examples are higher manufacturing costs of green building materials, electric vehicles, solar energy, and higher capital investment in metro, and other rail-based transport systems. As a result, business entities either do not come forward for investing in these alternatives or depend heavily on government subsidy. Technology, and R&D are playing an integral role in making these solutions cost effective for businesses and end consumers. Government policies and other institutions must support and provide an eco-system for more R&D leading to sustainable and technology driven solutions.

While the trade-off between economic growth and environmental sustainability is well established, government policies must strike a balance between economic development, social well-being and the environment.

The five research papers presented in this section address various aspects of environmental sustainability. The first paper examines the COVID-19 infection pattern and the subsequent government response in ten countries. It brings out that timely interventions and administrative initiatives can make enormous difference in outcomes, beyond environmental sustainability. The second paper has developed a research-based ranking framework based on multi criteria decision making method for solar energy sector. The third paper has evaluated the sustainability of buildings using a system dynamics approach. The framework enables the incorporation of dynamic temporal characteristics such as a change in the building's average energy consumption throughout its operation period, ignoring which could lead to underestimating of actual impacts. The fourth paper has reviewed the Indian Government policies on electric vehicles. It suggests that car purchase tax and feebate policies are most effective in accelerating low carbon technology uptake and reducing life cycle greenhouse gas emissions. The fifth paper reviews the impact of renewable energy for their effectiveness. It emphasizes on technological advancements, R&D and right policy enforcement to encourage and enhance renewable energies.

REFERENCES

Aggarwal, M. (2021, August 25). Retrieved from Mongabay: https://india.mongabay.com/2019/09/control-import-of-waste-tyres-into-india-ngt-tells-pollution-board/

Atkins et al. (2017). *What's wrong with infrastructure decision making? - Conclusions from six UK case studies.* Institute for Government.

GIZ. (2021). *Status quo analysis of various segments of electric mobility and low carbon passenger road transport in India.* Deutsche Gesellschaft für Internationale Zusammenarbeit (GIZ) GmbH.

Sims R *et al.*, (2014). *Transport. In: Climate Change 2014: Mitigation of Climate Change. Contribution of Working Group III to the Fifth Assessment Report of the Intergovernmental Panel on Climate Change.* Cambridge, United Kingdom and New York, NY, USA: Cambridge University Press.

Statista. (2021, August 30). Retrieved from Statista: https://www.statista.com/statistics/1185559/carbon-footprint-of-travel-per-kilometer-by-mode-of-transport/

The World Bank. (2018). *Low-Carbon Infrastructure - Private Participation in Infrastructure (PPI).* World Bank Group.

UNEP. (2011). *Towards a Life Cycle Sustainability Assessment: Making informed choices on products.*

WBCSD. (2008). *Managing End-of-Life Tires.* World Business Council for Sustainable Development.

Around the World in Eighty Days: Some Insights for Health Policies from Early Incidence, Fatality, and Recovery Data of Covid-19

Ajeet N. Mathur[1]
Professor Emeritus
New Delhi Institute of Management

Sandhya Sreekumar[2]
Assistant Professor
MIT World Peace University, Pune

Abstract: Covid-19 is different from previous pandemics in many respects and singularly striking for an exceptionally unique phenomenon. Never before has an infection gone around the world to 216 countries in a short span of eighty days. This paper compares the incidence, fatality and recovery from Covid-19 data to discern patterns, examine differences in approach and draw lessons for health policy and health systems with data of first eighty days from the first infection in each country. The purpose of this paper is threefold: first, to compare responses of high income and low income countries from the perspective of spread, control measures, containment, tracing and treatment; second, to examine whether greater societal development or prosperity is associated with better outcomes for recovery of infected patients or lower fatality; and thirdly, to consider institutional differences that may explain differences in outcomes. For the study, we included countries with high infection rates [United States of America (USA), United Kingdom (UK), Italy, China, and Saudi Arabia] and also those with low infection rates (Vietnam, Japan, South Korea, New Zealand, and India). We conclude that health systems in high-income countries can learn to be resilient from the experience of other high income countries and also from low-income countries. Timely interventions and administrative initiatives can bring about an enormous difference in outcomes.

Keywords: Health Care Systems, Public Health Risk, Pandemic, Prevention and Control, and Institutions

1. INTRODUCTION

When the French Novelist Jules Verne wrote about the escapades of Phileas Fogg and his valet Passepartout in 1872 and how they circumnavigated the globe in eighty days, it was considered something of a marvel. With the growth of air traffic, a microorganism, the Covid-19, has spread through contagion to 216 countries in eighty days across all latitudes and longitudes (WHO, 2020a). Coronaviruses are enveloped, positive-sense, single-stranded RNA viruses that can transmit a disease to both human and animal species (Chu et al., 2020). The virus was first noticed in December 2019 in Wuhan province of China (WHO, 2020b; Huang et al., 2020). On 30 January 2020, the World Health Organization (WHO) announced the COVID-19 epidemic as a 'public health emergency of international concern' (WHO, 2020c). In Wuhan, where the outbreak first raged, it left thousands dead but over 90% of patients afflicted by the disease recovered. By May 2020 the number of persons infected by Covid-19 in China had dropped to a miniscule number and China featured neither in the top ten countries in terms of total infection incidence nor in the number of active cases or deaths. A particular way of limiting the spread with a strict regional lockdown prevented the spread to other parts of China. Several other countries have struggled to keep infections down through testing, tracing and treating infected patients. There was a variety of responses in different countries at national and sub-national levels.

[1] Former Professor, Indian Institute of Management Ahmedabad

[2] Former Research Officer, Adani Institute of Infrastructure Management, Ahmedabad

Are there insights to be gained from the experience and outcomes of different country responses of the first eighty days? Might there be clues to alternative strategies so that such a pandemic is better coped in the future? Are there lessons of resilience from the experiences of countries for health systems and public health elsewhere? This was especially intriguing because there were hardly any models that inspired confidence.

1.1 Pandemics and Health Policies

The motivation for this inquiry arose from the importance of augmenting what we know about pandemics and early response to them. There are differences in how public health systems are organized (Madsen, 2016; Gray, 1974) and public health interventions from previous studies (Abbott et al., 2017; Brieba, 2018). From adversities that have accompanied pandemics previously, it is possible to learn and mitigate setbacks with better policies and interventions (Bhattamishra & Barrett, 2010; Zarychta, 2020). From what is known about the effectiveness of health care spending and priorities, it may also be possible to examine whether more health expenditures always yield better public health (Ssozi & Amlani, 2015). Solutions must be found for controlling the devasting impact of pandemics that affect the developed world (Huizer, 2015) and isolated small environments such as Bhutan, Sikkim, Maldives (Prior & Stanhope, 1980).

Countries like China and South Korea relied on technologies and engaged in 'aggressive-mass-testing'. Facial recognition cameras, Quick Response Code (QRS) technology and drones were used to track movements of citizens in China. South Korea used Global Positioning System (GPS) data from mobile phone networks, credit card information from transactions, and video images to scope the spread of coronavirus (Nay, 2020). This helped South Korea with contact-tracing which would otherwise have been expensive and inaccurate (Ferretti et al., 2020; Sun & Viboud, 2020). These tracking technologies helped national and local governments to foresee health threats and prepare well in advance accordingly.

South Korea managed to suppress its outbreak early on due to a concerted effort to test and trace based on expert guidelines, whereas in Japan, early grassroot-level response saved the day. Japan's contract local tracers, who are part of public health centers, acted fast due to their previous experiences with tracing other common infections such as influenza and tuberculosis. After successfully tracing initial infections found in January, they focused on detecting bunch of infections from a single site like hospitals or slums, to prevent a rapid increase in cases. Therefore, these public health centers could efficiently act as local centers for disease control (Du & Hang, 2020). Japan and South Korea acted with alacrity based on experience of Severe Acute Respiratory Syndrome (SARS) and learnings from that (Shaw et al., 2020).

South Korea, Singapore, Italy, Spain, India, and the UK opted for lockdowns. South Korea, Singapore and India did better than Italy, Spain, and the UK on both incidence and fatality, adjusted for population. What accounts for the difference? Countries for instance, Sweden and Brazil did not introduce lockdowns. Such a strategy based partly on precautions and partly aimed at eventually cultivating 'herd immunity' was associated with higher fatality rates in both Sweden and Brazil. Sweden as a prosperous developed country with well-resourced public healthcare coped better than Brazil raising questions about how capacities to respond to public health pandemics may have something to do with economic development, or health systems. Some countries had more infections than others, but their recovery rates were high and fatality rates lower. Vietnam, Saudi Arabia, Japan had very low fatality rates. Countries such as Italy, Spain, UK, USA experienced both high rates of incidence and fatality. While the incidence denoting the spread of the disease can be influenced by the severity of lockdowns, testing and tracing, and the prevalent common sense in a population educated enough to maintain good personal hygiene and social distancing, once infected, the fatality or recovery has mainly two contributing factors. First, the comorbidity factors such as age (the older, the more vulnerable), pre-existing conditions such as diabetes, cardiac ailments etc. may be different among those infected as a population group. Secondly, the robustness of a country's healthcare system and well-endowed properly resourced hospitals with adequate infrastructure and sufficiency of competent medical professionals could make a difference. The only way to know is to analyse and compare what happened to incidence, recovery and fatality in different countries from the day the first infections were reported in each of them and examine the two-way causality between the level of development and the capacity to deal with the pandemic. This paper concludes by bringing focus to the intricacies of the issues discussed and observing that in the short run, medium term and long-term policy problems cannot be telescoped. Development indicators are not a predictor of how effective responses to public health emergencies would be organized. There is scope for learning in high-income countries from countries of all income levels. The first infections were confirmed on different dates in different countries. For a meaningful comparison, responses of countries from the first so-called 'index case' onwards can be taken for the same number of days.

New Zealand adopted a different approach, an elimination strategy, instead of a mitigation model. The first case of coronavirus was reported on 28 February 2020 in New Zealand. Flights from China were banned from 3 February 2020. It focused on effectively regulating borders, and conducted wide testing, surveillance and contact tracing. With a small population of only five million, more than 1,50,000 were tested for Covid-19 since 22 January. These tests not only covered people with symptoms but also their casual and close contacts (Cousins, 2020). New Zealand learned lessons from the struggles of Italy, Spain, and the UK with Covid and initiated a new four-level 'Alert System' and its last stage was implemented immediately on March 23 with just 102 cases and zero deaths (Trevatt, 2020; Wilson, 2020). Later, the Ministry of Health specifically arranged tests for specific communities like the aged in residential care and health-care workers, who were at higher risk of infection (Cousins, 2020).

Another high-income nation, France, did not succeed like New Zealand. Recommendations given by WHO for community-wide testing, social distancing and contact tracing were not followed early as was done in South Korea where the first case was detected on 1 February 2020, like France. Timely implementation of non-pharmaceutical measures was critical and late lockdowns in Italy (March 9) and France (March 17) aggravated the situation. Due to the shortage of both, authorized laboratories (only 45 in public facilities) and RT-PCR kits, France lacked the logistic capacity for mass testing (Godeluck, 2020; Nature, 2020; Moatti, 2020).

Responses of countries USA and UK were also fairly delayed, and the situation got out of control. USA's fight against coronavirus suffered from various factors including uncoordinated actions between states and the centre, absence of transparency and trust in communications from the nation's highest office levels, political leaders disregarding expert-based advice and uneven lockdowns across the country (Hatcher, 2020; Gondi et al., 2020; Van Dorn et al., 2020). The situation degraded due to underinvestment in public health infrastructure and emergency preparedness and over dependence on international suppliers for medical supplies which manifested as the dearth of personal protective equipment (PPE) kits (e.g. gloves, masks and gowns etc.). Similarly, the UK government introduced lockdowns on 23 March 2018 long after the detection of the first case on 31 January 2020 (Banerjee et al., 2020; WHO, 2020c).

Vietnam, with no deaths due to coronavirus, till the 80th Day and even beyond stood out as having imbibed useful insights from an outbreak of SARS in 2003. Vietnamese health authorities gave special attention to the management of hospitals and quickly setup temporary hospitals well before an increasing number of Covid patients could overwhelm the capacity for health management. With the help of experts from South Korea, mass testing was established with testing kiosks at hotspots (Ohara, 2004; Nguyen & Chau, 2020; La et al., 2020; Xuan, 2020).

India adopted a graded action plan with point-of-entry surveillance, community wide testing, scaling up of laboratory and hospital surge capacities, and regular spread of technical guidelines on administering various aspects of the infection's outbreak. These steps helped India be one of the lowest in the world with respect to the total number of Covid cases per million population, which as compare to the world average of 1,453.25, was 505.37 on 7 July 2020. With additional amenities of oxygen support, ICU and ventilator facilities, India scaled up infrastructure in government hospitals (Press Trust of India, 2020). The government established a comprehensive Covid portal to provide updates at the national and state levels through various applications like Aarogya Setu and ITIHAS, a mobile-based tracking technology used for surveillance and detection of potential clusters of infection, applications for testing and keeping track of patients undergoing treatment and current hospital bed capacities. All the orders and demand for hospital supplies including oxygen cylinders, ventilators, PPE kits and N-95 and N-99 masks were met by new 'Make in India' initiatives (Press Information Bureau, 2020a). With an enhanced focus on 'Test, Trace, Treat', India conducted more than 5 lakh tests per day (Press Information Bureau, 2020b). In India, Kerala did exceptionally well in containing the outbreak having learnt from the experience with the Nipah virus in 2018 (Chetterje, 2020).

2. MATERIALS AND METHODS

This paper analyses the data of incidence, fatality and recovery from Covid-19 infections in ten countries for their respective first eighty days from the first infection in each country. With the help of trend analysis, we compared the differences in Covid-19 scenarios of high and low-infection rate countries. And we observed differences among the high and low-infection rate countries.

Since one of the main aims was to compare the experience of the first eighty days across countries, country level data of the incidence of infections was first clustered across all countries from low infection incidence to high infection incidence.

We then selected countries with high infection rates [United States of America (USA), United Kingdom (UK), Italy, China, and Saudi Arabia] and some with low infection rates (Vietnam, Japan, South Korea, New Zealand, and India). There were countries with lower infection rates such as Lebanon, Ghana, Costa Rica, and Georgi (WHO, 2020d), but we excluded them because their demographic characteristics and development ranks by the Human Development Index (UNDP, 2019) rendered them unsuitable for purposes of comparison at the lower end of the spectrum.

To understand movements along the curve of infection, we noted the daily cumulative cases of COVID-19, for the first 80 days starting from Day 0 (when the first case of infection was confirmed) for 10 different countries, sourcing our data from the Center for Systems Science and Engineering (CSSE) of Johns Hopkins University (CSSE, 2020). For collecting information on China, the repository of the European Centre for Disease Prevention and Control (ECDC) was referred (ECDC, 2020) as the data on China by CSSE is available only from 22 January 2020 onwards but cases of coronavirus had previously been reported before that (WHO, 2020b; Huang et al., 2020). Cases of death and recovery were also obtained from the same source and included in the data set corresponding to the infection incidence cumulatively.

For comparison, the infection incidence was adjusted for the population size by taking cumulative cases per million of the population for each of the first eighty days for all ten countries. Then instead of taking incidence of infection for every day, we took the cumulative numbers every fourth day and plotted them in tables.

The trend was analysed by plotting data of Covid cases of China and USA to compare recovery and death rates as they were both in the category of countries with high numbers of Covid infections. For similar reasons data related to Covid cases of low incidence countries (such as Vietnam and India) were plotted to study trends. The differences in patterns among the two different groups at each end of the spectrum from low incidence to high incidence were also studied.

3. FINDINGS

The five countries with high infection rates included in our study suffered a lot due to the Covid outbreak, but their struggles with the pandemic were not similar to one another. Figure 1 shows trend lines based on moving averages for total confirmed cases, active cases, recovered cases and deaths in China. This indicates that even though China had a high number of confirmed Covid cases, majority of them recovered and only a few remained as active cases. Further, the situation seems to in control as the incidence trend curve and the actual curve flattened after the 56th day (since the first case of Covid was confirmed) and did not rise any further.

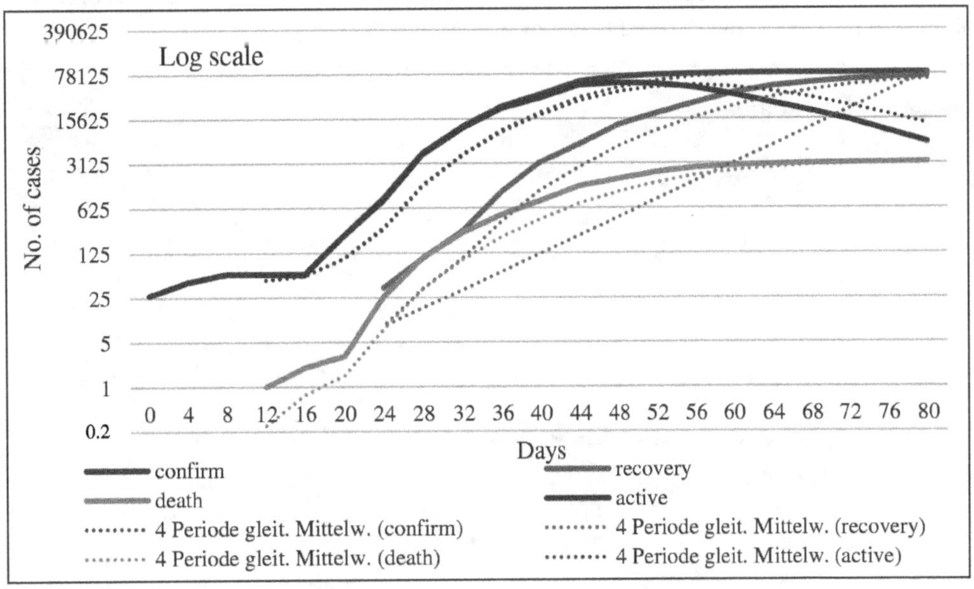

Fig. 1 Trend analysis of Covid cases in China

(This image appears in colour at the end of the compendium).

The situation in the USA reveals a different trend than in China, despite being a country with a comparable high infection rate (see Figure 2).

The trend line of confirmed cases is lower than the actual cases of Covid and the actual and trend curves of incidence of USA do not flatten but kept moving upwards aggressively even after the 40th day. Further, trend lines and real lines of both confirmed and active cases were quite close to each other indicating that most of the confirmed cases did not recover and remained active. Therefore, the situation in the USA was much worse than the one prevailing in China.

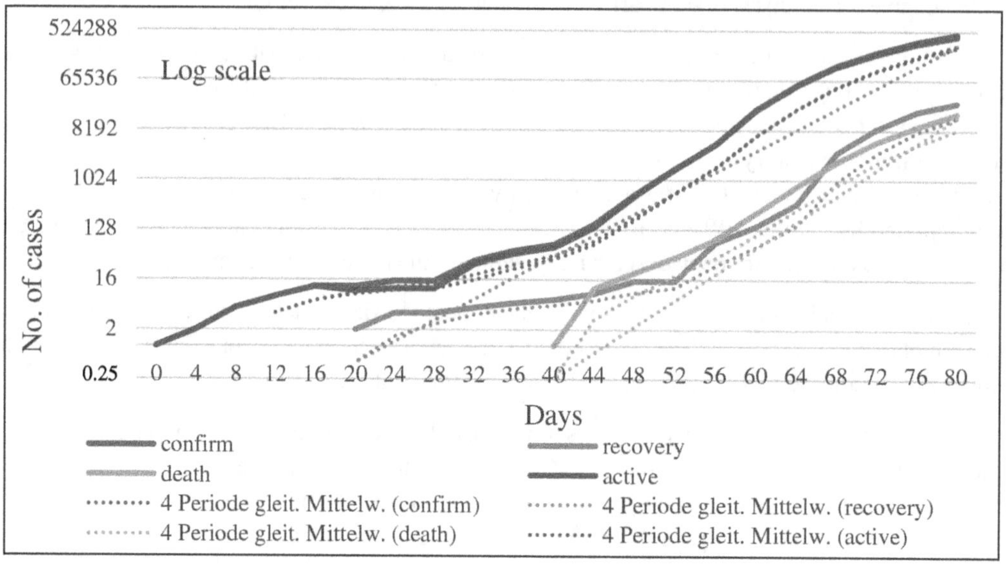

Fig. 2 Trend analysis of Covid cases in USA

(This image appears in colour at the end of the compendium).

Next, we examine varying scenarios of Covid cases in countries with low infection rates - India and Vietnam. In Figure 3, both the trend lines and real lines for confirmed and active cases in India are quite close to each other, which shows that many people detected with coronavirus did not recover quickly and remained as active cases. Further, the actual number of confirmed and active cases is plotted above their respective trend lines, which indicates a similar struggle with Covid infection in India as in USA. Here too, the actual infection incidence curve and its trend line did not show any signs of flattening even on the 80th day. This steep growth in India does not augur well for the period ahead. By our estimates, the total number of infections in India could exceed Brazil by end-August 2020.

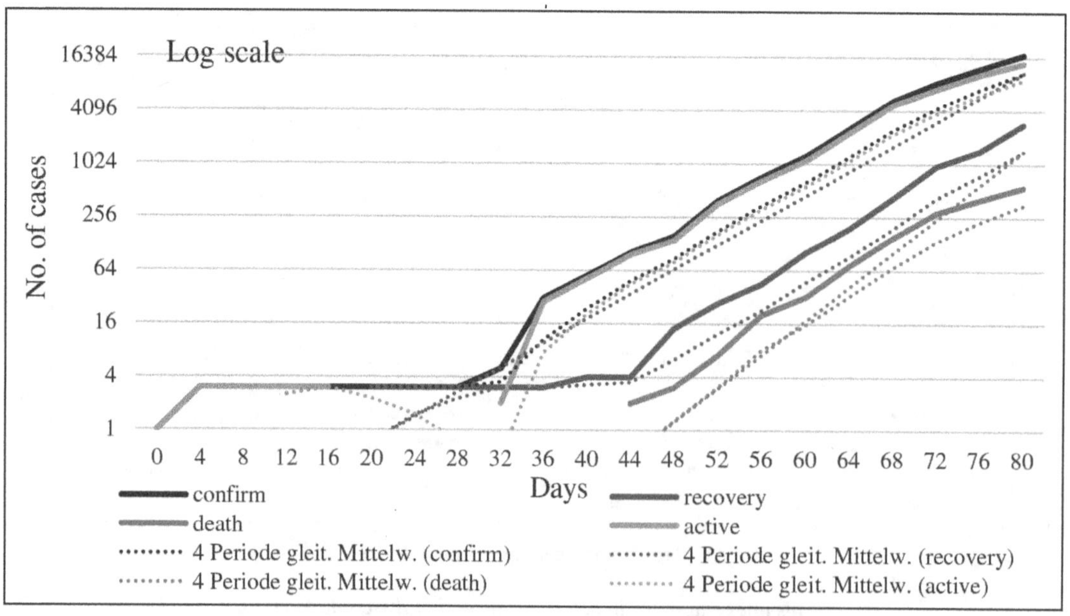

Fig. 3 Trend analysis of Covid cases in India

(This image appears in colour at the end of the compendium).

In contrast, among the low infection countries, Vietnam did not register a single death due to Covid-19 last week of July 2020 (CSSE, 2020). Figure 4 shows a positive picture where the gap between the trend lines of confirmed and active cases is wide and the actual curve of recovered patients shows an upward trend and is placed above its corresponding trend line. Therefore, despite being bracketed in the same group with India, Vietnam was in better control of the Covid pandemic than India during the first eighty days.

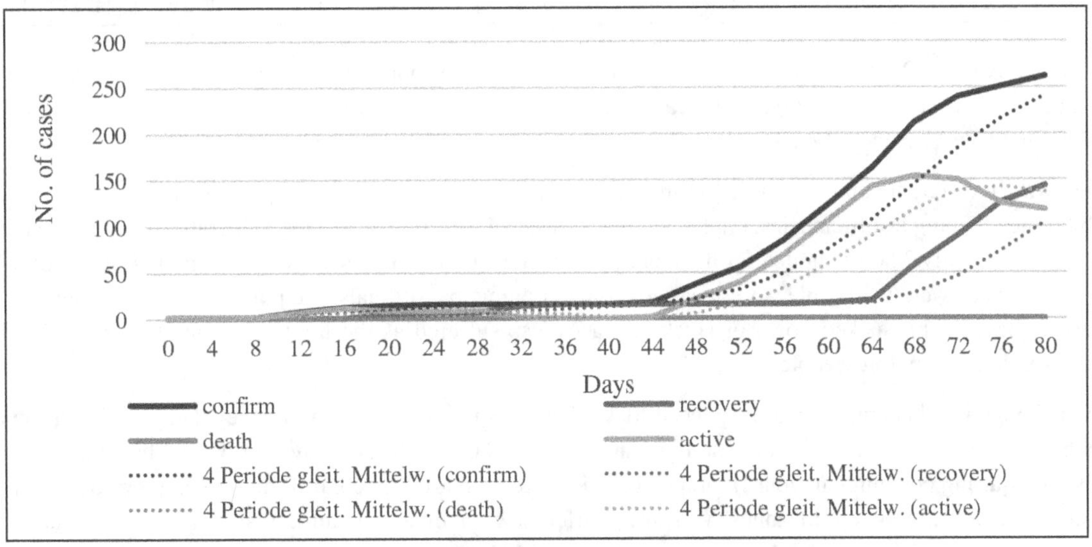

Fig. 4 Trend analysis of Covid cases in Vietnam

(This image appears in colour at the end of the compendium).

The pattern of infection incidence over the 80 eighty days is quite revealing. Table 1 shows the cumulative increase per million of the population for ten countries over the first eighty days.

Table 1 COVID-19 Infection Incidence (per million of population)

Day	China	India	Italy	Japan	New Zealand	Saudi Arabia	South Korea	UK	USA	Vietnam
Day '0' in each country	31-12-2019	30-01-2020	31-01-2020	22-01-2020	28-02-2020	02-03-2020	20-01-2020	31-01-2020	21-01-2020	23-01-2020
0	0.02	0.001	0.03	0.02	0.2	0.03	0.02	0.03	0.003	0.02
4	0.03	0.002	0.03	0.03	0.2	0.15	0.06	0.03	0.006	0.02
8	0.04	0.002	0.05	0.09	1.02	0.59	0.08	0.05	0.01	0.02
12	0.04	0.002	0.05	0.16	1.02	3.06	0.29	0.14	0.02	0.08
16	0.04	0.002	0.05	0.2	1.64	5.07	0.47	0.14	0.03	0.14
20	0.17	0.002	0.05	0.21	5.73	15.16	0.54	0.14	0.03	0.16
24	0.63	0.002	3.79	0.34	20.86	30.03	0.54	0.2	0.04	0.17
28	3.25	0.002	14.7	0.66	75.26	43.12	0.6	0.3	0.04	0.17
32	8.48	0.003	41.42	1.16	132.31	60.5	11.67	0.77	0.11	0.17
36	17.46	0.02	97.4	1.69	194.27	82.94	34.22	3.09	0.16	0.17
40	26.73	0.04	206.32	2.17	247.44	119.67	84.01	6.85	0.21	0.17
44	42.98	0.08	409.72	3.32	271.98	173.95	127.77	17.12	0.48	0.19
48	50.71	0.12	679.39	4.59	286.5	277.8	145.6	40.38	1.69	0.4
52	54.24	0.29	1058.39	6.11	294.48	413.35	156.71	99.85	5.07	0.59
56	55.83	0.54	1432.09	7.03	298.77	558.19	163.04	218.36	14.2	0.89
60	56.98	0.92	1751.52	8.7	301.43	715.04	173.66	377.63	59.79	1.29

64	57.72	1.9	2063.44	10.96	304.09	897.66	179.09	629.17	168.28	1.71
68	58.03	3.93	2308.31	14.75	304.5	1101.96	187.23	911.91	379.84	2.22
72	58.11	6.24	2588.79	20.69	306.13	1330.27	195	1265.45	660.33	2.51
76	58.17	9.11	2797.04	30.88	306.34	1624.69	200.21	1547.94	1028.75	2.63
80	58.32	13.02	3000.46	47.47	306.54	1931.07	203.1	1873.02	1419.97	2.74

On their respective 80th Days, the incidence of infection per million of population, Vietnam (2.74), India (13.02), Japan (47.47), China (58.32) and South Korea (203) can be contrasted with Italy (over 3000), Saudi Arabia (1931) UK (1873), USA (1420) and New Zealand (306.54).

The lockdowns in different countries varied in their scope and strictness. In India, implementation of the lockdown was marred by some planning insufficiencies, unplanned outcomes, and surprises. The most vulnerable people were the migrant workers who got merely 3 hours' notice for the lockdown from the time of the government's announcement on 24 March. Regional differences were noticeable were local government/municipal officials, the police and local community leaders had a part to play. People locked down or stuck at places also suffered as the flow of essential supplies for them was sluggish, disrupted, and unforeseeable.

The first challenge in all countries that introduced lockdowns was monitoring the frequency and severity of the outbreak with zoning. One solution was to use a traffic light analogy and classify all areas into red (Covid-hotspots of community transmission requiring containment zones), orange (Covid affected but under control) and green (very little or no Covid) and administer these three kinds of zones with three different guidelines. Dynamic mapping with granularity was not feasible with zoning by three colours due to the well-known problem called 'The four-colour conjecture' (Wilson, 2003). Since proper mapping and demarcation for monitoring the spread of the Covid-19 infections required a minimum of four colours and there was a need to use a fifth colour for transitional, indeterminate zones, a solution was proposed accordingly (Mathur, 2020). Geographically, a country could be marked into five types of regions/zones, each assigned by a colour to simplify identification, and furthermore to observe the alteration in status with time:

Zone I (WHITE ZONE) A lockdown of different nature which would be entirely lifted inside but entry and exit could still be controlled for States/districts with no active cases (such as Sikkim in India). Such a solution was attempted only in New Zealand, South Korea, Vietnam, and Singapore. In U.S.A. communities protested over their rights to equality in freedom of movement.

Zone II (GREEN ZONE) States/territories/districts where the death rate was low. For example, Goa, Tamil Nadu, Kerala, and Ladakh in India despite some infections demonstrated robustness in their healthcare infrastructure and patients were well cared for in a timely manner with low fatality rates. In such states/territories/districts relief from the lockdown could be practised with closing zones only for specific containment areas to be marked. Countries such as Japan and Saudi Arabia with a well-resourced and abundant capacity of healthcare could easily keep most of their territory green zoned.

Zone III (PURPLE ZONE) States/Territories/Districts/Areas could need to be momentarily placed in a category if the circumstance were uncertain and entry and exit here vital to be monitored with more testing. This was the situation in Sicily (Italy), West Bengal (India), Chicago (USA).

Zone IV (ORANGE ZONE) Cluster Outbreak regions where containment processes were ongoing and the situation was meandering between community spread and cluster outburst as in Milan (Italy), Delhi (India), Florida (USA) and Edinburgh (UK) required a very different kind of control. Here the balance between loss of lives and loss of livelihoods could require partial lockdowns with permissions for certain economic activities with due precautions.

Zone V (RED ZONE) In USA, New York was a red zone and in Italy, Milan remained a red zone for a long time. States like Maharashtra and Gujarat in India, especially with slum areas like Dharavi and Gulbai Tekra (where social distancing was impossible) were dangerous hotspots where the peak may not be reached for a long time and the situation needed constant alerts for reviewing.

A five-zone solution would have the topographical possibility of colour mapping not only at a country level but also at a disaggregated level for regions, towns, local communities, and neighbourhoods. For every zone, the decentralised systems for supply chains, vital supplies, mass testing, preventing, tracing, and treating could be managed differently in a more humanely and productive manner. This would prevent from spreading the much-needed human resources thin, instead direct them to critical zones without disturbing lives in safe areas.

Table 2 (Supplementary Table 1) is even more revealing because it shows up the fatality rate on the 80th day for each of the ten countries selected for this study.

Vietnam did not lose anybody to the Covid-19 infection. Saudi Arabia, New Zealand, Japan and South Korea had a remarkably low fatality rate. Was this due to better organized public health administration? Or was this due to well-endowed medical systems? India (with 3.17%) USA (3.58%) and China (with 4%) represent the average fatality rate of all Covid-19 infections in the world. At the subnational level, these figures reveal sharp differences. In USA, the fatality rate in New York was almost double the national average. In India, the fatality rates in Mumbai and Ahmedabad were distinctly higher compared to Chennai, Delhi and Kolkata. Despite a National Health Service, the UK had the highest fatality followed by Italy. Let's turn to recovery rates in Table 3.

Recovery rates are not sensitive indicators because they rise slowly and recovering patients may remain unrecovered for long periods. There can also be periods where recovery rates rise but the rise is then later followed by a decline. But the relative differences between them across the ten countries show up another important detail-the duration of hospital stay or medical supervision needed for the same Covid-19.

The two-way causality between pandemic diseases and development also merits attention. In the case of infectious diseases such as Malaria, the poor sleeping in the open without mosquito nets are more susceptible than others. It is similar to Covid-19. People sharing overcrowded housing space and common toilet facilities are more vulnerable than others. A working adult in a poor family who catches Covid-19 may die before getting tested or may get tested positive and be quarantined in poorly resourced overcrowded facilities without much possibility of being transferred to intensive care if need were to arise. Yet, the state of affluence in a country or its level of human development does not seem to affect the pandemic liability of incidence and fatality. Table 4 presents certain indicators.

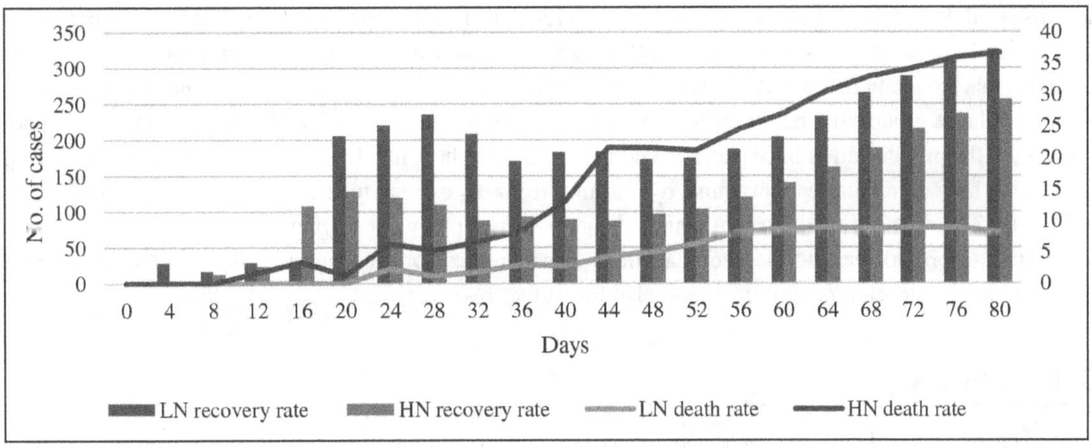

Fig. 5 Comparative analysis of recovery rates and death rates of nations with high infection rates (HN) and low infection rates (LN)

(This image appears in colour at the end of the compendium).

Figure 5 charts combined recovery rates and death rates of all ten countries with high and low rates of infection. Recovery rates of high incidence countries are relatively much lower than the recovery rates of low incidence countries and the gap seems to widen after the 56th day narrowing slightly on the 80th day. This is preliminary evidence to investigate deeply how health systems begin to lose their efficiency when the pressure on their capacities mounts. There is also a stark difference between the death rates of high and low incidence countries and is pronounced more towards the 80th day starting from the 52nd day. This analysis of recovery and death rates highlights the efficiency of the healthcare systems functioning in low incidence countries like Vietnam (118th rank in HDI index, 5.53% of GDP as health expenditure) and India (129th rank in HDI index, 3.53% of GDP as health expenditure) which helped them outperform countries like USA (15th rank in HDI index, 17.06% of GDP spent as health expenditure) and Italy (29th rank in HDI index, 8.84% of GDP spent as health expenditure) (see Supplementary 3 for Table 4 with Development Indicators).

Despite higher health expenditures in the USA and the UK, they suffered a higher incidence of Covid-19 and a higher fatality rate. New Zealand, the UK and the USA were comparable in Human Development Index (ranked 14 and 15 respectively) but the outcomes on Covid-19 were far better for New Zealand. Saudi Arabia with a lower per capita GDP than Italy, UK, USA and New Zealand and a lower HDI than all of them responded better to the Covid-19 pandemic with lower fatality.

4. DISCUSSION

In this study, the recovery rate and the cumulative death rate on the 80th day from first infection were examined which gives an idea of the healthcare infrastructure and medical resources of the countries in our sample in two different ways. First, it provides a rough indication of the robustness of the healthcare systems to offer care. Secondly, the rate of recovery also indicates how long it took to recover.

This study did not find economic prosperity or the level of human development capable of explaining country responses to the Covid-19 pandemic and the outcomes measured by incidence of the disease and its striking power for causing fatalities. The nuances of 'good governance' seemed to involve the capacities of communities and institutions consistent with what was observed in Indonesia (Fossati, 2016) and Bangladesh (Lewis, 2018) in other comparable situations. Essential public health functions require anchoring in social development as in Kerala (Singh, 2011) and citizen-led initiatives as in Guatemala (Hernández et. al. 2019). One could make a case for rights-based health policies (Joshi, 2017) but the models that evolve in each country would have to depend on institutions that can be mandated and which become sustainable because medical models are rarely transportable. China was the first country to eradicate small-pox but no other country could import the Chinese model and each country had to develop its own (Lampton, 1978). This is a huge challenge for the WHO because universal policy prescriptions may not work without regard to institutional differences.

It is possible that after the first eighty days that this study covered, the ten countries studied may exhibit a different pattern than what was so far observed and analysed. The cumulative peaks had not been reached in some countries such as India and the incremental increases were reduced only in New Zealand, China and Vietnam among the ten countries studied. Our findings suggest that the relationships between responses to health policies and systems are intermediated by several factors. The behaviour of large groups, the nature of institutions each country has evolved with, and the motives and powerbases of all the actors in the private and public spaces collectively influence how much setbacks would be suffered in a pandemic situation and also how communities reorganise by learning from experience to strengthen healthcare availability, access and affordability. The connections between achievements of development as evidenced by HDI and the capacity of the healthcare system to provide care to the needy at times of pandemics appear tenuous. This counter-intuitive insight has several implications for development policies and also for further research.

5. CONCLUSION

In near future, health policy decisions would need to consider various parameters at the national as well as regional levels, including rights to wellbeing, trade and advancement. But this is not easy. International regimes and national policies and can fail to achieve balance among these arrays of rights. There is also the danger that there could be a conflict between equality as a right and equality as a policy.

In the long term, creative solutions will be required to build and sustain arrangements between nations, while existing institutions will need reinforcements given the absence of consensus within and among countries regarding the rights stated above. Questions over privacy and data protection and surveillance would require resolving and actions. For the formation and interpretation of healthcare trade rules and laws including dispute settlement, self-governing healthcare standards and regulatory bodies/agencies must be introduced. A new trans-national collaboration of regulators, under the aegis of the WHO or United Nations, could be created. These health workers could also work in the same capacity as peacekeepers. This could also be done at the EU level by the EU-28 countries. The North-South divide in health policy, priorities, preferences, and perceptions needs bridging (Sabat et al., 2020). The conception of international insurance markets in opposition to regulatory failure also deserves attention. The task of overseeing healthcare could be restricted, with the help of WHO, to liberal democracies who are willing to adhere to acceptable rules of governance and provide financial guarantees in favour of autonomous international bodies like global health banks. With proper safeguards, health banks could finance the identification and distribution of genetic information to the general population.

The inescapable Covid-19 adversity is an opportunity but overburdening it with idealistic expectations would be irrational. All the issues of the world will not disappear. The cost-benefit calculations that guide life-saving or prolonging endeavours are likely to remain. Creating and supporting local community organisations with internationally portable health security is a difficult task and will continue to be so.

Note

Table 1 was prepared using raw COVID 19 data on total infections sourced from the CSSE database of John Hopkins University (CSSE, 2020). For the sake of comparability, data for each country was taken for the first eighty days from the day of its first case.

Table 2 was prepared by taking the number of infections and deaths cumulatively noted in the Covid-19 data sourced from the CSSE (CSSE, 2020).

Table 3 was prepared from raw data of the COVID-19 database of the CSSE (CSSE, 2020).

REFERENCES

Abbott, P., Sapsford, R., & Binagwaho, A. (2017). Learning from success: how Rwanda achieved the millennium development goals for health. World Development, 92, 103–116.

Banerjee, A., Pasea, L., Harris, S., Gonzalez-Izquierdo, A., Torralbo, A., Shallcross, L., ... & Pagel, C. (2020). Estimating excess 1-year mortality associated with the COVID-19 pandemic according to underlying conditions and age: a population-based cohort study. The Lancet, 395(10238), 1715–1725.

Bhattamishra, R., & Barrett, C. B. (2010). Community-based risk management arrangements: A review. World Development, 38(7), 923–932.

Brieba, D. (2018). State capacity and health outcomes: Comparing Argentina's and Chile's reduction of infant and maternal mortality, 1960–2013. World Development, 101, 37–53.

Center for Systems Science and Engineering (CSSE), John Hopkins University. (2020). COVID-19 data. https://www.arcgis.com/apps/opsdashboard/index.html#/bda7594740fd40299423467b48e9ecf6

Chetterje, P. (2020). Gaps in India's preparedness for COVID-19 control. The Lancet Infectious Diseases, 20(5), 544.

Chu, H., Chan, J., Yuen, T., Shuai, H., Yuan, S., ... Yuen, K., 2020. Comparative tropism, replication kinetics, and cell damage profiling of SARS-CoV-2 and SARS-CoV with implications for clinical manifestations, transmissibility, and laboratory studies of COVID-19: an observational study. The Lancet Microbe, 1(1), 14–23. https://www.thelancet.com/journals/lanmic/article/PIIS2666-5247(20)30004-5/fulltext

Conceição, P. (2019). Human Development Report 2019: beyond income, beyond averages, beyond today: inequalities in human development in the 21st century. United Nations Development Programme. http://hdr.undp.org/sites/default/files/hdr2019.pdf

Cousins, S. (2020). New Zealand eliminates COVID-19. The Lancet, 395(10235), 1474.

Du, L., & HUANG, G. (2020). Did Japan Just Beat the Virus Without Lockdowns or Mass Testing. Economic Times. https://economictimes.indiatimes.com/news/international/world-news/did-japan-just-beat-the-virus-without-lockdowns-or-mass-testing/articleshow/75911339.cms?utm_source=contentofinterest&utm_medium=text&utm_campaign=cppst

European Centre for Disease Prevention and Control (ECDC). (2020). COVID-19 data. https://www.ecdc.europa.eu/en/covid-19-pandemic

Ferretti, L., Wymant, C., Kendall, M., Zhao, L., Nurtay, A., Abeler-Dörner, L., ... & Fraser, C. (2020). Quantifying SARS-CoV-2 transmission suggests epidemic control with digital contact tracing. Science, 368(6491).

Fossati, D. (2016). Beyond "good governance": The multi-level politics of health insurance for the poor in Indonesia. World Development, 87, 291–306.

Godeluck, S. (2020). Coronavirus: France commits to a massive screening strategy. Les Echos. Retrieved from https://www.lesechos.fr/economie-france/social/coronavirus-la-france-sengage-dans-une-strategie-de-depistage-massif-1190362

Gondi, S., Beckman, A. L., Deveau, N., Raja, A. S., Ranney, M. L., Popkin, R., & He, S. (2020). Personal protective equipment needs in the USA during the COVID-19 pandemic. The Lancet, 395(10237), 90–91.

Gray, R. H. (1974). An estimate of the demographic effects of malaria control: A case study of Sri Lanka. World Development, 2(2), 19–21.

Hatcher, W. (2020). A failure of political communication not a failure of bureaucracy: The danger of presidential misinformation during the COVID-19 pandemic. The American Review of Public Administration, 50(6-7), 614–620.

Hernández, A., Ruano, A. L., Hurtig, A. K., Goicolea, I., San Sebastián, M., & Flores, W. (2019). Pathways to accountability in rural Guatemala: A qualitative comparative analysis of citizen-led initiatives for the right to health of indigenous populations. World Development, 113, 392–401.

Huang C., Wang, Y., Li, X., Ren, L., Zhao, J., ... Cao, B. (2020). Clinical features of patients infected with 2019 novel coronavirus in Wuhan, China. The Lancet, 395(10223), 497–506.

Huizer, Y. L., Kraaij-Dirkzwager, M. M., Timen, A., Schuitmaker, T. J., & van Steenbergen, J. E. (2015). Context analysis for epidemic control in the Netherlands. Health Policy, 119(1), 66–73.

Joshi, A. (2017). Legal empowerment and social accountability: Complementary strategies toward rights-based development in health? World Development, 99, 160–172.

Lampton, D. M. (1978). Development and health care: Is China's medical programme exportable? World Development, 6(5), 621–630.

La, V. P., Pham, T. H., Ho, M. T., Nguyen, M. H., P Nguyen, K. L., Vuong, T. T., ... & Vuong, Q. H. (2020). Policy Response, Social Media and Science Journalism for the Sustainability of the Public Health System Amid the COVID-19 Outbreak: The Vietnam Lessons. Sustainablity, 12(7), 2931–2958. https://www.arcgis.com/apps/opsdashboard/index.html#/bda7594740fd40299423467b48e9ecf6

Lewis, D. (2018). Peopling policy processes? Methodological populism in the Bangladesh health and education sectors. World Development, 108, 16–27.

Madsen, J. B. (2016). Barriers to prosperity: Parasitic and infectious diseases, IQ, and economic development. World Development, 78, 172–187.

Mathur, A. (2020). Strategies for solving wicked problems of true uncertainty: Tackling pandemics like COVID-19. https://web.iima.ac.in/assets/snippets/workingpaperpdf/12502768892020-04-03.pdf

Moatti, J. P. (2020). The French response to COVID-19: intrinsic difficulties at the interface of science, public health, and policy. The Lancet Public Health, 5(5), e255.

Nature. (2020). COVID-19: what science advisers must do now. Nature, 579, 319–20.

Nay, O. (2020). Can a virus undermine human rights? The Lancet Public Health, 5(5), 238–239.

Nguyen, Q, Chau, M. (2020). Vietnam Province Isolates 10,600 People Amid Virus: Tuoi Tre. Retrieved from https://www.bloomberg.com/news/articles/2020-02-13/vietnam-province-isolates-10-600-people-amid-virus-tuoi-tre

Ohara, H. (2004). Experience and review of SARS control in Vietnam and China. Tropical medicine and health, 32(3), 235–240.

Press Information Bureau. (2020a). No shortage of ventilators, oxygen cylinders, PPE, N-95 and N-99 masks, RT-PCR kits: Chairman, Empowered Group 3. Retrieved from https://pib.gov.in/PressReleseDetailm.aspx?PRID=1620073

Press Information Bureau. (2020b). More than 10 lakh patients in India recover from COVID-19; recovery rate is continuously rising, while fatality rate is decreasing: Health Ministry. Retrieved from https://pib.gov.in/PressReleseDetail.aspx?PRID=1642394

Press Trust of India. (2020). India's COVID-19 tally, fatality rate per million population lowest in world: Health Ministry. The Hindu. 2020. Retrieved from https://www.thehindu.com/news/national/coronavirus-indias-covid-19-tally-fatality-rate-per-million-population-lowest-in-world-health-ministry/article32012829.ece#

Prior, I., & Stanhope, J. (1980). Epidemics, health and disease in a small, isolated environment. World Development, 8, 995–1016.

Sabat, I., Neuman-Böhme, S., Varghese, N. E., Barros, P. P., Brouwer, W., van Exel, J., Schreyögg J., & Stargardt, T. (2020). United but divided: Policy responses and people's perceptions in the EU during the COVID-19 outbreak. Health Policy, 124(9), 909–918. https://doi.org/10.1016/j.healthpol.2020.06.009

Shaw, R., Kim, Y. K., & Hua, J. (2020). Governance, technology and citizen behavior in pandemic: Lessons from COVID-19 in East Asia. Progress in Disaster Science. https://www.sciencedirect.com/science/article/pii/S2590061720300272?via%3Dihub

Singh, P. (2011). Wellness and welfare: A longitudinal analysis of social development in Kerala, India. World Development, 39(2), 282–293.

Ssozi, J., & Amlani, S. (2015). The effectiveness of health expenditure on the proximate and ultimate goals of healthcare in Sub-Saharan Africa. World Development, 76, 165–179.

Sun, K., & Viboud, C. (2020). Impact of contact tracing on SARS-CoV-2 transmission. The Lancet Infectious Diseases. https://www.thelancet.com/journals/laninf/article/PIIS1473-3099(20)30357-1/fulltext

The World Bank. (2020). World Bank Open Data. https://data.worldbank.org/

Trevatt, C. (2020). COVID-19 coronavirus: Prime Minister Jacinda Ardern's week in a pandemic. The New Zealand Herald. Retrieved from www.nzherald.co.nz/nz/news/article.cfm?c_id=1&objectid=12320198

United Nations Development Programme (UNDP). (2019). Human Development Report, Beyond income, beyond averages, beyond today: Inequalities in human development in the 21st century. Retrieved from http://hdr.undp.org/sites/default/files/hdr2019.pdf

Van Dorn, A., Cooney, R. E., & Sabin, M. L. (2020). COVID-19 exacerbating inequalities in the US. The Lancet, 395(10232), 1243–1244.

WHO. (2020a). Novel Coronavirus (2019-nCoV) situation report-12. Retrieved from https://www.who.int/docs/default-source/coronaviruse/situation-reports/20200201-sitrep-12-ncov.pdf?sfvrsn=273c5d35_2

WHO. (2020b). Novel Coronavirus – China. Retrieved from https://www.who.int/csr/don/12-january-2020-novel-coronavirus-china/en/

WHO. (2020c). Rolling updates on coronavirus disease (COVID-19). Retrieved from https://www.who.int/emergencies/diseases/novel-coronavirus-2019/events-as-they-happen

WHO. (2020d). Novel coronavirus disease (COVID-19) situation report-117. Retrieved from https://www.who.int/docs/default-source/coronaviruse/situation-reports/20200516-covid-19-sitrep-117.pdf?sfvrsn=8f562cc_2

Wilson, R. (2003). Four Colours Suffice. London: Penguin.

Wilson, S. (2020). Pandemic leadership: lessons from New Zealand's approach to COVID-19. Leadership, 16(3), 279–293.

Xuan, L. (2020) Hanoi Begins Quick Testing COVID-19 in Public, Results Come in 10 Minutes. Retrieved from https://tuoitre.vn/ha-noi-bat-dau-xet-nghiem-nhanh-covid-19-ngoai-cong-dong-co-ket-qua-trong-10-phut-20200330140703285.htm

Zarychta, A. (2020). Making social services work better for the poor: Evidence from a natural experiment with health sector decentralization in Honduras. World Development, 133, 104996. https://doi.org/10.1016/j.worlddev.2020.104996

Zhu, N., Zhang, D., Wang, W., Li, X., Yang, B., Song, J., ... & Tan, W. (2020). A novel coronavirus from patients with pneumonia in China, 2019. New England journal of medicine, 382, 727–733.

Data Envelopment Analysis Based Fuzzy TOPSIS and Fuzzy COPRAS Techniques for Selection of Solar Energy Projects

Harsh S. Dhiman
Assistant Professor
Adani Institute of Infrastructure Engineering, Ahmedabad

Samudra Sen
Assistant Professor, Energy and Public Policy
Adani Institute of Infrastructure Management, Ahmedabad

Abstract: With increasing awareness about the negative effects of industrialization, the world is moving from non-renewable to renewable sources of energy. All over the world, there is stress on finding cheap and widely available sources of power. Solar energy is the leader in renewable sources of energy the world over. As countries and corporates are participating in installing more solar projects than ever, it becomes important to evaluate the efficacy of resources used in the solar projects. In this paper, we devise a novel methodology to compare solar energy projects on the basis of a few relevant parameters. We integrate Data Envelopment Analysis (DEA) and Fuzzy TOPSIS and DEA-Fuzzy COPRAS to shortlist and rank solar energy projects. First, DEA is used to identify energy projects which lie at the technology frontier in terms of efficiency. Thereafter, shortlisted efficient projects are separately ranked using Fuzzy TOPSIS and Fuzzy COPRAS to identify projects which use the resources in the best possible manner. Using two different methodologies in the second stage separately enables us to compare and validate our ranking system. Our methodology can also be adapted to evaluate other types of energy sources.

Keywords: Solar energy, renewable energy, Data Envelopment Analysis, TOPSIS, COPRAS

1. INTRODUCTION

Access to green electricity is considered as a meritorious asset for a developing and developed country (Kumar, Sah, Singh, Deng, He, Kumar & Bansal, 2017). However, access to electricity remains a key challenge where the demand for the same keeps increasing exponentially. Traditional means of power generation lead to an increased depletion of ozone layer and balance in an ecosystem. Sustainable energy development for power consumption and industrial use is considered a major goal for many United Nation countries (Köksalan, Wallenius, & Zionts, 2011). In order to address the critical environmental issues coming in the path of sustainable development, the green energy resources can play an important role. Hence, for developing countries to thrive on the path of sustainable development, renewable energy sources can be proved to be beneficial (Dhiman, Deb, Muresan & Unguresan, 2019; Dhiman & Deb, 2020).

Currently, clean operation functioning has made alternative energy source to gain more importance. With limited nuclear resources and fossil fuels, wind and Solar Energy technologies have showed their importance in the market. Given its rich sustainability, a renewable energy power portfolio strengthens the economic condition of our country (Dhiman, Deb, Muyeen & Kamwa, 2021). Worldwide employment opportunities are created from the wind energy along with its positive environmental impact. The functioning and control of renewable energy sources have become important with the increase in the penetration of the resources (Dhiman, Deb, Carroll, Muresan & Unguresan, 2020). Wind turbines are tested under wide range of dynamic phenomenon. Wind farms are commissioned to fulfil the cost effectiveness obtained from its operations. The objective is to help the operator by minimizing its losses and providing accurate forecasting schemes knowing the unambiguous nature of wind speeds. However, system of batteries operating at an investment cost are capable enough to suffice the power in the grid. An optimum operational strategy is selected that will increases the reliability of the power system and will lower the system cost.

In order to select the best alternative from the slot Multi-Criteria Decision Making (MCDM), a mathematical decision approach is used. These mathematical models may not always indicate the best "choice" that were considered best. The outranking methods and compensatory methods are the two prominent categories of the MCDM approach. A nominal trade-off between the alternatives is witnessed, as the compensatory method includes choices that shows positive characteristics over the negative ones. It also includes Analytical Hierarchical Process (AHP) and Fuzzy Logic Decision Making (FLDM). It is practically applied in the field of water resources, like evaluation of rural water supply, resilience in water scarcity, and evaluation of desalination plants. On the other hand, a sequence of logical decision-making steps based on weights assigned to an individual criterion is followed by outranking methods. Outranking methods such as weighted sum and product methods like, the Technique for Order or Preference by Similarity to Ideal Solution (TOPSIS), the Complex Proportional Assessment (COPRAS) method, the Preference Ranking Organization Method for Enrichment Evaluation (PROMETHEE), and Elimination Et Choix Traduisant la Realite Method (ELECTREE) are commonly used (Kumar et al., 2017). However, there is a problem of rank reversal in the PROMETHEE method, this method puts decision maker into dilemma of choosing the best alternatives when compared with other methods (Hwang & Yoon, 1981).

Several science and engineering applications utilizes MCDM methods for finding the best alternatives using questionnaires and surveys to collect qualitative and quantitative information. successful application of the MCDM methods in the renewable energy field are into energy planning, transportation energy management, utility planning, and building energy management (Haralambopoulos & Polatidis, 2003). The methods such as AHP and PROMETHEE were discussed by Georgiou, Mohammed & Rozakis (2015) in selecting an efficient energy topology for a reverse osmosis desalination plant and social, economic, and environmental impact were considered while ranking five such topologies (Georgiou et al., 2015). MCDM methods were further explored by Kundakc (2018) using two outranking methods in selecting the best boiler for a dye-house in the textile industry. The two outranking methods are Measuring Attractiveness by a Categorical-Based Evaluation Technique (MACBETH) and Evaluation based on Distance from Average Solution (EDAS) (Kundakc, 2018). Lee, Hung, Kang & Pearn (2012) explored that Multi-criteria decision making can be used to select suitable wind turbines for developing a wind farm using Interpretive Structural Modeling (ISM) and the Fuzzy Analytical Hierarchical Process (FAHP). A binary matrix indicating the relationship between them is created after identifying criterion and a sub-criterion. Geographical Information System (GIS)-based AHP technique used in Egypt was used to identify the offshore wind energy potential considering several factors like wind, water depth, and distance from shore (Mahdy & Bahaj, 2018).

Kolios, Rodriguez-Tsouroukdissian & Salonitis (2016) have studied the MCDM approach under stochastic inputs where factors like environmental impact, depth compatibility, cost of installation, and maintenance cost were considered as criteria in terms of selecting offshore turbine structures. Discussion by Garni, Kassem, Awasthi, Komljenovic, & Al-Haddad (2016) on MCDM approach for evaluating renewable power sources for Saudi Arabia using the AHP method, found that solar thermal technology is less preferred than solar PV technology. Considering criteria such as environmental, socio-cultural, and political impact. The selection process was also influenced by the effect of the normalization of beneficial and non-beneficial criteria." A comprehensive review of normalization techniques used for streamlining the decision-making process was presented by Jahan & Edwards (2015).

2. METHODOLOGY

The performance of each alternative is translated into a single aggregated value using an MCDM approach to rank the alternatives. With available information and problem characteristics, the selection of methods is done by the Decision Makers (DMs) as there is single mode of analysis which is inadequate to deal with complex decision-making problems. Moreover, there should be a universal agreement in forming a distinct aggregation method that can be used in any kind of decision problem. The main aim of this paper is to make the decision-making process trouble free and to be well suited to most of the situations by applying suitable multi-beneficial MCDM methods by analysing suitable criteria. We approach the problem as per the steps mentioned in figure 1. First, we compute technical efficiency of each solar power project (a 'decision making unit' or DMU in this case) through DEA. If there is a single DMU which is efficient, then the ranking is already complete. If there are several efficient DMUs, then we separately use Fuzzy TOPSIS and Fuzzy COPRAS to rank the efficient DMUs in the second stage to rank only the efficient solar power projects. We use two different MCDM methodology to compare the rankings from the two methods instead of relying on one method. The objective behind using two different methodologies for ranking the solar power projects is to compare rankings of the projects and draw robust insights from the results.

There are many methodologies available for evaluation and comparison of power projects. However, these methodologies are technology specific, capable of evaluating only power projects of any specific type. Further, existing methodologies require technical specification data which may not be always available for all projects. Therefore, not all power projects may be evaluated using existing methods. In such a context, the novelty of our methodology lies on two fronts. First, our methodology does not require extensive data for analysis and comparison of power projects. Our methodology can be used with basic data regarding the projects. Second, our methodology can be used to compare any power project with other power projects irrespective of the technology involved in the project. For example, solar power projects may be compared with wind or hydro power projects or any other type of power projects.

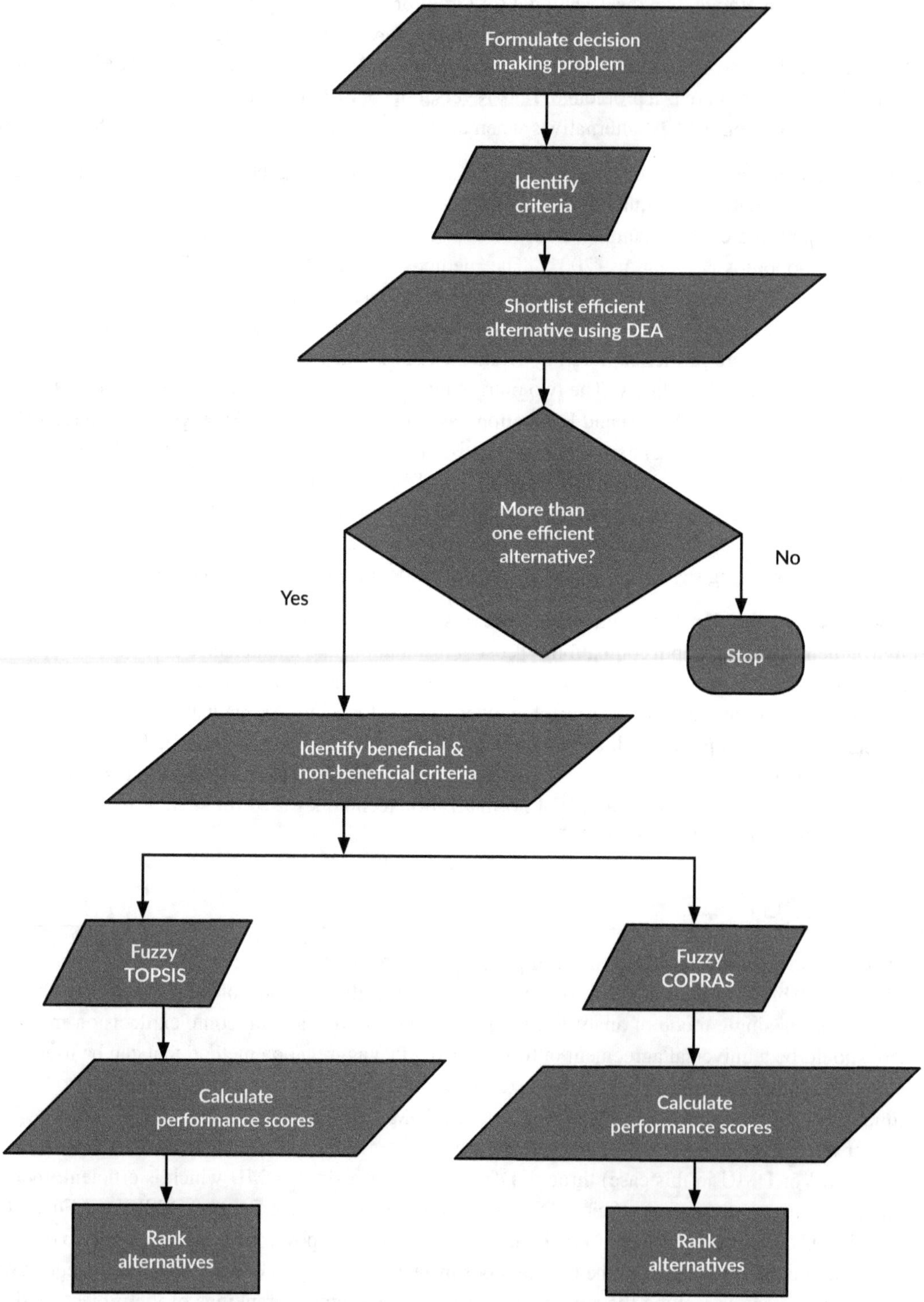

Fig. 1 Flowchart for ranking of solar power projects

2.1 Data Envelopment Analysis (DEA)

DEA is a linear programming methodology which is used to evaluate the efficiency of individual decision making units (DMUs) (Charnes, Cooper & Rhodes, 1978). Efficiency is understood as a relative measure of performance, relative to the performance of a peer group of similar units constituting an efficient production frontier (also known as efficient technology frontier). This frontier can be determined through various parametric and nonparametric methods. DEA is an appropriate and widely used nonparametric methodology for such evaluation in different sectors. In this paper, we use the terms efficiency and productivity interchangeably. We use input-oriented model since inputs are the only attributes which can be controlled at will for any project. Once the output is specified, it cannot be altered, so that an output-oriented model is not suitable for evaluation of such projects. Further, we do not want to make any apriori assumption regarding the returns to scale. Therefore, we resort to a variable returns to scale (VRS) model. Technical efficiency score (TE_t) of DMU_t is computed by solving the following linear programming duality problem, on the basis of an input-oriented VRS model:

$$
\begin{aligned}
&\text{Minimize } \delta_t \\
&\textit{subject to}: \sum_{i=1}^{N} \lambda_i x_{ik} \le \delta_t x_{tk} \\
&\sum_{i=1}^{N} \lambda_i y_{ij} \ge y_{tj} \\
&\sum_{i=1}^{N} \lambda_i = 1 \\
&\lambda_i \ge 0
\end{aligned} \tag{12}
$$

where λ_i is the weight applied to input x_i and output y_i of each DMU, $i = 1, ..., N$ (index for each of N DMUs), $j = 1, ..., m$ (index for each of q outputs) $k = 1, ..., n$ (index for each of p inputs), t = index for the DMU being evaluated.

The three inputs for our DEA model are: area of the land on which the solar power project is located in acres, cost of the project in million US$, time since the construction of the project till its commissioning in months. The lone output parameter of our evaluation is installed capacity of the power plant in megawatts. Any production process is bound to be influenced by a host of variables. Including many variables in the DEA model is possible but is not recommended. Increase in the number of variables decreases the discriminatory power of DEA models (Kempkes et al., 2010, footnote 4, p. 5). Therefore, researchers have suggested a limit on the number of input and output variables that may be included in a DEA model. This maximum number of variables is guided by the number of DMUs in the data. As per Cooper, Seiford & Tone (2000) and widely accepted in the research community, this limit is expressed as:

$$N \ge \max\{p \times q, 2(p + q)\}$$

Our data consists of 25 large solar power projects from around the world. We use three inputs and one output for our DEA model. Thus, our data and model satisfy the above equation and DEA methodology can be appropriately used in evaluating DMUs.

2.2 Fuzzy TOPSIS

"Chen (2000) has put forward a method based on fuzzy logic that translates TOPSIS method in its original form to a fuzzy domain. Fuzzy decision making or a normal decision-making process is best carried out with a variety of surveys that vary from candidate to candidate. The intuitionistic fuzzy numbers (IFS) based TOPSIS model is capable of reflecting approval or rejection, and ambiguity displayed by decision-makers through the consideration of real-life uncertainties and linguistic human decisions. Fuzzy TOPSIS is performed among q decision-makers with each decision-maker presenting their decision matrix. Following steps are followed for evaluating decision-making problem with fuzzy TOPSIS:

- The performance scores assigned by q decision makers and denoted as $(\bar{h}_{ij})$ for alternatives A_i $(i = 1, 2,..., m)$ corresponding to C_j $(j = 1,2,..., n)$, are aggregated with $(\bar{w}_{ij})$ weights, stated as

$$\bar{w}_{ij} = \frac{1}{q}\left(\bar{w}_{ij}^1 + \bar{w}_{ij}^2 + ... + \bar{w}_{ij}^q\right),\ \bar{h}_{ij} = \frac{1}{q}\left(\bar{h}_{ij}^1 + \bar{h}_{ij}^2 + ... + \bar{h}_{ij}^q\right) \tag{1}$$

- From (1), we can establish H, an aggregate matrix as

$$H = \begin{pmatrix} C_1 & C_2 & \cdots & C_n \\ \bar{h}_{11} & \bar{h}_{12} & \cdots & \bar{h}_{1j} \\ \bar{h}_{21} & \bar{h}_{22} & \cdots & h_{2j} \\ \vdots & \vdots & & \vdots \\ h_{i1} & \cdots & \cdots & \bar{h}_{ij} \end{pmatrix} \begin{matrix} \\ A_1 \\ A_2 \\ \vdots \\ A_m \end{matrix}$$

- Further, we can establish a normalized matrix D having elements as $\bar{z}_{ij}$ for criteria C_j as

$$z_{ij} = \left(\frac{l_{ij}}{n_j^+}, \frac{m_{ij}}{n_j^+}, \frac{n_{ij}}{n_j^+} \right); n_j^+ = \max n_{ij} \tag{2}$$

$$z_{ij} = \left(\frac{l_j^-}{n_{ij}}, \frac{l_j^-}{m_{ij}}, \frac{l_j^-}{l_{ij}} \right); e_j^- = \min l_{ij} \tag{3}$$

- Further, based on the weights $\bar{w}_{ij}$ for each criterion, a weighted matrix is constructed as

$$\bar{H} = [h\bar{h}_{ij}]_{m \times n} = \bar{w}_{ij} \times \bar{z}_{ij} \tag{4}$$

where $h\bar{h}_{ij}$ is the element corresponding to weighted normalized matrix.

- Now, the fuzzy positive (FPIS) and negative ideal solution (FNIS) are established for decision making and are given as

$$GG^+ = \{h\bar{h}_1^+, h\bar{h}_2^+, ..., h\bar{h}_m^+\}, \; GG^- = \{h\bar{h}_1^-, h\bar{h}_2^-, ..., h\bar{h}_m^-\} \tag{5}$$

Based on the euclidean distances zz_i+ and zz_i- from their respective FPIS and FNIS, given by

$$zz_i^+ = \sum_{j=1}^{n} zz_p(h\bar{h}_{ij}, h\bar{h}_j^+), \; zz_j^- = \sum_{j=1}^{n} zz_p(h\bar{h}_{ij}, h\bar{h}_j^-),$$

$$zz_p(xx, yy) = \sqrt{\frac{1}{3}(l_{xx} - l_{yy})^2 + (m_{xx} - m_{yy})^2 + (n_{xx} - n_{yy})^2} \tag{6}$$

and xx – (l_{xx}, m_{xx}, n_{xx}) and yy = (l_{yy}, m_{yy}, n_{yy}) as two different TFNs and zz_p(xx, yy) being the euclidean distance based on vertex method, for each alternative, we obtain the performance score (FF_i) given by

$$FF_i = \frac{zz_j^-}{zz_i^- + zz_i^+} \tag{7}$$

and rank them in descending order.

We use Fuzzy TOPSIS in the second stage of our analysis to rank those solar power projects which, using DEA, were found to be efficient in the first stage. In this stage, we rank them based on beneficial criteria and non-beneficial criteria to arrive at a closeness coefficient (performance score) as described above. In this case, the sole beneficial criteria used is installed capacity of the project. Three non-beneficial criteria used are: area of the project (hectares), time taken to complete installation of the project (months) and construction cost of the project (US$ in millions).

2.3 Fuzzy COPRAS

Fuzzy COPRAS is an extension of the COPRAS method that is used actively in various disciplines of decision making.

- "MCDM problem is formulated based on alternatives (A_i, i = 1, 2,……, m) and criteria (C_j, j = 1,2, …, n) and a fuzzy decision matrix is developed.
- A normalized decision matrix using (2) and (3) as seen in fuzzy TOPSIS method is then obtained.
- Aggregate beneficial and non-beneficial indices $\bar{T}_i^+$ and $\bar{T}_i^-$ are then evaluated for each alternative A_i as

$$T_i^+ = \left\{ \sum_{j=1}^{t} h\bar{h}_{ij}^l, \; \sum_{j=1}^{t} h\bar{h}_{ij}^m, \; \sum_{j=1}^{t} h\bar{h}_{ij}^n \right\} \tag{8}$$

$$T_i^- = \left\{ \sum_{j=t+1}^{n} \overline{hh}_{ij}^{l}, \sum_{j=t+1}^{n} \overline{hh}_{ij}^{m}, \sum_{j=t+1}^{n} \overline{hh}_{ij}^{n} \right\} \tag{9}$$

where $j = 1, 2,\ldots, t$ represent beneficial criteria and $j = t + 1, t + 2,\ldots, n$ represent non-beneficial criteria.

- The crisp values $V(\bar{A})$ for each alternative A_i and $\alpha \in [0, 1]$ from the fuzzy numbers ($\bar{A} = (l, m, n)$) are determined as

$$V(\bar{A}) = 2e(1-\alpha) + \frac{n-m}{2}(1-\alpha)^2 \tag{10}$$

- Finally, the performance scores are obtained and the alternatives are ranked accordingly: "

$$XCC_i = \frac{V_i}{V_{\max}} \times 100\% \tag{11}$$

where V_i and $V_{\max}$ represent i^{th} crisp value and maximum crisp value for each alternative.

3. RESULTS & DISCUSSION

25 solar power projects from around the world are evaluated on their efficiency based on different criteria. Using DEA, first the projects are evaluated to shortlist efficient power projects. Figure 2 illustrates solar power projects with their installed capacity considered for DEA problem.

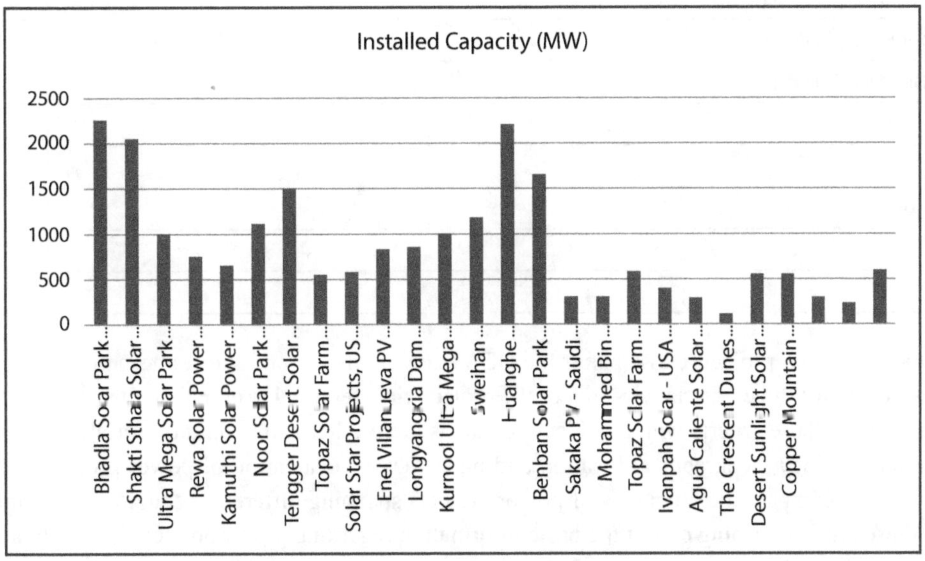

Fig. 2 Solar projects with their installed capacity

The solar projects are scrutinized based on installed capacity, area covered, completion time, and construction cost. Eight projects are found to lie at the efficiency frontier with technical efficiency of one. The average technical efficiency is found to be 0.625 with a standard deviation of 0.293. Table 1 depicts the technical efficiencies obtained for solar projects using DEA.

Table 1 Technical Efficiency of Solar Power Projects

Project	Tech. Efficiency (VRS)
Bhadla Solar Park	1
Shakti Sthala solar power project	1
Ultra Mega Solar Park	0.419
Rewa Solar Power Project	1
Kamuthi solar power plant	1
Noor Solar Park (Morocco)	0.222

Tengger Desert Solar Park (China)	1
Topaz Solar Farm and Desert Sunlight Solar Farm, US	0.333
Solar Star Projects, US	0.333
Enel Villanueva PV Plant, Mexico	0.451
Longyangxia Dam Solar Park, China	0.405
Kurnool Ultra Mega Solar Park, India	0.399
Sweihan Photovoltaic Independent Power Project, UAE	0.595
Huanghe Hydropower Hainan Solar Park, China	1
Benban Solar Park, Egypt	0.738
Mohammed bin Rashid Al Maktoum Solar Park	0.855
Topaz Solar Farm - USA	0.680
Ivanpah Solar - USA	0.253
Agua Caliente Solar Project - USA	0.314
The Crescent Dunes Solar Energy Project, Nevada	0.528
Desert Sunlight Solar Farm – Desert Center, California	0.332
Copper Mountain Solar Facility – Boulder City, Nevada	1
California Valley Solar Ranch, California	0.358
Antelope Valley Solar Ranch, California	0.405
Mount Signal Solar, Calexico, California	1
Average	**0.625**
Standard Deviation	**0.293**
Minimum	**0.222**
Maximum	**1**

Table 2 depicts the eight solar projects chosen after the DEA study. In the second stage, alternatives in form of eight solar projects are assessed against three criteria, viz. area of the project, time required to complete the project, and project cost in million USD. We choose these criteria with an objective that as these criteria are common for all types of power projects irrespective of the technology, geographical location and other factors, evaluation of power projects using these criteria would enable oneself to compare the efficiency of power projects spanning different technology, location and such other factors. Further, these criteria forming part of the basic information regarding power projects are easily available, it would become possible to evaluate different power project which are otherwise not possible to evaluate for want of technical data.

The essence of fuzzy based decision making arrives from the uncertainty involved in constructing decision matrix. In this case, the fuzzy decision matrix (FDM) is constructed based on triangular numbers. Tables 3 and 4 depict the performance indices for decision matrix and weights for criteria respectively.

Table 2 Eight solar projects as alternatives

Solar Project	Alternative
Bhadla Solar Park	A_1
Shakti Sthala solar power project A2	A_2
Rewa Solar Power Project A3	A_3
Kamuthi solar power plant A4	A_4
Tengger Desert Solar Park (China) A5	A_5
Huanghe Hydropower Hainan Solar Park, China A6	A_6
Copper Mountain Solar Facility { Boulder City, Nevada	A_7
Mount Signal Solar, Calexico, California A8	A_8

Table 3 Performance indices for decision matrix

Preference	LS as per AHP
Equal (EP)	(1,1,3)
Moderate (MP)	(1,3,5)
Strong (SP)	(3,5,7)
Very strong (VSP)	(5,7,9)
Extreme (XP)	(7,9,9)

Table 4 Weights for criteria

Preference	LS
Very Low (VL)	(1,1,3)
Low (L)	(1,3,5)
Average (AVG)	(3,5,7)
High (H)	(5,7,9)
Very High (VH)	(7,9,9)

Based on scores listed in table 3, the fuzzy decision matrix (FDM) is

$$H = \begin{matrix} & \begin{matrix} C_1 & C_2 & C_3 \end{matrix} & \\ & \begin{pmatrix} SP & SP & EP \\ SP & EP & MP \\ XP & XP & EP \\ XP & SP & XP \\ XP & XP & XP \\ MP & MP & SP \\ SP & XP & SP \\ SP & SP & MP \end{pmatrix} & \begin{matrix} A_1 \\ A_2 \\ A_3 \\ A_4 \\ A_5 \\ A_6 \\ A_7 \\ A_8. \end{matrix} \end{matrix}$$

The decision matrix is given as

$$H = \begin{matrix} & \begin{matrix} Area & Cost & Time \end{matrix} & \\ & \begin{pmatrix} (3,5,7) & (3,5,7) & (1,1,3) \\ (3,5,7) & (1,1,3) & (1,3,5) \\ (7,9,9) & (7,9,9) & (1,1,3) \\ (7,9,9) & (3,5,7) & (7,9,9) \\ (7,9,9) & (7,9,9) & (7,9,9) \\ (1,3,5) & (1,3,5) & (3,5,7) \\ (3,5,7) & (7,9,9) & (3,5,7) \\ (3,5,7) & (3,5,7) & (1,3,5) \end{pmatrix} & \begin{matrix} A1 \\ A2 \\ A3 \\ A4 \\ A5 \\ A6 \\ A7 \\ A8 \end{matrix} \end{matrix}$$

Table 5 Performance scores based on Fuzzy TOPSIS

Alternatives	zz+	zz–	FF	Rank
A_1	5.900	7.078	0.545	2
A_2	4.793	9.446	0.663	1
A_3	7.035	5.858	0.454	3
A_4	12.225	0.726	0.056	7
A_5	12.893	0.000	0.000	8

A_6	8.514	5.394	0.388	4
A_7	11.594	1.402	0.108	6
A_8	9.415	4.882	0.341	5
Average Performance Score			**0.319**	
Standard Deviation of Performance Score			**0.242**	

Table 6 Performance scores based on Fuzzy COPRAS

Alternatives	XCC	Rank
A_1	90.53	2
A_2	100.00	1
A_3	82.26	5
A_4	51.87	7
A_5	46.75	8
A_6	87.01	3
A_7	57.54	6
A_8	84.26	4
Average	**75.03**	
Standard Deviation	**19.95**	

Figure 3 illustrates the scores obtained for each alternative using fuzzy TOPSIS and fuzzy COPRAS. The average performance score for the eight solar power projects as per fuzzy TOPSIS is 0.319 with a standard deviation of 0.242. Evaluation of the solar power projects as per fuzzy COPRAS reveals that average performance score is about 75% with a standard deviation of 19.95%. Based on the analysis carried out using Fuzzy TOPSIS and Fuzzy COPRAS, and from tables 5 and 6, we find that alternative A2, i.e., Shakti Sthala solar power project is the best solar power project based on the criteria used for evaluation of the projects. It is worthwhile to note that according to both methodologies, A2 is the best alternative and A5 is the worst alternative amongst the eight alternatives. The robustness of our analysis is also revealed by the fact that Spearman's Rank Correlation Coefficient is 93% and only three alternatives experience a minor change in ranking as per the two methodologies.

The analysis is carried out based on important criteria that play a crucial role in project development. Both fuzzy TOPSIS and fuzzy COPRAS can be effectively used to arrive at the best alternative. The efficacy of this approach lies in ability of decision maker to assign matrix values using fuzzy approach.

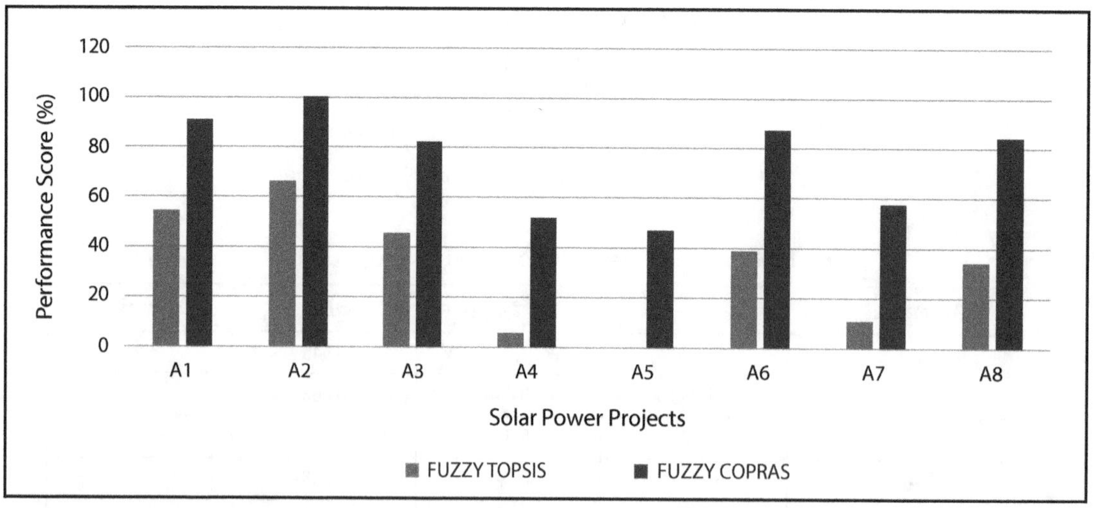

Fig. 3 Ranking of the eight solar projects as per Fuzzy TOPSIS and Fuzzy COPRAS

4. CONCLUSION

In this paper, we demonstrate how energy projects may be evaluated for their performance using integrated DEA-Fuzzy COPRAS and DEA-Fuzzy TOPSIS methodology. On the basis of DEA, we shortlisted solar power projects that are efficient. In the next stage, we ranked the shortlisted projects further using Fuzzy COPRAS. For the sake of fairness of the evaluation process, it may be a better idea to choose power projects which are similar in nature and technology. Since solar power projects depend on the availability of sunlight, projects which are located near each other or within the same region may be suitable for evaluation using our integrated methodology. Further, with availability of more data points, incorporating more of the technical aspects of solar projects would make this exercise more robust. We further expect that this methodology can also be used to evaluate any power project, given appropriate data is available and technicalities of the similar projects are considered. Since area, cost, time and installed capacity of projects are the parameters used for evaluating the projects, any energy project may be evaluated if data on these parameters is available.

5. ACKNOWLEDGMENT

Assistance of Harshil Dave, Academic Associate, Adani Institute of Infrastructure Management, Ahmedabad in preparing the manuscript is gratefully acknowledged.

REFERENCES

Charnes, A., Cooper, W.W., & Rhodes, E. (1978). Measuring the Efficiency of Decision Making Units. *European Journal of Operational Research, 2*, 429–444.

Chen, C. (2000). Extensions of the TOPSIS for group decision-making under fuzzy environment. *Fuzzy Sets and Systems, 114*(1), 1–9.

Cooper, W.W., Seiford, L.M. & Tone, K. (2000). *Data Envelopment Analysis: A Comprehensive Text with Models, Applications, References and DEA-Solver Software.* Kluwer Academic Publishers: Boston, MA.

Dhiman, H.S., Deb, D., Muyeen, S.M. & Kamwa, I. (2021). Wind Turbine Gearbox Anomaly Detection based on Adaptive Threshold and Twin Support Vector Machines. *IEEE Transactions on Energy Conversion.*

Dhiman, H.S., & Deb, D. (2020). Fuzzy TOPSIS and Fuzzy COPRAS based multicriteria decision making for hybrid wind farms. Energy, 202, 117755. https://doi.org/10.1016/j.energy.2020.117755

Dhiman, H.S., Deb, D., Carroll, J., Muresan, V. & Unguresan, M. (2020). Wind Turbine Gearbox Condition Monitoring Based on Class of Support Vector Regression Models and Residual Analysis. *Sensors, 20*(23): 6742.

Dhiman, H.S., Deb, D., Muresan, V. & Unguresan, M. (2019). Multi-Criteria Decision Making Approach for Hybrid Operation of Wind Farms. *Symmetry, 11*(5): 675. https://doi.org/10.3390/sym11050675

Garni, H.A., Kassem, A., Awasthi, A., Komljenovic, D. & Al-Haddad, K. (2016). A multicriteria decision making approach for evaluating renewable power generation sources in Saudi Arabia. *Sustainable Energy Technologies and Assessments,* 16: 137–150.

Georgiou, D., Mohammed, E.S. & Rozakis, S. (2015). Multi-criteria decision making on the energy supply configuration of autonomous desalination units. *Renewable Energy, 75,* 459–467.

Haralambopoulos, D.A., & Polatidis, H. (2003). Renewable energy projects: structuring a multi-criteria group decision-making framework. *Renewable Energy, 28*(6), 961–973.

Hwang, C., & Yoon, K. (1981). *Methods for Multiple Attribute Decision Making*, 58–191. Berlin, Heidelberg: Springer Berlin Heidelberg. https://doi.org/10.1007/978-3-642-48318-9_3

Jahan, A., & Edwards, K.L. (2015). A state-of-the-art survey on the influence of normalization techniques in ranking: Improving the materials selection process in engineering design. *Materials & Design, 65,* 335–342.

Kempkes, G., & Pohl, C. (2010). The Efficiency of German Universities – Some Evidence from Nonparametric and Parametric Methods. *Applied Economics, 42*(16), 2063–2079.

Kolios, A.J., Rodriguez-Tsouroukdissian, A. & Salonitis, K. (2016). Multi-criteria decision analysis of offshore wind turbines support structures under stochastic inputs. *Ships and Offshore Structures, 11*(1), 38–49.

Kumar, A., Sah, B., Singh, A.R., Deng, Y., He, X., Kumar, P. & Bansal, R.C. (2017). A review of multi criteria decision making (MCDM) towards sustainable renewable energy development. *Renewable and Sustainable Energy Reviews,* 69, 596–609. https://doi.org/10.1016/j.rser.2016.11.191

Kundakc, N. (2018). An integrated method using MACBETH and EDAS methods for evaluating steam boiler alternatives. *Journal of Multi-Criteria Decision Analysis.*

Lee, A.H.I., Hung, M., Kang, H., & Pearn, W.L. (2012). A wind turbine evaluation model under a multi-criteria decision making environment. *Energy Conversion and Management, 64,* 289–300.

Mahdy, M., & Bahaj, A.S. (2018). Multi criteria decision analysis for offshore wind energy potential in Egypt. *Renewable Energy, 118,* 278–289.

Kööksalan, M., Wallenius, J. & Zionts, S. (2011). *The early history of MCDM* in Multiple criteria decision making. *World Science,* 1–16.

Zavadskas, E.K., & Kaklauskas, A. (1996). The new method of multicriteria evaluation of projects. *Deutsch-Litauisch-Polnisches Kolloquim zum Baubetriebswesen. Hochschule fur Technik. Wirtschaft und Kultur in Leipzig. 3 Jahrgang. Sonderheft,* pp. 3–8.

A System Simulation Framework to Evaluate the Sustainability of Buildings

Ann Francis
Doctoral Research Scholar
Indian Institute of Technology Bombay

Albert Thomas
Assistant Professor
Indian Institute of Technology Bombay

Abstract: The development of building and infrastructure directly influences the economic and social growth of nations. However, they also negatively impact the environment through massive resource consumption, waste generation, and pressure on natural resources. Hence, buildings and infrastructure should embrace sustainable practices that minimize harmful environmental impacts and enhance economic growth and social well-being throughout its life-cycle. Therefore, sustainability assessment gains significant relevance in these sectors. However, on evaluating the existing sustainability assessment methods, it can be observed that they are primarily focused only on the environmental pillar and lacks a coherent and robust structure encompassing all the dimensions of sustainability. These tools and methods also ignore the interdependencies and interactions between the social, economic and environmental aspects. Further, conventional assessment methods adopt a static approach in their mode of evaluation by ignoring the external and internal changes that could occur with time in the building's long-life span. Therefore, this paper proposes a system dynamics-based modelling approach for sustainability evaluation that is capable of evaluating buildings by capturing the interdependencies between the pillars of sustainability as well as accommodating the dynamic temporal changes that occur in a building life cycle. A case study project from the Indian context demonstrates the features of the framework and its capabilities. Sustainability evaluation using this framework showed that currently, buildings need to focus on reducing energy consumption apart from achieving material efficiency. Similarly, it also demonstrates the importance of a dynamic sustainability assessment framework by illustrating the underestimation of emissions by about 50% when a static approach is adopted in terms of the building's energy consumption. Therefore, this integrated framework could serve as a means to achieve sustainable development targets envisaged by nations.

Keywords: Sustainability Assessment, Systems thinking, System dynamics, Life Cycle Sustainability Assessment (LCSA)

1. INTRODUCTION

The concept of sustainable development highlighted the necessity to direct attention to the protection of the environment with due consideration to the economic development and social growth of the countries (Keeble, 1988; Murray & Cotgrave, 2007). Unlike developed nations, ensuring sustainability for developing countries becomes a challenge due to the aggravating problems of rapid urbanization, growing inequality, and the plight to meet the basic needs and amenities demanded by their ever-growing population (Lohani et al., 1997). Their economic and social growth is directly influenced by the development of infrastructure and buildings (Srinivasu et al., 2013). However, constructing buildings and infrastructure causes massive resource consumption and significant environmental impacts (Yu et al., 2018). Therefore, it becomes essential to assess the level of impact of buildings and infrastructure on the environmental, social and economic parameters to understand its contribution to sustainable development. In this background, Sustainability Assessment (SA) has garnered significant attention.

Several practices and tools were developed worldwide for assessing the sustainability of buildings, such as indicators, impact assessment methods, rating systems, energy evaluation methods and other scoring-based approaches (Liu et al., 2013). Most of these tools focus primarily on environmental sustainability. However, sustainability in a holistic sense requires all dimensions to be balanced and given equal importance (ISO 15392:2019, (2019)). Further, most of the existing tools have ignored the interdependencies associated with these sustainability elements. For example, the economic impact of a building project which employs local suppliers and material can create local employment and change in the social status of the surrounding society. Further, the increase of reuse and recycling as part of influencing the environmental pillar can affect the economic pillar by influencing the costs. Similarly, most of these tools ignore the effect of time induced changes on a product such as a building with a long-life span of about 50-70 years. A building's sustainability performance could be significantly influenced by temporal factors such as a change in the electricity mix, technology up-gradation, change in standards and bye-laws, change in energy consumption due to material deterioration, occupant behaviour, and change in external surroundings (Collinge, 2013; Sohn et al., 2017; Su et al., 2019).

Therefore, an integrated sustainability assessment system that attempts to balance the tradeoffs between the pillars of sustainability and captures their interdependencies along with accounting for the temporal influences is vital for building assessment. Such a multi-faceted sustainability assessment approach would have several inherent complexities, requiring a computational modelling and simulation-based method for dynamic evaluation. Systems thinking provides an ideal platform to evaluate such complex multi-dimensional systems such as sustainability (Sterman, 2012). System dynamics is a branch of systems thinking that provides a suitable computational platform to develop frameworks to analyze complex systems that include numerous elements and interlinked dependencies. Further, this integrated tool/method developed should enable decision-makers to take suitable decisions oriented towards sustainable development while planning building projects. Therefore, this study demonstrates the development of such a framework capable of capturing the inherent dependencies among the social, economic and environmental aspects of buildings and the temporal and dynamic characteristics of a building's sustainability performance. For this, a sustainability assessment framework based on a system dynamics-based approach is proposed in the study.

2. LITERATURE REVIEW

2.1 A glimpse into the different sustainability assessment tools

Figure 1 below shows a glimpse of the various available tools for sustainability evaluation as compiled from various literature (Bendewald & John, 2013; Bragança et al., 2010; Hoogmartens et al., 2014; Mahmoud et al., 2019; Ness et al., 2007; Onat et al., 2014; Reed et al., 2011) and the phases of a building project they primarily impact. It can be observed that most of these tools are applied during the design and operation phase. The emphasis on sustainability is relatively imperceptible during the initial stages of planning. Further, most of these tools evaluate sustainability only from an environmental perspective. However, sustainability assessment should encompass social and economic influences while capturing environmental impacts. Additionally, it is also essential to understand the deep interconnections between social, economic, and environmental sustainability pillars from the buildings' perspective.

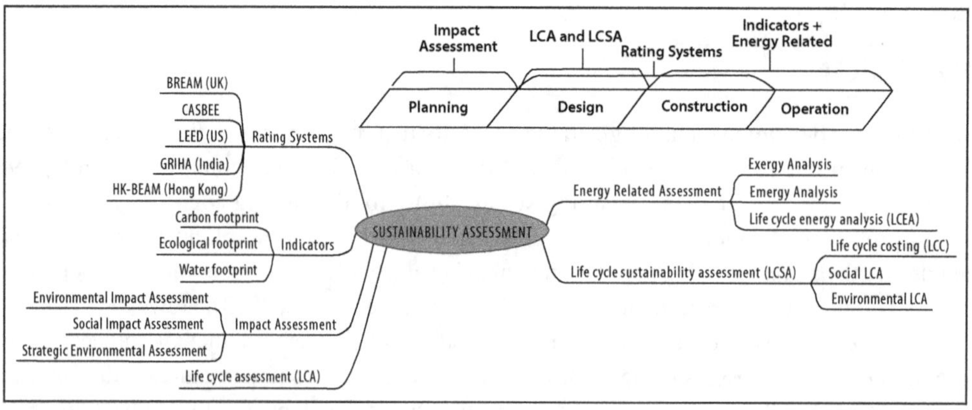

Fig. 1 Overview of various categories of sustainability assessment tools available

Although the science of environmental sustainability is well-established with the presence of tools such as LCA, it needs to progress to accommodate the modern complexities, and multi-functionalities demanded for overall sustainable development. LCA takes a cradle to grave environmental performance assessment approach by considering the life-cycle impacts of a product or activity from raw materials procurement to its final demolition and disposal(Guinée et al., 2001). However, emerging research in LCA propagates the incorporation of social and economic aspects of sustainability into its core principles by proposing the concept of LCSA (Guinee et al., 2011; Kloepffer, 2008; Valdivia et al., 2013). LCSA intends to address economic aspects through performing a Life Cycle Costing (LCC) that accounts for all the costs incurred from the inception to the demolition of the building. Social Life Cycle Assessment (S-LCA), is the other branch of LCSA that aims to address the social aspects related to human well-being and safety.Although LCSA appeared as a promising comprehensive sustainability assessment tool, a major drawback in its existing structure is the discrete consideration of the individual tenets of LCC, LCA and S-LCA, without accounting for their mutual interdependencies.

2.2 Sustainability pillars and their interactions from the context of built-environment

Singh et al. (2009) suggested that sustainability is a broader concept that should account for the interlinkages and dynamics created in the system due to social, economic, and environmental interactions. Therefore, it is significant to understand such possible linkages between the pillars of sustainability for meaningful evaluation. Figure 2 below is a representative graphic of the possible influences between each of the pillars of sustainability in the setting of a building or construction project development as compiled from various literature (Gibberd, 2005; Liu et al., 2013; Mahmoud et al., 2019; Shen et al., 2016; Ugwu et al., 2006). It shows a matrix that describes the salient parameters within each pillar of sustainability and metrics which interlink each of these pillars. It is not an exhaustive matrix of all the possible mutual influences existing between the dimensions but a fair depiction that these could influence the project's overall sustainability performance. For example, the health and safety of workers are a social aspect. However, when health is impacted by environmental degradation, it can lead to productivity loss and hence, economic loss in terms of costs. These interdependencies advocate the need for a framework that accommodates all three dimensions of sustainability and their mutual influences to assess projects.

	ECONOMIC	SOCIAL	ENVIRONMENTAL
ECONOMIC	• Internal rate of return • Benefit/Cost Ratio • Construction costs • Local economic development through employing local suppliers and materials • Time span of construction vs. profits	• Creation of local employment. • Employing local suppliers enhances local economy. • Income generating opportunities generated. • Increased affordability through lower costs through local supply.	• Use of local materials/suppliers reduces carbon footpring of transportation. • Travelling for basic needs and employment influences carbon footprint.
SOCIAL	• Poor health and unsafe practices increases the cost of construction • Increase in productivity due to better work conditions and health	• Safe working environment and conditions for workers. • Protection from Health hazards. • Proportion of women employed (gender disparity). • Consideration for people with specific needs. • Presence of heritage and culturally relevant sites. • Access to basic amenities.	• Accessibility to public transport affects environment. • Demographic changes can influence the environment. • Brown Field development creates lesser impact on land-use pattern.
ENVIRONMENTAL	• Influence of Energy costs. • Cost savings due to recycling and re-use. • Impact on Initial costs due to green technology	• Better indoor air quality leading to improved comfort and heath. • Resilience to extreme weather conditions influence the social nature • Minimize noise pollution to reduces mental stress • Public green spaces for better social development. • Change in ecology can influence livelihoods of people.	• Efficient use of resources. • Eliminates of wastes. • Recycling and reuse. • Reduce emissions. • Reduce pollution. • Improve water use efficiency. • Protect Biodiversity.

Fig. 2 Matrix showing the three pillars of sustainability and some of their interactions

2.3 Need for dynamic thinking and computational modelling methods for sustainability assessment

Evaluating sustainability by considering such interrelationships will help achieve a more holistic and coherent form of sustainability evaluation. However, it is also essential toconsider the time dependence of a product's different characteristics over its life cycle. (Su et al., 2017). For buildings and construction projects with a long life cycle, categories of environmental impacts such a greenhouse gas emissions, global warming, and water use could be significantly influenced by time-related factors (Fouquet et al., 2015; Sonnemann et al., 2013). Therefore, there arises a need to incorporate dynamic temporal aspects into sustainability evaluation to avoid erroneous impact prediction and forecasting, leading to inefficient policies and strategies being implemented.

To facilitate such a dynamic and comprehensive sustainability evaluation,a computational modelling-based approach is essential. Modelling is a process of replicating real-life instances with mathematical formulas to predict the future trends or behaviour of a phenomenon. The use of a computer-based modelling approach in environmental assessment has been proposed since the early 1990s (Fedra, 1990) owing to the flexibility and visualization provided by modelling platforms. However, the scale of application of modelling to improve the environment is found to be limited.

According to Hansmann et al. (2012), the simultaneous outcomes of economy, society, and environment can be produced through a system thinking approach.System dynamics is a computational modelling application of systems thinking which captures the non-linear behaviour of complex systems.SD developed by Jay Forrester aids in the analysis of complex and dynamic feedback systems (Forrester, 1970). Therefore, analyzing interdependencies between social, economic, and environmental impacts can be easily facilitated through a system dynamics based framework. Hence, system dynamics modelsenable the study of the interrelationship and interactions between different sustainability indicators and simulate their behaviour in time, which is not possible with individual observations alone (Huang and Chen 1999). Therefore, using a tool like system dynamics enables forecasting impacts, optimizing the strategies such that all the aspects are balanced and deriving the best strategies for the building under consideration.

3. METHODOLOGY

Figure 3 below shows the broad methodology adopted for the study. To develop a sustainability assessment framework encompassing all three pillars of sustainability, the first step is to identify the most suitable indicators for sustainability. Such a framework demands easily quantifiable andwell-established sustainability elements that are not subjective in nature. Hence, the indicators chosen should be such that they are easily measurable and can be sufficiently validated. The indicators considered in this particular study are the footprint family described by Galli et al. (2012), life cycle energy, life cycle cost, accessibility and social cost of carbon.They are described in brief,along with the different sub-model details elaborated in section 3.1.

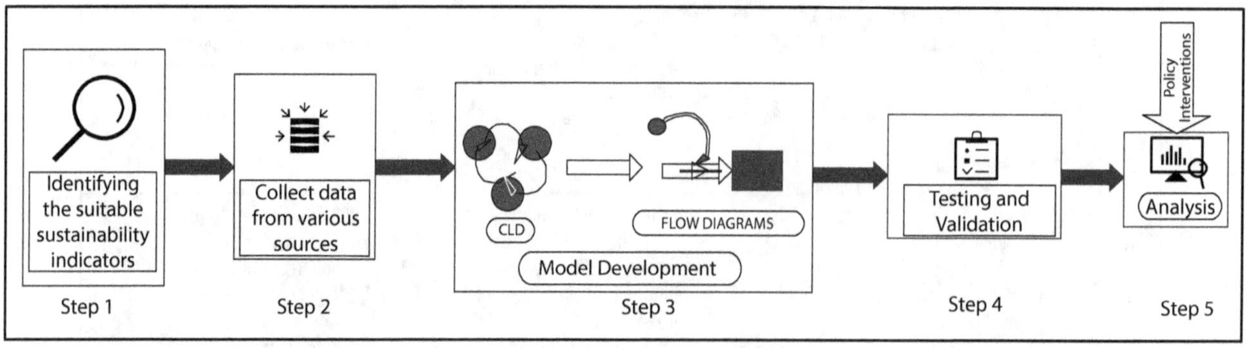

Fig. 3 Research Methodology

The second step involves data collection from various sources about the building's average resource consumption, namely materials, water, energy and waste generated. Additionally, the multiple factors associated with converting these processes into different types of impacts are to be sourced from different reliable documents or sources. These are vital for model creation and analysis. The details of the area, materials, time period of various phases of a building project, number of stakeholders and location would serve as important inputs for the framework.

The third step in the overall framework is model development. The system dynamics framework for sustainability assessment of buildings is developed in a software tool called Anylogic(Version 8.5.2), a java-based platform for multi-method simulation. It enables the creation of various models with interconnected elements that can be used to run multiple simulations to understand complex systems' behaviour. Model development consists of two parts. The first part involves creating causal loop diagrams (CLD),an integral part of the systems thinking approach that depicts the interactions between the various sustainability elements associated with building projects. Figure 4 below shows a CLD depicting the various sustainability elements of the project. The representation on the left of the figure summarizes the overall CLD shown on the right. When the sustainability of the project is low, the pressure to improve sustainability is high. Therefore, the need for policy interventions to improve sustainability increases. The improvement measures will lower the impacts of the indicators, thereby enhancing sustainability and reducing the pressure to introduce stringent measures. This overall feedback system, as captured with various sustainability elements,is shown in CLD developed in the right of figure 4.

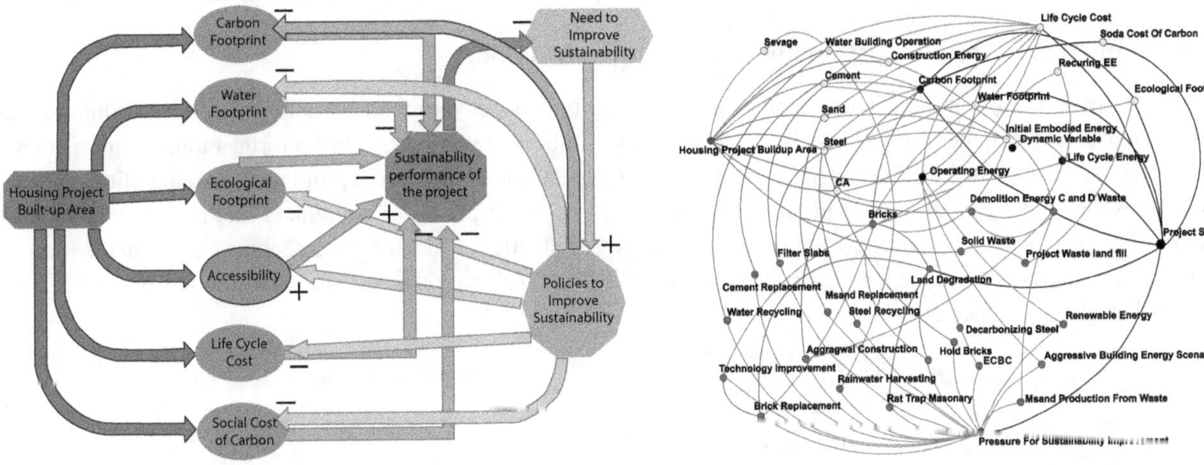

Fig. 4 Causal Loop Diagram (CLD) showing the interactions between various sustainability attributes

While the CLD qualitatively transfers the relationships associated with the sustainability elements, it is essential to capture the mathematical relationship between them to effectively quantify the concerned building's sustainability. This can be done with the help of stock and flow diagrams (SFD) that represent the interrelationship between various sub-models and captures their interactions using different mathematical formula. A flow diagram usually consists of stocks, flows and auxiliary variables. Stocks represent the accumulations after a fixed time step, while flow variables control the inflow rate and outflow of stocks. The general equation of flow diagrams adopted from Sterman (2012) is applied in the system dynamics interface. The relationship between stocks and flows are defined using the auxiliary variables and different parameter values. Several pre-defined parameters and variables are already input in the framework. Further several sub-models are developed for the framework to quantify and assess sustainability. Their combined behaviour and interactions influence the system's overall performance. These sub-models can be categorized into basic sub-models and sustainability indicator sub-models. The basic sub-models and their features along with the sub-models they interact with are briefly described in Table 1 below. The sustainability indicator sub-models are described in section 3.1.

Table 1 Basic Sub-Models in the framework

Sub-Model	Important Characteristics	Sub-Models it is directly linked with
Material Sub-model	It serves as the basis to quantify the environmental impacts resulting from material manufacturing and its transportation. The resulting sustainability impacts are accounted to the material procurement period to facilitate the computation from the life-cycle perspective.	Water, Energy, Transport,
Water Sub-model	The water sub-model quantifies water consumption across the different phases of the life cycle of the building. For this, water consumed while manufacturing materials, water use during the construction phase, and water consumption during the building use period are computed from the data collected in step 2.	Energy, Waste
Energy Sub-model	This sub-model calculates each phase's energy requirements, facilitating quantifying the life cycle energy and emissions resulting from energy use. It accounts for the energy spent in the manufacturing of materials, transportation, construction, operation and even demolition	Water, Waste, Transport.
Transport Sub-model	The transport sub-model accounts for all the transportation associated with the building project, which could significantly impact greenhouse emissions. It accounts for the transportation of raw materials from factories to the construction site and within the construction site	Energy,
Waste Sub-Model	The wastes generated from the building are quantified in the sub-model. Therefore, the construction-related wastes, general solid waste generated during building operation and demolition waste is computed. Sewage generated is also accounted for as a factor of water consumption as per standards	Energy, Transport,

3.1 Development of various sustainability indicator sub-models

The sustainability indicator sub-models capture the different impacts across environmental, social and economic dimensions and the tradeoffs between them. Environmental sustainability can be represented by the footprint family comprising of carbon, water and ecological footprint and life cycle energy (LCE). Carbon Footprint is a prominent sustainability indicator that quantifies the total greenhouse gas emissions released during different phases of a product or a process, expressed as kilograms of carbon dioxide equivalent ($kgCO_2e$) (Pandey & Agrawal, 2011). Quantifying greenhouse gases in the form of carbon footprint helps to reduce the long term impacts of the building on climate change. The carbon footprint for the study is computed as given in Equation 1 below.

$$\int_0^{ProcPeriod}\left[E_{materialproc}\right]ds+\text{stock}(0)+\int_{ProcPeriod}^{ConstuctionPeriod}\left[E_{construction}\right]ds+\text{stock}(ProcPeriod)+ \quad (1)$$
$$\int_{ConstuctionPeriod}^{BuildingUsePeriod}\left[E_{Use}\right]ds+\text{stock}(ConstructionPeriod)+$$
$$\int_{BuildingUsePeriod}^{DemolitionPeriod}\left[E_{dem}\right]ds+\text{stock}(BuildingUsePeriod)$$

where E represents the Emissions at different stages of the building project

Water Footprintis an indicator primarily developed to quantify freshwater consumption and conservation (Galli et al., 2012). It implies all the direct and indirect water consumed in the process of creating the product (IS 14046, 2014). In this study, the blue water footprint is onlyconsidered, whichis the volume of freshwater (surface and groundwater) consumed by the process or product throughout its lifespan (Bonamente et al., 2016). Quantifying the water footprint of proposed building projects helps in understanding their influence on the water resources and promotes water conservation. It is computed using the following equation 2. Figure 5 below shows a glimpse of a part of the system dynamics model developed.

$$\int_0^{ProcPeriod}\left[W_{materialproc}\right]ds+\text{stock}(0)+\int_{ProcPeriod}^{ConstuctionPeriod}\left[W_{construction}\right]ds+\text{stock}(ProcPeriod)+ \quad (2)$$
$$\int_{ConstuctionPeriod}^{BuildingUsePeriod}\left[W_{Use}\right]ds+\text{stock}(ConstructionPeriod)$$

where W represents the water consumption at different stages of the building project.

Similarly, Ecological Footprint is a unique indicator of sustainability developed by Wackernagel, and it is defined as the amount of land required to generate resources needed for humanity and that to assimilate the emissions and wastes generated (Wackernagel & Rees, 1998). It is represented in units of area in the form of global hectares of land (gha), describing it as an aspect of the carrying capacity of the earth. The ecological footprint accounts for the impact on land resources due to emissions, wastes, water, and project built-up land as a whole (Lin, 2019). The major components of ecological footprint are Ecological footprint of built-land ($EF_{built-land}$), Ecological footprint of water (EF_{water}), Ecological footprint of carbon emissions (EF_{CO2}) and Ecological footprint of waste (EF_{waste}). Therefore, it takes inputs from the carbon footprint, wastes and water sub-models. The ecological footprint is calculated as the sum of $EF_{built-land}$, EF_{water}, EF_{CO2} and EF_{waste}. Therefore, computing the proposed building's ecological footprint will provide a life-cycle perspective on land resources' impact.

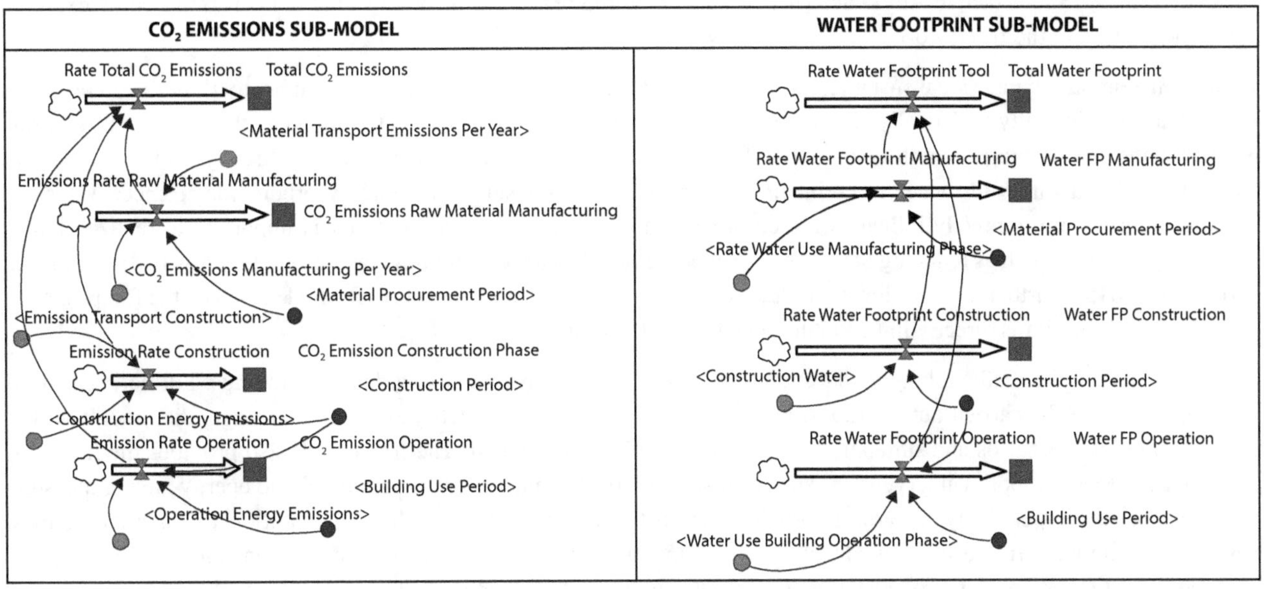

Fig. 5 Carbon and Water Footprint Sub-model

LCE of a building implies all the energy use in the building associated with all the project phases.It includes embodied energy, construction energy, operational energy, recurring embodied energy and demolition energy. Embodied energy is a significant part of life-cycle energy and can be classified into two categories. Initial Embodied Energy (IEE) and Recurring Embodied Energy (REE) (Dixit et al., 2014). IEE energy refers to the energy associated with the extraction of materials, manufacturing, and energy spent to converttheminto useful products. REE is the energy incurred in the repair, maintenance, or refurbishment of materials during the building's service life. Demolition energy includes the energy incurred to demolish the building and transport the debris; however, studies report its contribution to the overall life-cycle energy is very less and hence is ignored in most circumstance (Devi & Palaniappan, 2014; Praseeda et al., 2016; Ramesh et al., 2010). However, in this study, the recurring embodied energy and demolition energy is accounted for at a rate between 1-5% of the LCE to complete the building life-cycle phases. Total LCE will be the sum total of all these components.

According to Rebitzer and Hunkeler (2003), when a project is found to be acceptable in terms of environmental and social performance, it is also essential that it is sustainable from the economic sense as well, and LCC can act as a suitable indicator. LCC accounts for all the costs incurred during the lifetime of a product or process (Gluch & Baumann, 2004). However, more advanced economic indicators of sustainability need to be developed to provide insights into the economic effects due to environmental damage. Therefore the social cost of carbon is chosen as another indicator of economic sustainability. It represents the damage done to the global ecosystem of the future due to emissions of greenhouse gases today and is expressed in dollar per tonne of CO_2 emitted (Pearce, 2003). Higher values of the social cost of carbon demand better conservation measures of the environment. India is reported to have a very high social cost of carbon at the value of 86$ per tonne of CO_2 and is expected to be adversely affected by climate change effects (Ricke et al., 2018). Ricke et al. (2018) also report that, countries with higher social costs of carbon could face a severe impact on the economy due to CO_2 emissions.

Accounting social impacts due to a building are quite challenging, owing to the indicators' subjective nature. Although health, safety and security are broad terms that could be included in the analysis of social impacts, they are influenced by several multiple factors. The domain of Social-LCA is also fairly underdeveloped. Given this context, this study preliminarily explores a few easily measurable elements such as accessibility to basic amenities from building projects as a social indicator. Accessibility is considered both a social and an economic indicator of interest in sustainability (Grol, 2005). However, when accessibility is considered as an economic parameter, it primarily refers to the ease of transport, whereas from the social perspective, it pertains more to the desirability and nature of opportunities available for access to society.The cumulative measures method is one of the popular and simplest measures of accessibility. It takes into account both distance and the purpose of the trip (Bhat et al., 2018). A distance threshold is defined, and the number of potential facilities in that threshold is defined as accessibility. In this particular framework, accessibility of buildings to schools, bus stops, supermarkets, parks, and hospitals is considered a measure of social sustainability with the help of the GIS interface in Anylogic. This being an ongoing research few other social indicators are being explored for incorporation in the framework.

Apart from computing individual sustainability indicators, it is essential to understand these indicators' mutual interactions to compute sustainability holistically. The carbon footprint and water footprint directly influence the ecological footprint. Similarly, the carbon footprint will be directly affected by LCE because energy consumption directly impacts emissions. LCE also holds a link with water footprint in the form of water consumed for energy production. Hence, water and carbon footprints are indirectly influencing each other. Similarly, analyzing accessibility is important to realize broader sustainability goals, such as reducing emissions by reducing long-distance commuting and promoting low carbon transport (Ford et al., 2015). Further, LCC is directly influenced by water, energy, and transport sub-models, hence the footprints and LCE. Carbon footprint is directly linked to the social cost of carbon.

The fourth step in the methodology is to test and validate the model using existing data of buildings. Further, sensitivity analysis could also be carried out for robust results. Following this, in the methodology's final stage, the models will be run, and multiple scenarios and simulations as required would be generated. The framework also provides the flexibility to introduce necessary policy interventions such as material replacement, water conservation, and energy-saving measures that can contribute positively towards improving the sustainability of the building. In addition to quantifying these sustainability impacts, it is also essential that some dynamic impacts such as changes in energy consumption, varying laws and codes, and technology improvementthat occur with time in a building are suitably incorporated. These changes can be easily incorporated into the simulation framework with the help of different functions in Anylogic. The next section discusses a case study that demonstrates the potential of this framework.

3.2 Case study

The study considers the sustainability evaluation from the Indian perspective. Alarge scale low-cost housing in Maharashtra with the features as in Table 2 is considered. Further, the study considers only the basic materials, namely cement, sand, aggregate, steel, and bricks, for evaluation. This is because these materials are predominately known to contribute to the residential buildings' life-cycle energy from the perspective of building materials (Bansal et al., 2014; Reddy & Jagadish, 2003). Further, the sources of the various factorsused in the model framework for this case study based on the Indian scenario is provided in Appendix 1. Additionally, the case study also considers a scenario for varying energy consumption to account for temporal changes in the buildings energy profile during the building operation phase. Appendix 2 provides the details of this dynamic variation.

The relevant inputs are then provided into the framework, and on simulation, the life cycle impacts across each indicator can be observed. A few policy interventions are also introduced for the project in the form of replacement of cement, sand or steel, along with a few energy-saving measures to understand their influence on the overall sustainability. Such a large scale project is considered for case study evaluation to improve the understanding of the massive impact of such projects on the environment, economy and society.

Table 2 Case study Attributes

Project built-up area	160000 square meters
Cement quantity	8000 Metric Tonnes
Fine Aggregate	15000 Metric Tonnes
Coarse Aggregate	20000 Metric Tonnes
Steel	1000 Metric Tonnes
Bricks	9000 Metric Tonnes
Number of workers	600 nos
Households	2000 nos
Occupants	11000 nos

4. RESULTS

The major results are summarised below through the figures below. The main outputs from the system dynamics simulation are the values of sustainability indicators associated with the building evaluated across its entire life span. Once the inputs of the building to be analyzed are provided, the base case (building as planned) simulation results are obtained. Figure 6 below shows the simulation results associated with the carbon and water footprint. The rate diagrams show the rate of these footprints per year and the cumulative diagrams represent the stock values at end of life for each indicator. For example, in the rate of carbon footprint, it can be seen that the initial peak of emissions is quite high owing to the material procurement phase into which all the emissions due to material production is accounted. Further, the sudden dip and increase correspond to the transition from the construction phase to the operation phase. The use and maintenance phase exhibits a gradual increase in emissions due to the change in average household electricity use per year, and finally, the rate drops to zero after the end of life. Similar trends can be observed for the other impact indicators as well. Figure 7 below shows the graphs generated from the Anylogic interface that show the base case results of other cumulative sustainability indicators.

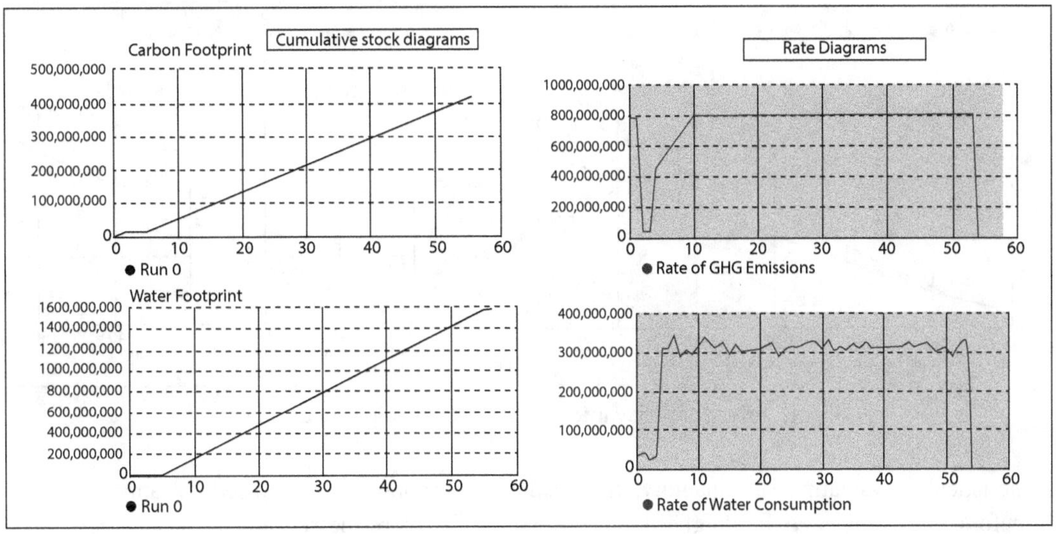

Fig. 6 Carbon and Water footprint and their stock and rate diagrams of the case study building

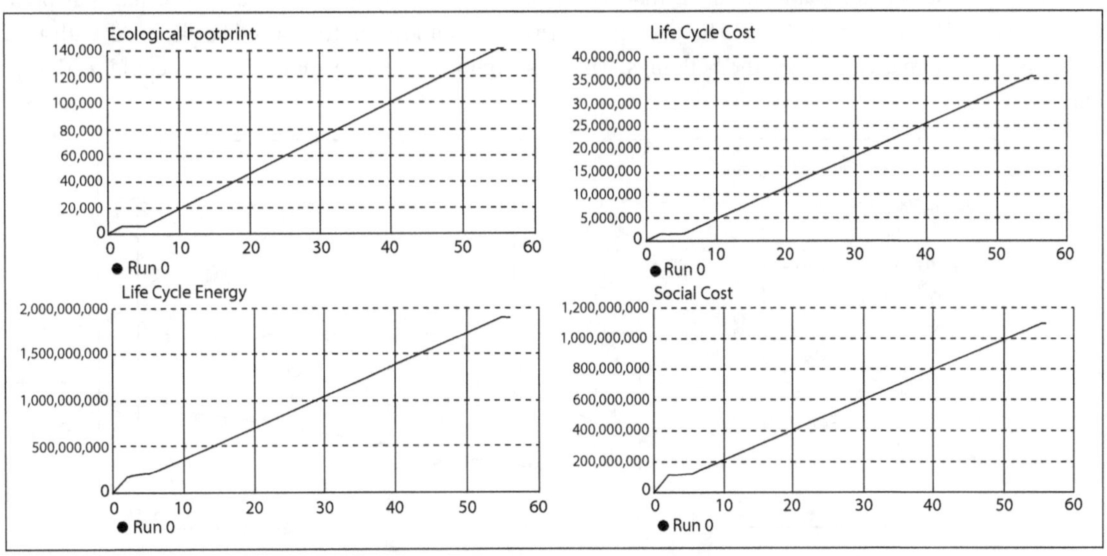

Fig. 7 Cumulative Diagrams of other indicators

Further, the framework is equipped to perform different policy analysis by introducing material, energy and water-related interventions. In this study, the influence of strategies such as replacing cement, sand, steel, bricks with other complementary materials is analyzed. Further, moderate policies related to energy savings are also available. Accordingly, Figure 8 below shows the effect of the following scenario of base case (Run 0), cement replacement by 50% (Run 1) or brick replacement with AAC by 50 % (Run 2) or the introduction of decarbonizing technology in steel manufacturing (Run 3) or moderately intensive energy reduction strategies (Run 4) on Ecological footprint, LCE, LCC and social cost.

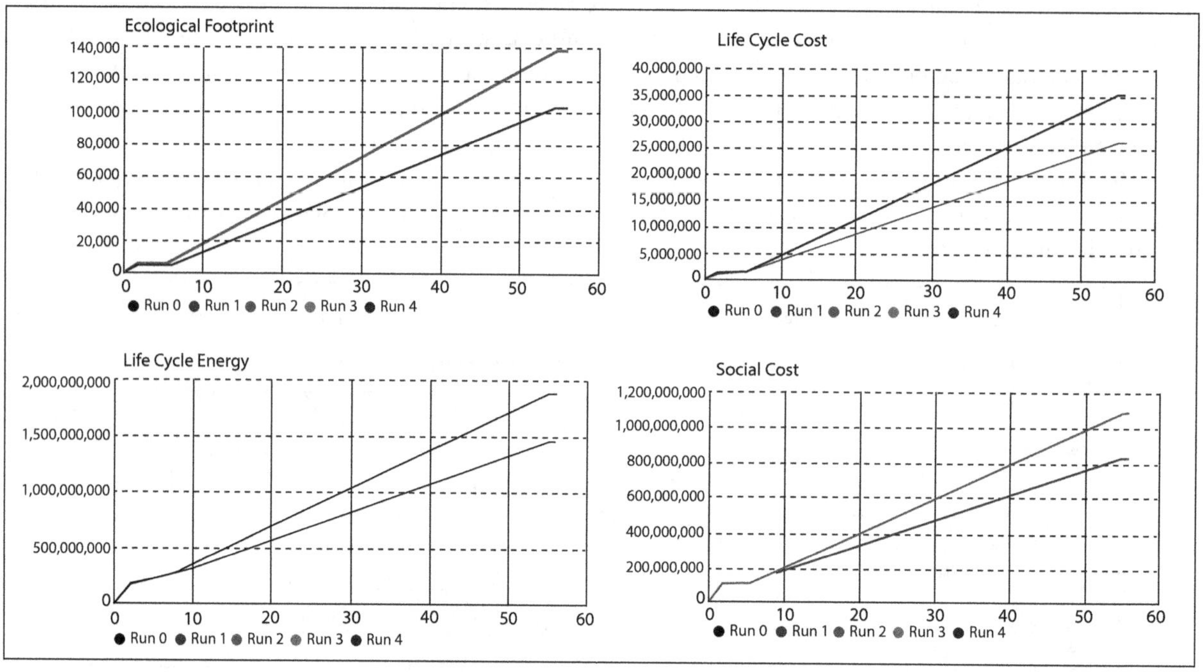

Fig. 8 Effect of policy interventions on building sustainability

Apart from holistically evaluating sustainability, the need to incorporate time induced dynamic changes is already emphasized before in this paper. Accordingly, it is worthwhile to explore the scenario in which such changes are not considered for evaluation. For the same case study, figure 9 below shows the carbon footprint graph for the same building where run 0 corresponds to the scenario where the average energy consumption is considered as a constant value throughout the 50 years life span. However, that is not the actual scenario. Run 1 corresponds to the actual scenario as predicted for Indian conditions by Rawal et al. (2014). The average energy consumption is forecasted to increase with time due to various external and internal changes in the buildings. Therefore ignoring such dynamic changes could lead to erroneous evaluation.

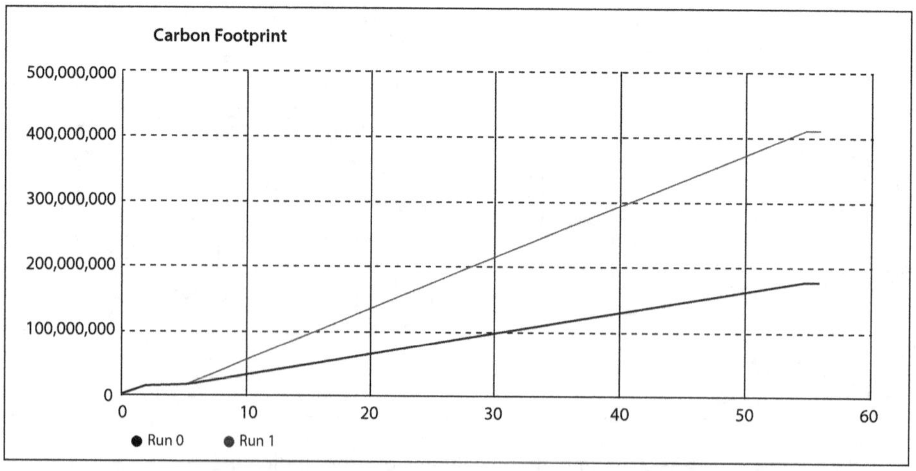

Fig. 9 Carbon footprint while considering temporal variations

5. DISCUSSION

The life cycle energy as obtained from the analysis for the building is 7.43 GJ/sqm which is in the range of 2.54–12.54 GJ/m^2 as reported for urban dwellings in India by Pal et al. (2017). It can be reduced to about 50% with suitable energy reduction strategies alone. The ecological footprint is 0.55gha/sqm and comparable results are found for a building reported in Husain (2019). Preliminary observations show that energy-related policies bring about significant improvement in building sustainability as opposed to material related interventions. However, anticipating a future where net-zero energy buildings or low energy buildings would be promoted on a broader scale in India, measures and strategies that promote material efficiency would gain relevance. Another major understanding of this study is that it is essential to accommodate the changes in building characteristics with time as much as they can be forecasted accurately. The ignorance of such changes as in energy consumption could result in reporting about 50 per cent lower value for an indicator such as carbon footprint or the corresponding global warming potential. This could lead to poor planning and policy formulation of projects and further delay India's attempts to achieve a 35% reduction in emission intensity by 2030.

6. CONCLUSION

The growing need to embrace sustainability in the building sector has led to the increased emphasis on the need for a comprehensive sustainability assessment framework. The study evaluates the flaws in the existing methods and proposes a novel method based on a systems thinking approach to assess the sustainability of buildings. A system dynamics framework is proposed to evaluate the interdependencies between the pillars of sustainability and provide a platform for multiple simulations and scenario analysis. Results show that significant sustainability improvement could be achieved by focusing on relevant policy measures particularly related to building energy. The framework also enables the incorporation of dynamic temporal characteristics such as a change in the buildings' average energy consumption throughout its operation period. Results show that ignoring such time-induced changes could lead to underestimating actual impacts such as emissionsby about 50%, leading to poor planning and sustainable practices. Future scope aims to increase the framework's robustness by incorporating relevant LCA indicators for environmental evaluation and improved decision-making capabilities of the framework through multi-criteria decision-making (MCDM).

7. APPENDICES

Table A.1 Relevant Factors required for the framework development and their sources.

Material Embodied energy and emission factors	(Indicators & Version, 2017)
Water conversion factors	(Weekly, 2007)
Transportation emission factors	(Consultation, n.d.)
Equipment related information	(Devi & Palaniappan, 2014)

Table A.2 Average Energy consumption in kWh per household per year under Business as Usual and Moderate, Scenarios as sourced from Rawal et al. (2014).

Year	BAU	MODERATE
2000	668	668
2005	708	708
2010	855	855
2011	954	954
2012	1002	1002
2013	1008	1008
2014	1079	1079
2020	1200	1100
2030	2000	1500

REFERENCES

15392:2019. (2019). INTERNATIONAL STANDARD Sustainability in buildings and principles. *ISO 15392:2019. Sustainability in Buildings and Civil Engineering Works – General Principles. ISO Geneva, Switzerland, 2019.*

Bansal, D., Singh, R., & Sawhney, R. L. (2014). Effect of construction materials on embodied energy and cost of buildings—A case study of residential houses in India up to 60 m^2 of plinth area. *Energy and Buildings, 69*, 260–266.

Bendewald, M., & John, Z. (2013). Using carrying capacity as a baseline for building sustainability assessment. *Habitat International, 37*, 22–32. https://doi.org/10.1016/j.habitatint.2011.12.021

Bhat, C., Handy, S., Kockelman, K., Mahmassani, H., Chen, Q., & Weston, L. (2000). Urban accessibility index: literature review. *Center of Transportation Research, University of Texas at Austin, Springfield.*

Bonamente, E., Scrucca, F., Rinaldi, S., Cleofe, M., Asdrubali, F., & Lamastra, L. (2016). Science of the Total Environment Environmental impact of an Italian wine bottle: Carbon and water footprint assessment. *Science of the Total Environment, The, 560–561*, 274–283. https://doi.org/10.1016/j.scitotenv.2016.04.026

Bragança, L., Mateus, R., & Koukkari, H. (2010). Building sustainability assessment. *Sustainability, 2*(7), 2010–2023. https://doi.org/10.3390/su2072010

Collinge, W. O., Landis, A. E., Jones, A. K., Schaefer, L. A., & Bilec, M. M. (2013). Dynamic life cycle assessment: Framework and application to an institutional building. International Journal of Life Cycle Assessment, 18(3), 538–552. https://doi.org/10.1007/s11367-012-0528-2

Consultation, F.S., 2015. India Specific Road Transport Emission Factors. India GHG Program. https://shaktifoundation.in/wp-content/uploads/2017/06/WRI-2015-India-Specific-Road-Transport-Emission-Factors.pdf (Accessed on October 2019)

Devi, P., & Palaniappan, S. (2014). A case study on life cycle energy use of residential building in Southern India. *Energy and Buildings, 80*, 247–259.

Fedra, K. (1990). A Computer-based Approach to Environmental Impact Assessment. *Indicators and Indices for Environmental Impact Assessment and Risk Analysis, pp. 11–40. INTERNATIONAL, October*, 1–8. https://doi.org/10.1080/07349165.1982.9725447

Ford, A. C., Barr, S. L., Dawson, R. J., & James, P. (2015). Transport accessibility analysis using GIS: Assessing sustainable transport in London. *ISPRS International Journal of Geo-Information, 4*(1), 124–149. https://doi.org/10.3390/ijgi4010124

Fouquet, M., Levasseur, A., Margni, M., Lebert, A., Lasvaux, S., Souyri, B., Buhé, C., & Woloszyn, M. (2015). Methodological challenges and developments in LCA of low energy buildings: Application to biogenic carbon and global warming assessment. *Building and Environment, 90*, 51–59. https://doi.org/10.1016/j.buildenv.2015.03.022

Galli, A., Wiedmann, T., Ercin, E., Knoblauch, D., Ewing, B., & Giljum, S. (2012). Integrating Ecological, Carbon and Water footprint into a "Footprint Family" of indicators: Definition and role in tracking human pressure on the planet. *Ecological Indicators, 16*, 100–112. https://doi.org/10.1016/j.ecolind.2011.06.017

Gibberd, J. (2005). Assessing sustainable buildings in developing countries – the sustainable building assessment tool (SBAT) and the sustainable building lifecycle (SBL). *The 2005 World Sustainable Building Conference, Tokyo, 2005* (September), 1605–1612.

Gluch, P., & Baumann, H. (2004). The life cycle costing (LCC) approach: A conceptual discussion of its usefulness for environmental decision-making. *Building and Environment, 39*(5), 571–580. https://doi.org/10.1016/j.buildenv.2003.10.008

Grigoryev, I., & Ui, A. (n.d.). AnyLogic 7: New Features Overview. *Anylogic v8.5.2 [Computer Software]. XJ Technologies, Chicago.*

Guinee, J. B., Heijungs, R., Huppes, G., Zamagni, A., Masoni, P., Buonamici, R., Ekvall, T., & Rydberg, T. (2011). Life cycle assessment: past, present, and future. Environtal Science and Technology. 45, 1, 90–96. https://doi.org/10.1021/es101316v

Hansmann, R., Mieg, H. A., & Frischknecht, P. (2012). Principal sustainability components: Empirical analysis of synergies between the three pillars of sustainability. *International Journal of Sustainable Development and World Ecology, 19*(5), 451–459. https://doi.org/10.1080/13504509.2012.696220

Hoogmartens, R., Van Passel, S., Van Acker, K., & Dubois, M. (2014). Bridging the gap between LCA, LCC and CBA as sustainability assessment tools. *Environmental Impact Assessment Review, 48*, 27–33. https://doi.org/10.1016/j.eiar.2014.05.001

Husain, D., & Prakash, R. (2019). Life Cycle Ecological Footprint Assessment of an Academic Building. *Journal of The Institution of Engineers (India): Series A, 100*(1), 97–110. https://doi.org/10.1007/s40030-018-0334-3

Indicators, D. E., & Version, R. (2017). India Construction Materials Database of Embodied Energy and Global Warming Potential: Methodology Report. International Finance Corporation 1-100. https://www.edgebuildings.com/wp-content/uploads/2017/12/IFC-India-Construction-Materials-Database-Methodology-Report.pdf (Accessed in September 2019)

Keeble, B. R. (1988). The Brundtland report: 'Our common future.' *Medicine and War, 4*(1), 17–25.

Kloepffer, W. (2008). Life cycle sustainability assessment of products. *The International Journal of Life Cycle Assessment, 13*(2), 89.

Lin, D. (2019). Working Guidebook to the National Footprint and Biocapacity Accounts. *Oakland: Global Footprint Network Report [Https://Www.Footprintnetwork.Org/Content/Uploads/2019/05/National_Footprint_Accounts_Guidebook_2019.Pdf, 14.08. 2019].*

Liu, J., Ding, G. K. C., & Samali, B. (2013). Building Sustainable Score (BSS)—A Hybrid Process Approach for Sustainable Building Assessment in China. *Journal of Power and Energy Engineering, 01*(05), 58–62. https://doi.org/10.4236/jpee.2013.15009

Lohani, B. N., Evans, J. W., Everitt, R. R., Ludwig, H., Carpenter, R. A., & Tu, S.-L. (1997). *Environmental impact assessment for developing countries in Asia: Volume 1-overview*. Asian Development Bank.

Mahmoud, S., Zayed, T., & Fahmy, M. (2019). Development of sustainability assessment tool for existing buildings. *Sustainable Cities and Society, 44*(May 2017), 99–119. https://doi.org/10.1016/j.scs.2018.09.024

Murray, P. E., & Cotgrave, A. J. (2007). Sustainability literacy: The future paradigm for construction education? *Structural Survey, 25*(1), 7–23. https://doi.org/10.1108/02630800710740949

Ness, B., Urbel-Piirsalu, E., Anderberg, S., & Olsson, L. (2007). Categorising tools for sustainability assessment. *Ecological Economics, 60*(3), 498–508.

Onat, N. C., Kucukvar, M., & Tatari, O. (2014). Integrating triple bottom line input-output analysis into life cycle sustainability assessment framework: the case for US buildings. *The International Journal of Life Cycle Assessment, 19*(8), 1488–1505.

Pal, S. K., Takano, A., Alanne, K., & Siren, K. (2017). A life cycle approach to optimizing carbon footprint and costs of a residential building. *Building and Environment, 123*, 146–162.

Pandey, D., & Agrawal, M. (2011). *Carbon footprint : current methods of estimation*. 135–160. https://doi.org/10.1007/s10661-010-1678-y

Pearce, D. (2003). The social cost of carbon and its policy implications. *Oxford Review of Economic Policy, 19*(3), 362–384.

Praseeda, K. I., Reddy, B. V. V., & Mani, M. (2016). Embodied and operational energy of urban residential buildings in India. *Energy and Buildings, 110*, 211–219.

Ramesh, T., Prakash, R., & Shukla, K. K. (2010). Life cycle energy analysis of buildings: An overview. *Energy and Buildings, 42*(10), 1592–1600.

Rawal, R., Shukla, Y., Didwania, S., Singh, M. and Maweda, V. (2014). *Residential Buildings in India: Energy Use Projections and Savings Potentials. Global Buildings Performance Network (GBPN): Paris, France, September.*

Rebitzer, G., & Hunkeler, D. (2003). Life cycle costing in LCM: Ambitions, opportunities, and limitations - Discussing a framework. *International Journal of Life Cycle Assessment, 8*(5), 253–256. https://doi.org/10.1007/BF02978913

Reddy, B. V. V., & Jagadish, K. S. (2003). Embodied energy of common and alternative building materials and technologies. *Energy and Buildings, 35*(2), 129–137.

Reed, R., Wilkinson, S., Bilos, A., & Schulte, K.-W. (2011). A Comparison of International Sustainable Building Tools – An Update. *The 17th Annual Pacific Rim Real Estate Society Conference*.

Ricke, K., Drouet, L., Caldeira, K., & Tavoni, M. (2018). Country-level social cost of carbon. *Nature Climate Change, 8*(10), 895–900.

Shen, L., Tam, V. W. Y., Gan, L., Ye, K., & Zhao, Z. (2016). Improving sustainability performance for public-private-partnership (PPP) projects. *Sustainability (Switzerland), 8*(3). https://doi.org/10.3390/su8030289

Sohn, J. L., Kalbar, P. P., Banta, G. T., & Birkved, M. (2017). Life-cycle based dynamic assessment of mineral wool insulation in a Danish residential building application. *Journal of Cleaner Production, 142*, 3243–3253. https://doi.org/10.1016/j.jclepro.2016.10.145

Sonnemann, G., Vigon, B., Rack, M., & Valdivia, S. (2013). Global guidance principles for life cycle assessment databases: development of training material and other implementation activities on the publication. *The International Journal of Life Cycle Assessment, 18*(5), 1169–1172.

Srinivasu, B., Professor, A., & Srinivasa Rao, P. (2013). Infrastructure Development and Economic growth: Prospects and Perspective. *Journal of Business Management & Social Sciences Research.*

Sterman, J. D. (2012). Sustaining sustainability: creating a systems science in a fragmented academy and polarized world. In *Sustainability science* (pp. 21–58). Springer.

Su, S., Li, X., & Zhu, Y. (2019). Dynamic assessment elements and their prospective solutions in dynamic life cycle assessment of buildings. *Building and Environment, 158*(November 2018), 248–259. https://doi.org/10.1016/j.buildenv.2019.05.008

Su, S., Li, X., Zhu, Y., & Lin, B. (2017). Dynamic LCA framework for environmental impact assessment of buildings. *Energy and Buildings, 149*, 310–320.

Ugwu, O. O., Kumaraswamy, M. M., Wong, A., & Ng, S. T. (2006). Sustainability appraisal in infrastructure projects (SUSAIP): Part 1. Development of indicators and computational methods. *Automation in Construction, 15*(2), 239–251. https://doi.org/10.1016/j.autcon.2005.05.006

Valdivia, S., Ugaya, C. M. L., Hildenbrand, J., Traverso, M., Mazijn, B., & Sonnemann, G. (2013). A UNEP/SETAC approach towards a life cycle sustainability assessment—our contribution to Rio+ 20. *The International Journal of Life Cycle Assessment, 18*(9), 1673–1685.

Weekly, P. (2007). Shaban, A., Sharma, R. N., 2007. Water Consumption Patterns in Domestic Households in Major Cities Water Required for Different Activities. Economic and Political Weekly 2190–2197. https://www.jstor.org/stable/pdf/4419690.pdf (Accessed on February 2020).

Yu, W. Der, Cheng, S. T., Ho, W. C., & Chang, Y. H. (2018). Measuring the sustainability of construction projects throughout their lifecycle: A Taiwan Lesson. *Sustainability (Switzerland), 10*(5). https://doi.org/10.3390/su10051523

Evolution of Electric Mobility Policy in India: A Historical Analysis

Sarath KT
Doctoral Research Scholar
Indian Institute of Technology Bombay

Rangan Banerjee
Professor
Indian Institute of Technology Bombay

Abstract: The paper has analyzed initiatives and milestones that drove the evolution of EV policy in India, considering the economic and environmental context. The paper is divided into three phases: post-independence, post-liberalization, and active government initiative phase post-2010. The major EV policy drivers identified are: rising vehicular emission causing ambient air quality deterioration in urban areas, global climate change agreements, increasing crude oil import bills and demand for sustainable transport solutions in cities. The major government initiatives to increase EV demand are the MNRE incentive scheme, National Electric Mobility Mission Plan 2020 (NEMMP), Faster Adoption and Manufacturing of Electric Vehicle (FAME) Scheme Phase I and II. Through these initiatives, the government has indicated a clear inclination towards the electrification of the transport sector. The implementation was slow, subsidy access was limited, and it did not boost EV sales as predicted. There were gaps in policy planning and implementation timeframe due to stakeholder objections and lack of institutional mandate. The financing responsibility of EV charging infrastructure lack clarity, and it needs to be delegated to respective ministerial departments. India still does not have a National EV policy document, which is a major issue for upcoming investors in the EV industry and prospective consumers. The success story of China indicates how the top-down approach, along with city-level aggressive implementation strategies, can boost EV share. On the other hand, Norway cut the cost of EV by removing sales tax and provided non-fiscal incentives like exemption from road toll, parking fee, and road space restriction. There is a need to make the EV transition more practical and inclusive, considering the cost-conscious Indian market and phased implementation, making the transition economically viable. The paper has explored the EV policy evolution in India and its drivers. It also identifies contextual issues to suggest a more practical approach towards sustainable EV penetration.

Keywords: emission, electric vehicles, sustainable transport, policy, climate change

1. OBJECTIVES

- To trace the policies and initiatives regarding vehicular emissions till the electric mobility policy
- To critically analyze the electric mobility policy in India and assess other steps taken by the government towards electric mobility
- To study international best practice cases (China and Norway) regarding approach and implementation of EV policy

2. INTRODUCTION

The increasing automobile dependency in urban areas is causing congested traffic, poor ambient air quality and increasing GHG emissions, making a dent in the INDC emission pledge. Personal mobility in modern India has attracted the population mainly due to poor public transport and improved financing options for private vehicle purchase in the past couple of decades. The added dependency on imported crude oil for its energy needs is another issue the country faces regarding carbon emission and expenditures.

The vehicular emissions are increasing due to the rise in the number of vehicles in India's urban areas, where the two-wheeler market is strongest due to low median per capita income levels. Private car usage has also increased in the last two decades due to increased competition, technological advancements, and income levels. Although car usage is less in India than in developed countries, the high population of automobiles is causing major concern in Cities.

Even though energy efficiency and emission reduction technology have improved in the current generation of automobiles, it can still not catch up with the nullifying effect of the fast-growing automobile population. This is causing heavy air pollution in cities leading to health concern among citizens. There is an urgent need to have a faster transition towards greener and sustainable modes of transport through efficient EV policy and implementation.

It is essential to look at previous policy decisions and initiatives by the government and further identify the drivers and the changes in government stance. The increasing carbon emission, lower power demand, fuel security risks in the global market are the strategic imperatives for India to follow a sustainable green mobility path. Although on a nascent stage, electric mobility can get an overhaul with due policy and industry synergy in the right direction at the right time.

Methodology

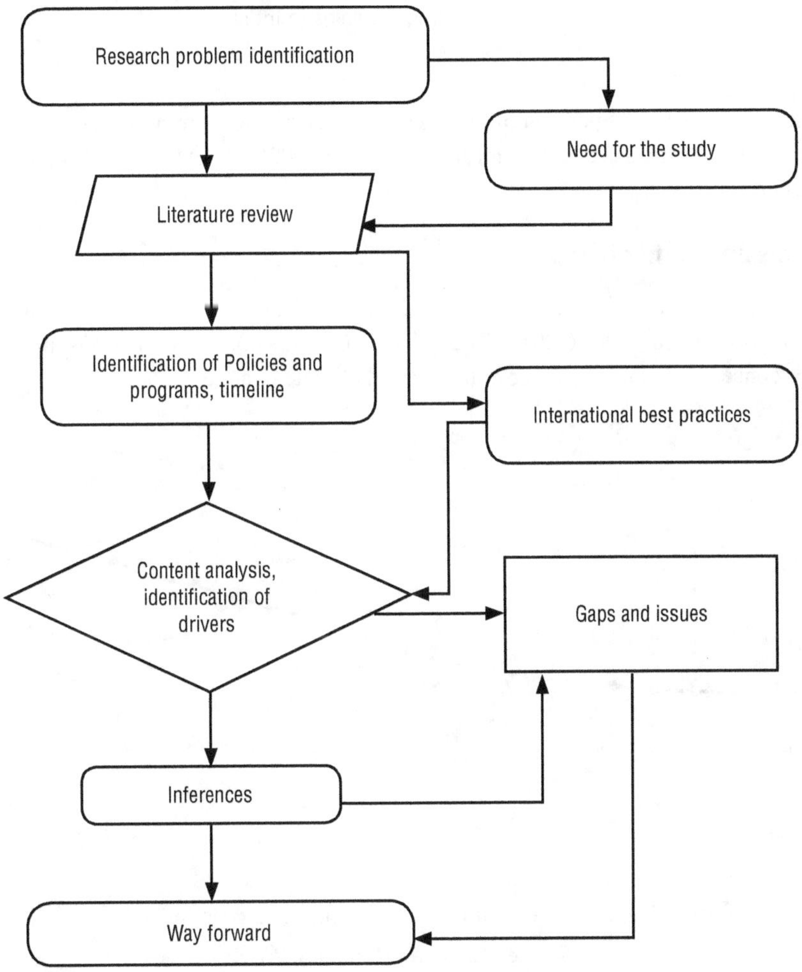

3. LITERATURE REVIEW

Indian automobile scenario

The number of registered automobiles have continuously increased in India from about 0.3 million in 1951 to 230 million by 2016. Post liberalization, India has seen rapid urbanization and economic growth, which has led to vehicular congestion in sprawling cities and a concerning deterioration of air quality. From 2015 to 2019, India's rate of urbanization increased from 32.78 per cent to 34.47 per cent, which further led to the road transport industry growing at a CAGR of 9.40 per cent.

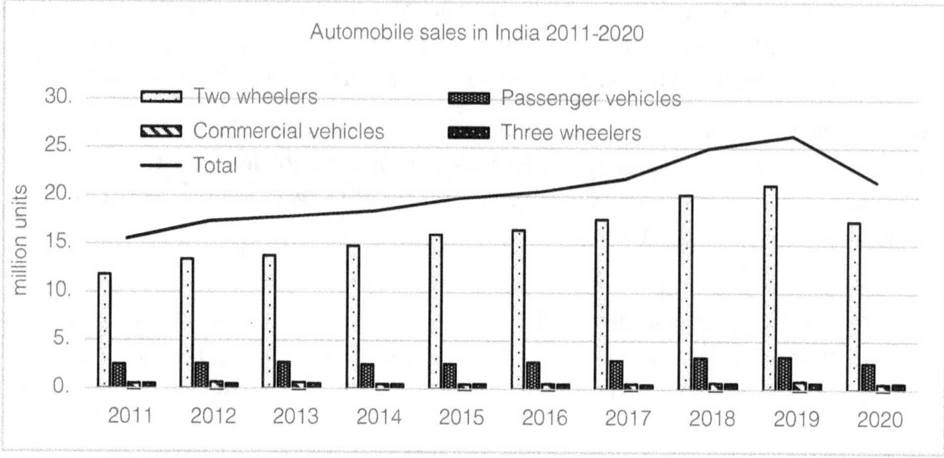

Fig. 1 Automobile sales in India
Source: (SIAM, siamindia.com, 2020)

The automobile industry accounts for 7.1 per cent of India's GDP and provides a numerous array of skilled and semi-skilled labour work. India recorded domestic sales of 21.5 million vehicles in 2020 (SIAM, SIAM Database, 2020) compared with 26.2 million a year earlier.

3.1 Automobile emissions and oil import

The energy sector (including electricity, transport, manufacturing, buildings) is the largest GHG emitter accounting for 73 per cent of global emission from 1990 to 2017. The annual CO_2 emission from the transport sector is doubling every 10 years and is a major concern causing severe air pollution and climate change.

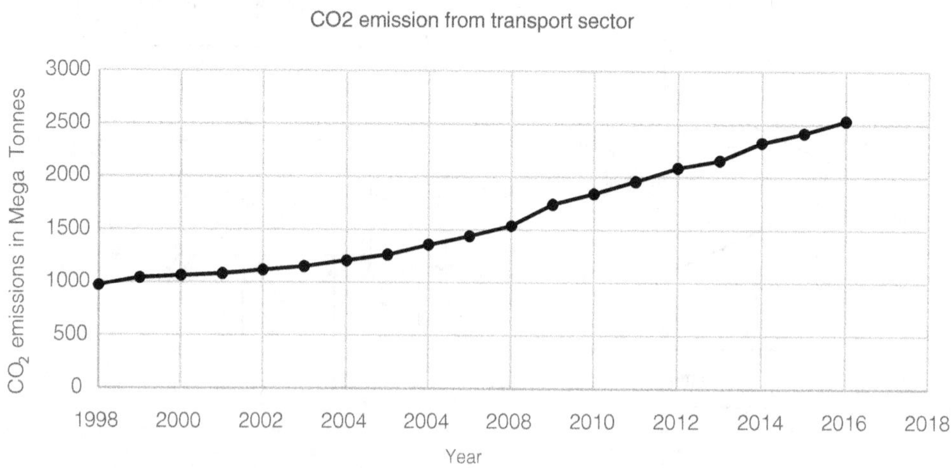

Fig. 2 CO_2 emission from transport sector in India
Source: Climatewatch data, 2018

With an overall population of 1.3 billion and a growing urban population, (460 million urban – 34 per cent) (MoHUA, 2019), India is facing a serious challenge in the sustainable transportation sector in the form of traffic congestion and emissions. With increased urbanization, travel demand and vehicle ownership are rising and passenger kilometer travelled is expected to increase 4.5 times by 2050 (Dhar, Subhash; Pathak, Minal; Shukla, P.R, 2018). Electric Vehicles are considered to be a key technology to de-carbonize transport sector and provide air quality benefits through zero tailpipe emissions (Shukla, Dhar, Pathak, & Bhaskar, 2014).

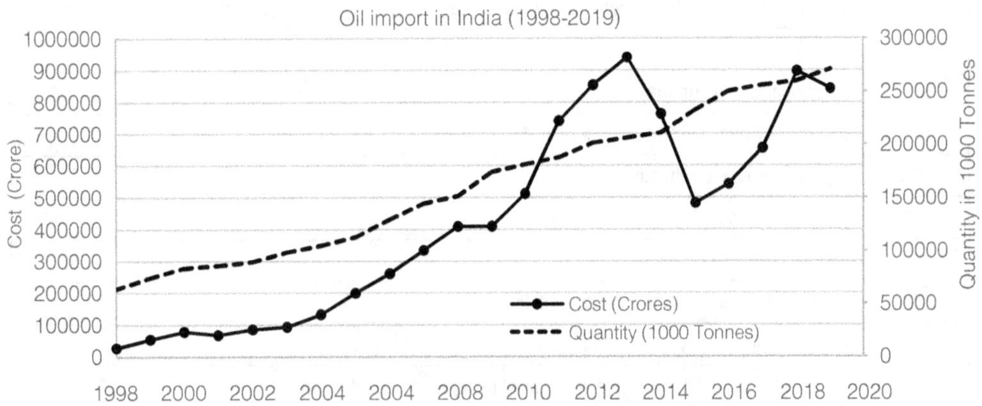

Fig. 3 Oil import data from 1998 till 2019

Source: PPAC data 2020

The crude oil import in India has reached nearly $90 Billion in 2019 and is rising continuously. The above graph indicates the fluctuating prices and increasing requirements of fossil fuel in the country. India is currently one of the world's largest energy user and require urgent attention to reduce fossil fuel dependency and promote EV. (NITI Aayog and Rocky Mountain Institute, 2017) has predicted a saving of 64 percent of road based energy demand and 37 percent carbon emission by 2030 through shared electric mobility initiatives.

The electric mobility policy in India has evolved through a series of iterative and periodic initiatives attributed to air pollution from vehicles and climate change threats. In India, formal efforts to promote Electric Vehicles (EV) did not surface till 2010. But the concern for air pollution from vehicles as a political agenda was prominent from 1990. The EV policy support was officially initiated after the announcement of National Electric Mobility Mission Plan aimed to accelerate the transition to EV. Subsequently, the financial support from Faster Adoption and Manufacturing of Electric vehicles (FAME) scheme gave momentum to demand creation and drove EV into contemporary mainstream research and policy discussion. The study is divided into three time periods: post-independence till 1991, post-liberalization till 2010, Active government initiatives from 2010 till 2020.

3.2 Policy Timeline

Table 1 Policy timeline

Year	Policy/Initiative
1981	AIR act
1988	Motor Vehicle Act
1990	Judicial activism (Supreme court)
1993	Rio Earth Summit
1994	Motor Vehicle Act amendment
1997	Kyoto protocol
2000	Emission standards (BS)
2001	Reva Car launched
2003	Auto Fuel Policy

Year	Policy/Initiative
2005	JnNURM
	Bharat Stage II nation wide
2006	National Urban Transport Policy
2008	National Action Plan for Climate Change
2010	MNRE incentive scheme, Alternate Fuels for Surface Transportation program
	BS 4
	National Green Tribunal
2011	National Council for Electric Mobility, National Board for Electric Mobility
2012	MNRE Incentive scheme ends
2013	National Electric Mobility Mission Plan
2014	Lima COP
	National Urban Transport Policy updated
2015	National Air Quality Index announced
	FAME-1 (Faster Adoption and Manufacturing of Electric and Hybrid Vehicles)
	Paris Climate Accord COP 21
	Smart City Mission Plan
	AMRUT
	Auto Fuel policy update
2016	Green Urban Mobility Initiative
	Bharat Stage IV
2017	Transit Oriented Development policy
	FAME-1 extended
2019	FAME-2
2020	Go Electric campaign
	Scrappage Policy
	Euro VI

Source: compiled by author from reports from MoF, MoRTH, MoHIPE, DST, MoHUA, MoP

3.3 Post-independence (1947-1991)

One of the earliest attempts to protect air as a natural resource and address its pollution post-independence came after the 1972 UN general assembly (UNCHE, 1973), which led to a consensus among countries, including India, regarding the urgent need to preserve natural resources, including air. It led to carbon emission became relevant to the politics post-independence in the year 1974, when the Central Pollution control board was formed under the Water (prevention and control of pollution) Act and later entrusted under the Air (Prevention and control of pollution) Act 1981. Its influence is evident in the 1981 Air Act document prepared during the Indira Gandhi regime. After the Air Act, there was an increase in the the number of legislations on environment pollution, indicating a positive shift of awareness among the public. With the introduction of AIR act to combat air pollution, the State Pollution Control Boards was given the power to ensure standards for emission from automobiles. State government could, direct the authorities in charge of registration of motor vehicles. It gave SPCBs the power to prohibit the usage of any fuel that may lead to air pollution.

The Motor Vehicle Act was formulated in 1988 by MoRTH (Ministry of Road Transport and Highways), regulates aspects of road transport, such as traffic regulations, registrations, permits etc. According to section 110, The Central Government could make rules regulating the construction, equipment and maintenance of motor vehicles regarding the emission and set required standards. This move indicated the shift of government priorities as the number of automobiles on the roads increased.

In 1985, an activist, M.C. Mehta, filed a petition in the supreme court regarding the severe problem of vehicular pollution in Delhi and its impact on common people. In response to Mehta's petition, the Supreme Court directed the Delhi administration to take steps towards reducing air pollution (Narain & Bell, 2005). The Supreme court held that environmental protection is the responsibility of the State and observed that the right to a clean environment was a basic human right and that included clean air (Misra, 1991).The case by MC Mehta and growing public uproar forced government action on curbing pollution from vehicles. This led to the setting up of the Environmental Pollution Prevention and Control Authority (EPCA) for Delhi region along with National Clean Air Program. Following which the central government set vehicular standards in 1990 on its initiative.

On the basis of the EPCA report, the Supreme Court ordered vehicles to be run on CNG fuel in Delhi. The government introduced mass emission norms for automobile tailpipe emission in 1991 and it was periodically made more stringent. The first emission norm was set for petrol vehicles in 1991, followed by catalytic convertors usage for petrol vehicles and introduction of unleaded petrol. The M.C Mehta case was dormant till 1996 when the supreme court ruled all government vehicles were to be converted to CNG. In 1998 the court passed an order mandating that all the buses must be converted from diesel fuel engines to CNG. In 2002 Supreme Court re-affirmed its decision to CNG conversion and passed strict orders to the governmental agencies to implement the same.

3.4 Post-liberalization (1991-2010)

With the liberalization of markets post-1991, multinational car manufacturers such as Suzuki, Toyota and Hyundai invested in the Indian market leading to a rise in the sale of automobiles. To regulate the registrations and safety of the increasing number of automobiles, government passed the Motor Vehicle Amendment Act in 1994 which included clauses to promote use of alternative fuels, like electric batteries through non fiscal incentives. The amendment encouraged alternative fuels by relaxing the permit requirements for alternate energy users. Even though these measures stayed on paper, this move indicated the government's formal initiative for reducing emission and encouraging alternative fuels.

Meanwhile, the international voice regarding the need to reduce carbon emission and act upon the climate change crisis grew louder by the end of the 20th century. The UNFCC COP (Conference of Parties) made efforts for consensus among the partner countries regarding actions against the threat of human-activity-induced climate change. After the Kyoto protocol in 1997, the group agreed that developed countries are predominantly responsible for high-level GHG emission and through the principle of '*common but differentiated responsibilities*', there could be an equitable solution to reduce emission intensity. Although Kyoto Protocol did not develop a binding international environmental law, it boosted the activities towards reducing emissions and improving air quality. Government of India decided to set up Activities Implemented Jointly (AIJ) working group under the MoEF and issued a set of guidelines for report submission to the government. A broad consensus emerged regarding Clean Development Mechanism Projects (CDM) as well among the nations. Indian government emphasized on technology transfer through CDM projects and co-benefits of pursuing CDM for the country.

After 2000, India adopted the European model of emission standards for its automobiles. The Indian emission standard India 2000 (BS I) was taken from EURO 1 emission standards as a reference. In 2001, the Mashelkar committee recommended a countrywide Auto Fuel Policy and a roadmap for emission norms implementation till 2010. The Auto Fuel Policy, created guidelines for fuels, reduction of pollution from vehicles and encouraged R&D for alternative fuels. The further tightening of emission norms like BS-I, II, III and IV was done periodically till 2010.

Table 2 Indian Fuel standards timeline

Standard	Date	Implemented Region
BS-I	2000	Nationwide
BS-II	2001	NCR, Mumbai, Kolkata, Chennai
BS-II	2005.04	Nationwide
BS-III	2005.04	NCR, 11 cities
BS-III	2010.04	Nationwide

Standard	Date	Implemented Region
BS-IV	2010.04	NCR, 13 cities
BS-IV	2017.04	Nationwide
BS-V	Skipped	–
BS-VI	2020.04	Nationwide

The 2003 Auto Fuel Policy had envisaged that the policy undergoes periodic revision considering changing technology and other factors to be incorporated in the policy framework. Auto fuel policy was updated three years after the previous policy lapsed and was renamed Auto Fuel Vision and Policy 2025. Compared to the international scenario where countries have permanent institutions which periodically study and revise emission standards, India has relied majorly on ad-hoc Expert Committees. The committee to formulate the policy was initiated only in 2012, 2 years after the previous policy horizon had ended. The gap of over three years was mostly due to a lack of consensus among government bodies, automobile manufacturers and oil refineries who pushed for continually delayed deadlines (Chattopadhyay, 2010).

In 2016, the government announced that BS-V was being withdrawn and instead the government, is considering leapfrogging to BS-VI, one of the world's most stringent emission norms. This was seen as a reactionary measure due to the air pollution crisis in Delhi. The BS-VI emissions standard is expected to result in up to a 40 per cent reduction in PM emissions and a 43 per cent reduction in NOx compared to BS-IV emission standards (Sharma, et al., 2020). Air quality increasingly became an influential political agenda, which also became a challenge for automobile manufacturers in compliance of the stricter emission standards.

The following years saw numerous developmental neo-liberal policies and programs introduced by the Manmohan Singh led government in line with the 11th Five Year Plan's recognition as infrastructure and urbanization as drivers of growth. JnNURM scheme (2005-2014) focused on urban renewal through central government funding for capacity building or urban infrastructure, transport and poverty alleviation. It mandated the preparation of City Development Plan for the fund release from the Central government, which brought attention to the poor condition of infrastructure in urban areas and the need for capacity building, especially in the public transport sector. The year 2005 also saw the introduction of the Automotive Mission Plan (2006-2016) by the Society of Indian Automobiles Manufacturers (SIAM) and GoI, which aimed at making India a global hub for small car and components manufacturing.

In 2004, the transport sector contributed over 23 per cent of the world's total GHG emissions (IPCC, 2007). Between 2001 and 2011, the urban population in India grew from 286 million to 377 million (Census, 2011), which led to traffic congestions and higher levels of emissions. Considering the situations, the government launched a National Urban Transport Policy in 2006. It was aimed to prioritize people over vehicles by developing better public transport systems and Non-motorized transport infrastructure through City Mobility Plans. It also suggested the benefits of alternative fuel usage and electric vehicles. Even though NUTP laid out a list of ideal suggestions for sustainable transport development, most of its implementation remained on paper due to a lack of clear execution plan. It was modified and published in 2014 after the suggestions of stakeholders but still failed to develop an efficient enforcement mechanism and was mostly ignored by states and ULBs.

As the global dialogue on climate change proceeded, the government initiated a National Action Plan for Climate Change (NAPCC) in 2008. The climate change policies in India were dictated by a pursuit for *co-benefits* that bring both climate and developmental gains to the country. NAPCC was put in place for political attention leading up to the Copenhagen COP of 2009 (Atteridge, Srivastava, Pahuja, & Upadhyay, 2012). Climate change was a central topic in high profile political meetings such as G8+5, which stimulated national action. Subsequently, in 2009, India issued an international pledge to decrease emissions by 20-25 per cent from 2005 levels by 2020. The NAPCC gave a jump start to the national climate change framework narrative, policy and institutional function. Through the consistent efforts and initiatives since 2005 till 2010, the emission intensity of GDP decreased by 12 per cent (Government of India, 2015)

3.5 Active government initiatives (2010-2020)

India made its first concrete decision to incentivize EVs in 2010, under a 95 Cr scheme by the Ministry of New and Renewable Energy through Alternative Fuels for Surface Transportation Programme. It supported battery technology

R&D for automobiles and provided a subsidy of 20 per cent with a cap (maximum Rs 1 lakh on car), till 2012. The scheme subsidized up to Rs 5000 for electric scooter, Rs 60000 for three-wheelers, Rs 100,000 for cars and Rs 400,000 for buses. The government also reduced the excise duty on electric vehicles from 8 per cent to 4 per cent. Some states removed the sales tax, and Delhi government provided various subsidies and rebates up to 29.5 per cent of the cost of the EV purchase. The MNRE incentive scheme resulted in a 200 per cent increase in the sale of EVs, huge growth in market share, and the industry finally began to grow in an organized form. But in 2012, this incentive scheme was discontinued due to the end of 5-year plan, resulting in a drop of 70 per cent in the EV sales, and permanent closure of numerous EV manufacturers.

In the case of institutions regarding EV policy, the Central government approved the proposal to set up a **National Mission for Electric Mobility (NMEM)** in 2011 to promote electric Mobility and the manufacture of electric vehicles in India. The government also approved the setting up of **National Board for Electric Mobility** to prepare future policies on electric vehicles in India. NBEM was incumbent to examine and propose the short-term and long-term plans on electric mobility and delegating the responsibilities of stakeholders involved. It brought together, under one umbrella, all the relevant department and ministries, and it led to the development of the National Electric Mobility Mission Plan in 2013.

In 2012, during the United Nations conference on sustainable development, then PM Manmohan Singh described how economic development, social inclusion and environmental sustainability act as equally critical components of sustainable development, and how every country should be able to develop according to its own national priorities and resources. *"Difficult though it may seem, we have to summon the imagination to balance the costs that we will incur in the present with the benefits that will accrue to future generations"* (Singh, 2012). He made it clear that inclusive economic growth and rise in per capita income was most important at the moment for developing countries. He also mentioned how increased economic activity can result in negative results, by local pollution or by the global impact of GHG emissions and there is a need to tackle both. This suggested the inclination of the government to invest further in domestic initiatives for emission reduction.

In 2013, the Department of Heavy Industry unveiled the **National Electric Mobility Mission Plan 2020** to provide an EV roadmap, objectives and framework. It aimed at faster adoption of electric and hybrid vehicles in the country through government-industry collaborations, incentives to mitigate national energy security issues, and adverse impacts of vehicular growth on the environment and issues of domestic EV manufacturing capabilities. It outlined an expenditure of Rs.13000-14000 crores (60 per cent by government) over the following eight years estimating a demand of over 7 million EVs (5 10 per cent) sale and thereby saving over 2.5 MT CO_2 emissions (1.3-1.5 per cent) by 2020

Though the scheme was to offer subsidies and create supporting infrastructure for EV, the plan mostly remained on papers till 2015. As the incentives from the MNRE scheme dried out in 2012, 2013-2014 saw 26 out of 35 major electric two wheeler manufacturers going out of business due to poor demand. Sale of Electric 2 wheeler dropped from 100,000 in 2011-12 to 42,000 in 2012-13 and 21,000 in 2013-14. It also meant a loss of over 10,000 direct and indirect jobs in the economy. This reflected the inefficient implementation of NEMMP by the government. Due to lack of efficient implementation of the recommendations, only 0.263 millions EVs were sold by 2019 (Department of Heavy Industry & Public Enterprises, 2019).

The 2015 Annual budget saw the government earmarking 75 Cr. Towards Faster Adoption and Manufacturing of Electric Vehicle (FAME) in 2015-16 period. The EV manufacturers appreciated this step as a good beginning. The government extended the concessional excise duty of 6% for another year. Society for Manufacturers of Electric vehicles (SMEV) quoted this as a 'lifesaver' to the EV industry, bleeding heavily without government support. The biggest beneficiaries of the scheme were EV 2 wheeler, and small electric car manufactures.

FAME-1 had an outlay of Rs 895 crore to be spent over two years (later extended to 4 years) on EV demand creation and charging infrastructure. It aimed at 30 per cent private vehicle EV and 100 per cent government vehicles EV penetration by 2030. The scheme incentivized the customers through upfront reduced purchase price to drive the demand. Phase 1 of the FAME scheme supported 2.8 Lakhs hybrid and electric vehicles through demand incentives (amounting to Rs 359 crores). By 2019, under the FAME I scheme, incentives worth Rs 529 crores was disbursed (Ministry of Heavy Industries & Public Enterprises, 2019). The overall outcome in the case of fuel savings and CO_2 reduction was significantly below the target. The phased implementation plan was very slow and showed limited progress. The subsidies and incentives were difficult to claim and several new EV manufacturers permanently closed (Padmanabhan & Reddy, 2017).

The newly elected NDA government had an infrastructure development rhetoric and introduced programs like Smart City mission, AMRUT scheme, Housing for All scheme, Green Urban Mobility Initiative, Sustainable Urban Transport Project, Policy and other development programs. Although these initiatives did not directly impact vehicular emission, they had indirect impacts in vehicle kilometers travelled and per capita emissions. In 2015, GoI launched the National Air Quality Index to calculate ambient air quality as a standardized unit. This improved the accessibility of public information on local air pollution levels.

In 2016, NDA government's demonetization move aimed at curbing black money hit the sale of electric vehicles as EVs were mostly purchased using cash due to the absence of a financing system for EV. In the same year, the government announced that the India aimed to attain 100 per cent electric mobility by 2030 through a National EV Policy. This caused unrest among the ICE automobile manufacturers who were not prepared for such a transition in an already declining sales scenario. This year also saw the government ratifying the Paris climate deal, pledging emission intensity reduction of its GDP by 33 to 35 per cent by 2030 below 2005 levels. This indicated a new, more active role for India in international climate policy through domestic level progress. But the early timeline was criticized in India as it seemed risky for India since the implication of the deal were uncertain. Another concern was that the climate change mitigation action could compete with development challenges due to lack of support from developed nations. The major policy drivers for India were technology transfers and financial support along with the need for improving ambient air quality. The tag for the world's largest emitter of GHG after USA and China would impact its international image and subsequently its investment ecosystem.

Meanwhile, the increasing air pollution in cities spiked to all-time high and was responsible for one in eight deaths in the country (Balakrishnan K, 2018). The population-weighted annual average concentration of PM2.5 for the country, was 91 $\mu gm/m^3$ in 2017, which was more than twice the national standards (Health Effects Institute, 2019). This forced the government to take quick actions to prevent and contain the impact of air pollution. Electric mobility was often dubbed as a quick solution to reduce ambient air quality deterioration by the government.

In 2018, the government announced that it had decided against formulating a National EV policy. The Union Minister of Road Transport announced that there was no need for a policy document since there is an action plan for the Electrification of the transport sector in place. He reasoned that implementing EV policy would make the rules and regulations rigid in a rapidly changing tech environment and would make it difficult for the government to change it later if required. This U-turn from its earlier position provided temporary relief to automobile manufacturers unprepared for such an abrupt shift to electric technology. The EV policy needed massive investments, and the government was unwilling to invest due to a shortage of funds. In other words, the government left the market, manufacturers and consumers to figure out the issues. This move indicated the governments increasing trust in open markets, sorting out the gaps for themselves. This approach was later proven ineffective as the EV sales dropped, and only less than one per cent of the objective was completed as of 2020.

The second phase FAME scheme announced in 2019 (**FAME 2**), focussed more on public transport and shared vehicle electrification. With a budget of Rs 10,000 Cr to be spent over three years, the scheme allotted 86 per cent of the fund towards demand incentives linked to battery capacity. Active participation of private players in charging infrastructure was expected with the FAME 2 scheme and localisation of manufacturing, which was missing in FAME 1. The 50 per cent localisation condition was deemed to be a deterrent for most manufacturers. For private vehicles, the government reduced incentives to Rs 10,000 per kWh of battery capacity from Rs 22,000 per kWh, given under the first phase of the FAME scheme. A reduction in incentive amount was expected to bring down the cost and drive demand. By July 2020, 44 per cent of the intended FAME-2 scheme duration had elapsed, while only 1.4 per cent of the incentives allocated for light vehicles (2W and 3W) and cars were utilised. While the initial sluggishness was due to manufacturing localisation requirements, strict qualification criteria continued to weigh down on adoption. To avail subsidies, EV sold needed to adhere to a specific minimum range, speed, energy consumption, acceleration and a warranty while not exceeding a certain battery capacity. (Eg: min 80 km range and a top speed of 40 kmph for Two Wheelers - 95 per cent of existing models will not qualify) This move was aimed to make the EV industry focus on efficiency but ended up being counterproductive as over 95 per cent of the two wheeler models in the market did not qualify for the subsidy.

GST on EV was reduced to 5 per cent from 12 per cent and electric chargers from 18 per cent to 5 per cent. This GST rate cut indicated that government prioritised reduction of vehicular pollution in urban areas and rising crude oil bill. The Central government had also directed state governments to draft State EV policy and provide additional fiscal and non-fiscal incentives to manufacturers and buyers. Currently, over 14 states have finalized EV policies with varying targets and objectives.

The government has since softened its approach on the timeframe to transition to EV. MoHIPE, MoRTH, MoP and NITI Aayog has agreed to pragmatic phase-wise approach. In this updated approach, highly polluted Cities would be targeted first for implementation of EV targets. This change in stance was due to strong resistance from automobile manufacturers over the government's plan to ban ICE 2 wheelers and 3 Wheelers by 2023 and 2025. The automobile industry argued that the decision would create unprecedented disruption in a market where EV infrastructure is nascent.

Despite numerous policies at the National, State and City level, India's current share of electric vehicles is relatively low (Society of Manufactureres of Electric Vehicles, 2019) (less than one per cent). The trends and government focus in EVs indicate an increase in EVs' share in the coming years. However, the quality of EVs, enabling framework, and environmental consequences need policy attention to ensure the sustainable transition to EVs. Other initiatives such as fuel efficiency standards and battery recycling can also help create more favourable enabling conditions for EV. India's enhanced focus on upscaling EV is evident in National targets and policies, specifically NEMMP and financial initiatives under FAME. But its ambitious aims are limited by financial constraints (Dhar, Subhash; Pathak, Minal; Shukla, Priyadarshi; Gupta, Anurag, 2020). Updating Building codes, charging infrastructure, and public transport policies aligned with EV targets can being a sizable upscaling of EV in Cities leading the country to a low-carbon sustainable path.

3.6 Key government actors in electric mobility

Table 3 Institutional actors and actions

<table>
<tr><th colspan="3">Actors</th><th>Actions</th></tr>
<tr><td rowspan="6">PMO</td><td rowspan="6">NITI Aayog</td><td>Ministry of heavy Industries and Public enterprises (Department of Heavy industries)</td><td>Launched NEMMP and manages FAME scheme to disburse financial incentives and non-fiscal measures</td></tr>
<tr><td>Ministry of Power</td><td>Launched National E-mobility program by procuring EVs and EVSE (Electric Vehicle supply equipment) through EESL (Energy Efficiency Services Limited)
Released notification declaring Charging is a service and not a commodity thereby providing tax benefits to operators of charging stations.
Declared guidelines for setting up charging stations</td></tr>
<tr><td>Ministry of Housing and Urban Affair</td><td>Residential and commercial complexes to allot 20% of parking spaces for EV charging facilities
Bringing various agencies and stakeholders in cities to facilitate development. (EY, Bureau of Energy Efficiency, 2019)</td></tr>
<tr><td>Ministry of Finance</td><td>In 2017 GST on EVs was reduced to 12 per cent. In 2019 GST was further reduced to 5%.
MoF updated customs duty for EV and components</td></tr>
<tr><td>Ministry of Roads and National Highways</td><td>Non fiscal policies and incentives of the EVs: lane access, parking infra etc.
Green license plates for EV.
Import of 2,500 electric vehicles compliant with international standards without homologation</td></tr>
<tr><td>Department of Science and Technology</td><td>Technology Platform for Electric Mobility(TPEM) Forming electric mobility standardization roadmap for India</td></tr>
</table>

4. INTERNATIONAL CASE STUDIES

Global drivers of EV adoption are the increasing issue of climate change, advances in renewable energy technology, rapid urbanization, battery technology, digital data capture and energy security. The cases of China and Norway have been hailed as few of the most successful case studies in the global electric mobility transition.

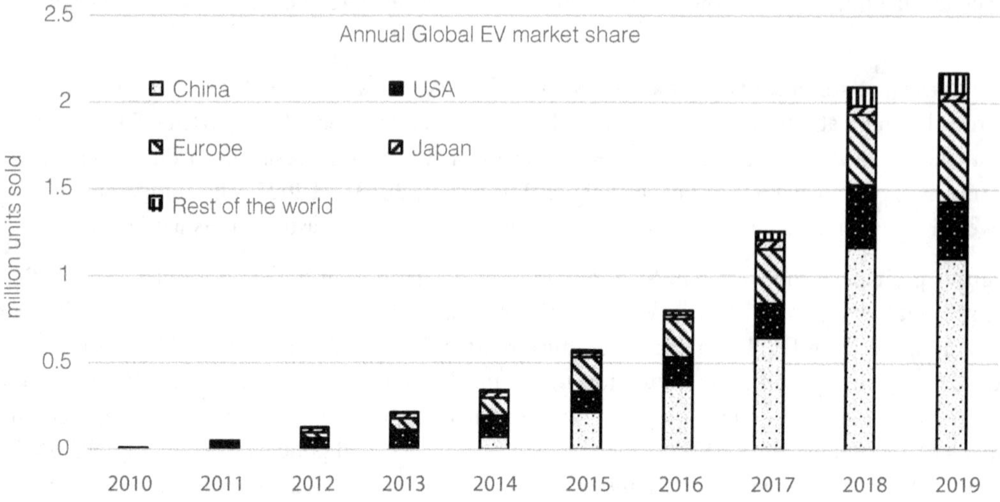

Fig. 4 Global annual EV market share

Source: (IEA, 2020)

4.1 China

In the international arena, China has become the world leader in EV manufacturing and sales surpassing USA in 2015. (Lingzhi Jin, 2021). In 2015, the Chinese government announced a China 2025 National Development Plan which highlighted the importance of electric mobility related industrial development and set goals for automobile manufacturers. The incentives for EV in China began in 2009 and was planned to be phased out by 2020 to be replaced with mandatory manufacturing goals for the automobile manufacturers. Financial penalties were imposed on manufacturers which did not comply with EV car production percentages which increased the efficacy of EV transition. The percentage mandate has become as much as 40 per cent of all car sales by 2030. The government further invested heavily in R&D for components, standardization and certification which resulted in more than 1 million EV production in 2018 which accounted for more than half of global EV sales (Lingzhi Jin, 2021). The implementation of EV policy in China is majorly centralized with cities playing a major role by providing substantial financial support on top of central government support making EV more affordable. (Stauffer, 2020). The alignment of industry with energy and environmental goals also helped the further coordinative efforts of the government.

4.2 Norway

Since the 1990s, Norwegian politics supported use of electric vehicles widely. The government decided to have a national goal of 100 percent electric vehicle sales by 2025. The sales tax of cars at a high 25 percent was waived off for EV which brought down the cost of EVs to ICE levels. Further, Non-fiscal incentives such as access to bus lanes, road toll exemption, free public parking, reduced income tax on company cars along with exemption of initial registration tax, VAT and annual circulation tax accelerated the growth of EV to 54 per cent in 2020. Norway focused on passenger electric cars and the funding is provided completely by the central government. The high tax policy aims to reduce the gap in price between electric vehicle and ICE vehicles by reducing the cost of EVs and increasing the cost of fossil fuel using vehicles through feebates. Currently, Norway, with a small population of 5 million, has over 464,000 EVs and over 10,000 public charging stations.

Table 4 Comparison of EV policies in China, Norway and India

Indicators	China	Norway	India
Annual GDP	$14.25 Trillion	$403 Billion	$2.86 Trillion
Population	1.398 Billion	5.3 million	1.366 Billion
EV investment	$60 Billion	$16.6 Billion	$1.3 Billion
Method of funding	Public	Fully public	Public and private
Active Time Period	2001	1990	2013
Aim	20% EV by 2025	100% EV by 2025	30% EV by 2030
Vehicle type focus	Taxi, bus	Private cars	2W, bus, 3W
Number of EVs	37,00,000 (6.3%)	464,000 (15%)	5,00,000 (0.88%)
Public Chargers	807,000	10,000	933
Approach	Top down planning, aligned interest of air quality, govt.-industry-academic partnerships, fiscal and non-fiscal incentives (road access, parking, charging), PPP in EV ride hailing fleets, selected cities focused - aggressive local policies,	Huge Tax incentives to make EV cheaper than ICE, road use, free tolls, higher road tolls for diesel cars, fully imported, non-peak hour charging incentives	Demand and supply incentives with strict criteria for subsidy, free market trust, non-binding regulations, implementation ratio is less, focus on shared mobility and 2 Wheeler

Source: Compiled by Author, World bank open data 2020, https://data.worldbank.org/, (Lingzhi Jin, 2021) https://www.smev.in/ev-industry

5. CONCLUSIONS AND WAY FORWARD

The historical evolution of electric mobility policy in India indicates how the concern over the rising import of crude oil and the severity of air pollution in cities have driven the policymaking process. This also showed how international climate agreements and treaties have influenced the government to act on emissions and sustainable development through domestic policies. India has taken periodic steps to curb air pollution from vehicles through the years.

5.1 Drivers of EV policy

(i) The rising usage of fossil fuel is a major concern for governments since 2000. The expenditure towards the import of crude oil has risen continuously which has also been a driver for policymakers to turn towards electrification of the transport sector. The government of India has repeatedly mentioned the financial benefit of saving fossil fuel usage and CO_2 emissions through Electric Mobility I nits announcements.

(ii) The increasing severity of air pollution and deterioration in air quality in urban areas has forced the government to adopt stricter emission norms and focus on electric mobility. To take the example of pollution in Delhi leading to Supreme court action on enactment of government regulation on vehicular emissions.

(iii) There has been a visible change in the stance of the government from being conservative regarding the emission cut initiatives in the International climate dialogues (UNFCCC) to being proactive in leading the sustainable transition movement in the last five years. The plans have been increasingly more ambitious and including more private player participation. To take the example of emission cut pledge, INDC has become 33-35 per cent by 2030 from 20-25 per cent by 2020 during the previous government in 2012. The emission norms were made stringent in Auto Fuel Policy Vision 2025, National Action Plan on Climate Change while benefiting the country by reducing air pollution and moving towards sustainable energy, also strengthened the country's case at climate negotiations.

5.2 Government EV initiatives

(i) The active government phase started in 2010 when MNRE initiated an upfront subsidy of 20 per cent for an EV purchase. This initiative was found to be highly successful and drove EV sales by 200 per cent. After removing the

MNRE scheme in 2012, the sales crashed 70 per cent, leading to fallout of EV manufacturers in the country. This event indicated upfront incentives are imperative to increase EV penetration.

(ii) National Electric Mobility Mission Plan in 2013 formalized the EV policy sector and gave an EV roadmap and objectives and strategies mainly through demand and supply incentives, Public-Private partnerships, and R&D on EV technology. The policy was not implemented till 2015 when the government came up with Faster Adoption for Manufacturing of Electric and Hybrid Vehicles scheme (FAME). The first phase allocated Rs 895 Cr to be spent over two years towards EV demand creation, technology platform, pilot project and charging infrastructure. Phase 1 of the FAME scheme supported 2.8 Lakhs hybrid and electric vehicles through demand incentives (amounting to Rs 359 Cr). The government further extended till 2019 due to low compliance rate and sales. By 2019, under the FAME I scheme, incentives worth only Rs 529 crores was disbursed. The phased implementation plan was very slow and showed limited progress.

(iii) The second phase of the FAME scheme had an increased budget of Rs 10,000 Cr and was focused more on Electrifying public transport and shared mobility. Active participation of private players in charging infrastructure was expected with the FAME 2 scheme and localization of manufacturing, which was missing in FAME 1. The subsidy amount was reduced compared to FAME 1, and the government tightened the criteria for eligibility of subsidies to improve the efficiency of the technology. With an objective of 6-7 million EV in India by 2020, India currently has only 0.263 million EVs (less than 1 per cent of target).

5.3 Gaps and issues in EV policy

(i) The gaps in policy announcement and implementation timeframe is a critical issue that has emerged from the historical analysis of EV policy in India. There is a need to ensure that there is no delay in updating the policy before the horizon period ends and ensuring the implementation follows up without delay. The stakeholder consultations and optimum solutions must be arrived at within the timeframe planned.

(ii) Although most of the Electric mobility initiative's objectives were not met, it has given momentum to the nascent EV industry, and upcoming policies could utilize this. There is a need to prepare the policies strictly on the timeframe, and the financing of charging infrastructure should be delegated to DISCOMS and relevant ministry/department as a mandate. The government has mentioned the dilemma of providing charging infrastructure first or letting consumers buy EVs first as a chicken and egg problem. In international EV success stories, the charging infrastructure is to be provided first as it gives confidence to prospective buyers. India still doesn't use the concept of *feebates*, in which the additional taxation on Internal Combustion Engine vehicles would be directed towards incentivizing EVs.

(iii) The lack of a national EV policy document is a major issue for EV manufacturers and consumers, as the periodic updating and changes bring uncertainty regarding infrastructure provision, battery mechanism, technology standardization and regulations. As of 2020, 14 states in India have developed state EV policies with varying objectives and focus areas. But there is no mandate to implement and doesn't have a monitoring agency.

5.4 International case studies

(i) In China, the government started providing generous subsidies for EV purchase in 2009. China had incentive and disincentive based dynamic policy regarding the percentage of EV manufactured annually (as much as 40 per cent). Cities play a major role in providing extra incentives and aggressive implementation strategies that positively impacted EV penetration.

(ii) As seen in Norway, it was proven that car purchase tax and feebate policies are effective in acceleration electric mobility transition and proper design of taxation can help customers with reduced tax burden and rationalized decision making regarding EV purchase leading to low carbon development. Non-fiscal incentives such as public transport lane use, free tolls, higher road tolls for diesel cars, and non-peak hour charging have also influenced the Norway EV market.

There is a need to make the EV transition in India practical and inclusive by using the existing institutional structure and infrastructure capacity building, thereby avoiding a radical policy change and making the transition economically viable.

India has made commendable efforts in the policy sphere to encourage faster EV adoption through various initiatives and incentive schemes. Still, compared to China and Norway's international case studies, India is lagging by a long margin. The primary issues that have surfaced from the research are the lack of government investment in charging infrastructure, policy mandate for departments and price difference between ICE vehicles and EVs. There is a need for a quick and integrated approach where the various departments of the governments at multiple levels and automobile manufacturers prioritise electrifying vehicles as a priority.

REFERENCES

Atteridge, A., Srivastava, M. K., Pahuja, N., & Upadhyay, H. (2012). *Climate Policy in India: What Shapes International, National and State Policy?* Ambio, 41(Suppl. 1).

Balakrishnan K, D. S. (2018, December). The impact of air pollution on deaths, disease burden, and life expectancy across the states of India: the Global Burden of Disease Study 2017. *The Lancet Planetary Health*, e26-239.

Bithal, S. (2015, November 30). *National Air Quality Index: A solution with too many problems*. Retrieved from www.downtoearth.org.in: https://www.downtoearth.org.in/blog/national-air-quality-index-a-solution-with-too-many-problems-49465

C, B., J, A., & M, T. (2012). *Accelerating the transformation to a low carbon passenger transport system: The role of car purchase taxes, feebates, road taxes and scrappage incentives in the UK.* Transportation Research Part A: Policy and Practice.

Census. (2011). Primary Census Abstracts, Registrar General of India. Ministry of Home Affairs, Government of India.

Chattopadhyay, V. (2010, June 15). *New auto emission norms delayed.* Retrieved from downtoearth.org.in: https://www.downtoearth.org.in/news/new-auto-emission-norms-delayed-644

Department of Heavy Industry. (2019, December 20). *Press Information Bureau.* Retrieved from https://pib.gov.in/PressReleseDetailm.aspx?PRID=1597099

Dhar, S., Pathak, M., & Shukla, P. (2018, January 20). *Transformation of India's transport sector under global warming of 2°C and 1.5°C scenario.* Elsevier.

Dhar, S., Pathak, M., & Shukla, P. (2018, January 20). Transformation of India's transport sector under global warming of 2°C and 1.5°C scenario. *Journal of Cleaner production, 172*, 417–427.

Dhar, S., Pathak, M., Shukla, P., & Gupta, A. (2020). Electric vehicles penetration in India for enhanced energy efficiency deployment in the transport sector. In *Energy Efficiency in Developing Countries.* Routledge.

EY, Bureau of Energy Efficiency. (2019). *Propelling Electric Vehicles in India: Technical Study of Electric Vehicles and Charging Infrastructure.* Bureau of Energy Efficiency. Ernst & Young LLP.

G. Bansal, A. Bandivadekar, (2013). Overview of India's vehicle emissions control program past successes and future prospects, ICCT.

Global electric car database. (2020). Retrieved from EV-volumes.com: http://www.ev-volumes.com/datacenter/

Government of India. (2015). *India: First Biennial Update Report to the United Nations Framework Convention on Climate Change.* Ministry of Environment, Forest and Climate Change. Government of India.

Health Effects Institute. (2019). State of Global Air 2019. Special Report. Boston, MA: Health Effects Institute. ISSN 2578-6873

IEA. (2020). Global electric car sales by key markets 2010-2020. *IEA*. Retrieved from https://www.iea.org/data-and-statistics/charts/global-electric-car-sales-by-key-markets-2015-2020

IPCC. (2007). *Climate Change 2007: Mitigation. Contribution of Working Group III to the Fourth Assessment Report of the Intergovernmental Panel on Climate Change.* IPCC. Cambridge University Press.

IQAir. (2020). *World air quality report.* IQ AIr.

I-Y.L. Hsieh and W.H. Green. (2020). "Transition to electric vehicles in China: Implications for total cost of ownership and cost to society." SAE International Journal of Sustainable Transportation, Energy, Environment, & Policy.

KPMG. (2020). Shifting gears: The evolving electric vehicle landscape in India, KPMG.

Lingzhi Jin, H. H. (2021). *Driving a green future: A retrospective review of China's electric vehicle development and outlook for the future.* China EV100. International Council on Clean Transportation (ICCT).

Ministry of Heavy Industries & Public Enterprises. (2019, July 09). *PIB Delhi.* Retrieved from https://pib.gov.in/PressReleasePage.aspx?PRID=1577880

Misra, R. (1991). *M.C. Mehta vs Union of India and Ors on 14 March, 1991.* SCR (1) 866, 1991 SCC(2) 353. New Delhi: Supreme Court.

MoHUA. (2019). *Handbook of Urban Statistics.* Ministry of Housing and Urban Affairs.

Narain, U., & Bell, R. G. (2005). *Who Changed Delhi's Air? The Roles of the Court and the Executive in Environmental Policymaking.* Washington: Resources for the future.

NITI Aayog and Rocky Mountain Institute. (2017). *India Leaps Ahead: Transformative mobility solutions for all.* NITI Aayog.

Padmanabhan, A., & Reddy, S. (2017, May 3). *Policy push to boost electric vehicle sales.* Retrieved from https://www.livemint.com/Opinion/24QvIByNFcKdpn1Rg1vhYK/Policy-push-to-boost-electric-vehicle-sales.html

RMI, NITI Aayog. (2019). *India's Electric Mobility Transformation: Progress to date and future opportunities.*

Sharma, S., Goel, A., Bhattachrya, S., Juneja, M., Bajpai, N., & Sharma, S. (2020). *Fleet Modernization: Solution to Achieve Better Air Quality.* The Energy and Resources Institute (TERI). New Delhi: The Energy and Resources Institute (TERI).

Shukla, P., Dhar, S., Pathak, M., & Bhaskar, K. (2014). *Electric Vehicle Scenario and Roadmap for India.* UNEP DTU Partnership.

SIAM. (2020). *SIAM Database.*

SIAM. (2020). *siamindia.com.*

Society of Manufactureres of Electric Vehicles. (2019). *EV market scenario India.*

Stauffer, N. W. (2020, November 25). *China's transition to electric vehicles.* Retrieved from MIT Energy initiative: https://energy.mit.edu/news/chinas-transition-to-electric-vehicles/

UNCHE. (1973). *Report of the United Nations Conference on the Human Environment, Stockholm, 5-16 June 1972.* New York: United Nations Publication.

Impact of Renewable Energy on Indian Economy: A Review

Bhaveshkumar Govindbhai Patel
Doctoral Research Scholar
Karnavati University, Uvarsad

Sunil Patel
Professor
Karnavati University, Uvarsad

Abstract: Renewable forms of energy are unconventional, need of hour sources of energy. The decline in production of green-house gases and multiple socioeconomic gains from clean energy sources in conjunction with fossil carbon fuels add a great deal. India deployed around 7.3 GW solar PV plant throughout the nation in 2019 and has developed itself as third leading solar sector in the world. As of 31 October 2020, the built power was 89.63 GW, of which 36.31 GW and 38.26 GW is solar and wind. The northern reason of India is projected as a centre for solar renewable energy in India with a potential capacity of 363 GW. This paper has attempted to illustrate the value of green energy, the effect on India's renewable solar energy economics of the international solar alliance and government policies to encourage and enhance renewable energies.

Keywords: **Energy, Renewable, Economy, Solar Photovoltaic System, International Solar Alliance**

1. INTRODUCTION

Energy is described as the ability to make an impact to do work. Energy was an essential factor in fulfilling people's daily needs. Human population is rapidly requiring resources for manufacturing, economic, residential, agricultural and transportation purposes. Energy is a basal utility element of socio-economic development. Different sources of energy are categorised as primary, secondary, commercial, non-commercial, sustainable and non-renewable energy.

Today in 21st century modern society development and it's nurturing only comes with 24 × 7 hr electricity at low cost. To achieve this socio-economic goal for stable and sustainable energy supply government should focus with zeal in area of energy policy.

The Paris Agreement, took further actions to prepare the international policy for renewable energy and their continues efforts to reduce risks and the impacts of climate change by limiting global warming to well below 2°C by 2100 relative to preindustrial levels.

2. SOLAR ENERGY

In the form of solar rays, the Earth absorbs solar energy. Such radiations are ultraviolet, visible and infrared. A variety of variables such as geographical position, time of day, season, land scope, and local weather depend on the amount of sunlight obtained by each location. The sun's ray hits the Earth at varying angles since it is round (ranging from 0 degree to 90 degree). The atmosphere of the earth receives full energy while the sun's rays are vertical.

Solar resources are available everywhere without any geopolitical conflicts over natural resources. In addition, solar power has few technological risks with the advantage of being able to provide decentralized power. As said, solar photovoltaic market has demonstrated a constant growth supported by favourable political aids and policy reforms in the energy transition context. The Solar Energy Technology prices have sharply reduced benefiting from economy of scale in recent years.

3. INTERNATIONAL SOLAR ALLIANCE

Resolution A/RES/36/193 of the UN General Assembly in 1981 demonstrated the need for collaboration between developing nations and the mobilisation of financial capital for modern and sustainable energy sources. After 2002 a range of lobbying groups, mostly to disseminate awareness of green energies, were set up after the UN Summit on Sustainable Development.

A particular entity does not handle the solar energy deployment needs of the countries that have a rich solar resource between the Tropical of Cancer and Capricorn Tropic. Geographically, the rest of these countries are for optimum sun ray absorption. There is a lot of sunshine all year round, with a strong insolation of about 300 bright days a year, contributing to cost-efficient solar power and other end applications. There are significant farming communities in most nations. Many countries face gaps in the future eco-system for solar energy development. Many rich countries are acquainted with the absence of universal electricity supply, energy equity, and affordability.

The International Solar Alliance (ISA) is a collaboration between India and France to unite high solar resource countries. The ISA is a collaborative partnership initiative. At Paris Climate Summit conducted in December last year, collaboration aimed at putting together some 120 countries with up to 300 days of sunlight in the Tropics of Cancer and Capricorn. In a very short period, it was a long voyage for the ISA. At the Paris Climate Change Conference 2015, India and France initiated a new project, the International Solar Alliance (ISA). The ISA is the first foreign agency located in India to encourage solar power in its sunshine belt primarily between the Capricorn Tropic and the Cancer Tropic. As a weapon of strategic power, one of the main goals of India to co-found ISA.

The ISA is conceived as an alliance of rich countries with solar resources that meet their special energy needs and is a forum to work together to address the defined gaps through a shared, negotiated strategy. They are not going to repeat or reproduce the efforts that are currently being put out by others (like the International Renewable Energy Agency, REN21, UN bodies and bilateral organisations, etc.), but rather create network and synergy growth, for model the International Renewable Energy Agency (IEA), and the International Renewable Energy Policy Network for the twenty-first century.

4. MISSION AND VISION

The ISA goal is to provide a forum for collaboration between rich solar energy countries to facilitate the usage of solar energy to meet ISA Member States' energy needs in a protected, healthy manner, through the use of bilateral and multilateral organisations, companies, industry and stakeholders.

5. INDIA RENEWABLE INDUSTRY

The Indian RE (Renewable Energy) sector is world's 4th most profitable RE industry. In 2018 India was classified as 5th in renewable energy capacity, 4th in wind power and 5th in solar PV power.

In recent years the installed potential for renewable energy output has gained momentum with a CAGR of 17.33% between fiscal year 16-20. The industry has been appealing from an investment point of view with rising government funding and strengthened economics. As India alone is looking to fulfil its own electricity demand of 15820 TWh by 2040, green energy would play a major role. By 2022, the government aims to produce 225 GW of renewables (including solar power addition of 114 GW and wind power of 67 GW) over the 175 GW goal set by the Paris Convention. The government aims to build a potential of 500 GW for renewable energy by 2030.

6. IMPACT OF RENEWABLE ENERGY ON INDIAN ECONOMY

Most analysts use a unit for the economy called the energy demand to calculate economic growth. According to current forecasts, the market for specific energies is projected to rise three times worldwide in the coming decades. The IEA reports forecast that India's overall energy scenario will increase due to population growth, rendering India by 2050. Another Greenpeace study outlines factors such as demographic gains and exponential GDP growth that impact the country's potential power needs, which raise demand more than 200 per cent by 2040-50. In the next several decades, these reports are likely to boost oil production and gas use. It is expected that the power grid of the world would have to quadruple in size to address this steep increase in electricity demand. While the studies show the potential growth in electricity consumption, they also display clean energies forecasts by 2050. The Greenpeace study anticipates a rise in photovoltaic systems worldwide with PV comprising 20-40 percent of renewables deployed across India.

Various factors affect the demand for adequate services in developing countries, such as income production, socioeconomic growth, severe health concerns arising from fuelwood usage, charcoal, etc. Historically, there has been a pattern that greenhouse gas levels for the developed economy are considerably higher than for emerging economies. Recent studies indicate, however, that the pattern is shifting. A tectonic transition from traditional energy sources to Non-conventional sources of energy include wind and solar, bio-energy and hydropower energy, was initiated to resolve energy poverty concerns and the adverse climate of conventional energy sources. The usage of gaseous fuels in different sectors, such as shipping, industry and residential industries, also increased. Hydropower and natural gas are the perfect renewables and power-generating resources. However, several concerns dampen the usage of such supplies, such as lack of provision, delays in clearing and public agitation.

India has also pushed on to green energy sources to fulfil their energy demands, maintain the world pattern. In 1974, India demanded a total of 16.7 GW of installed capacity, which was all held by the nationwide administrations. Around 51% operated by the coal burned, 42% by major hydro-project and 4% by nuclear energy and 2% by gas fuel, through renewable making up 0%. It was a pleasant shock for the government to convert coal to clean energy, as the oil crisis in the 1970ies pushed the emphasis. In combination with the financial crisis of the early 1990s and private-sector dedication to industrial growth induced by liberalisation and industrialisation in the Indian economy in 1991, the renewable energy sector expanded.

As a tropical region, India has plenty of solar energy. Its area makes a great deal of solar radiation in several regions during the year. The satellite-based and then ground-authenticated provision throughout the entire country reveals, with most of the regions obtaining 4 to 7 kWh/m2/day, that 500 000 TWh of electric power are obtained from Indian lands. In the states of Rajasthan and Gujarat, the highest global horizontal irradiance is obtained.

7. SOLAR PV MARKET IN INDIA

A modern and effective green energy technology is being moved ahead in the Paris Agreement on reducing GHG emissions. The first photovoltaic cells were very costly and effective, while coal energy was inexpensive and readily accessible. However, many analyses of the price of photovoltaic technology have shown an exponential decrease across the years. A research has shown that since 2009 alone solar panels rates have declined by up to 80%. As a consequence of this decline in costs and of the need for decarbonization of energy supply, PV plant has increased. The solar photovoltaics costs have seen a decrease in cost from USD/kWh 0.285 to USD/ kWh 0.126 in 2010 to 2015. A 2018 International Energy Organization study explains the low cost of PV tenders around the globe. Chile and Mexico's levelled energy prices were record low at a rate of 2.1 USD cents per kWh and of 5 USD cents/kWh in Europe. These factors allowed the country and worldwide demand for solar photovoltaics to grow.

As of 31 October 2020, the installed capacity was 89.63 GW, of which 36.31 GW and 38.26 GW is of solar and wind. 4.74 GW and 10.14 GW respectively served small hydropower and biomass. By December 2019, there had been an issuance of 15100 megawatts (MW) for wind power projects with projects with a potential of 12162.50 MW. In FY20 the production of total RE sources reached approximately 127.01 BU (billion units) in India.

India deployed around 7.3 GW solar PV plant throughout the nation in 2019 and has developed itself as third leading solar sector in the world. As October 2020, the built power was 89.63 GW, of which 36.31 GW and 38.26 GW is solar and wind. The northern reason of India is projected as a centre for India's renewable energies thanks to its potential ability of 363 GW and renewable energy policy.

8. INVESTMENTS / DEVELOPMENTS

From April to June 2020 in the Indian non-conventional energy market the FDI influx stood at US$9.56 billion, as per details available from the Department of Industry and Internal Trade Promotion (DPIIT). Since 2014-15, India's renewable industry has spent more than US$42 billion. Renewable energy expenditure in the world in 2018 was up to US$11.1 billion.

In the Indian clean energy industry, several big investments and innovations are:

- In November 2020 Sun Source Energy with the solar energy company (SECI), declared its plan to build a 4 MW floating solar pv grid-connection power plant with the 2 MW Battery storage device in the Andaman Nicobar Island.
- The Indian Airports Authority (AAI) signed a MoU in November 2020 on the usage of electric cars and the construction of solar energy plants at its airports with NTPC's Vidyut Vyapar Nigam subsidiary.
- Patel Engineering reported in October 2020 that its contract for the 2 GW Subansiri Lower Hydro Electro Project in state of Arunachal Pradesh had been ordered to Rs. 1564.42 crores ($ 211.15 million).
- From January to September 2020, India added 2.320 MW of solar energy.
- Tata Power announced in October 2020 its plans in Dholera, in Gujarat Solar Park, to build a 100 MW solar plant.
- NTPC formed a wholly-owned clean-energy firm, NTPC Renewable Energy Ltd, following NITI Aayog and its DIPAM approval in October 2020. By 2032, NTPC plans to produce approximately 30% or 39GW of its total renewable energy ability.
- The SECI has initiated large-scale solar park central auctions and has been contractually allocated to 47 parks with total potential reaching 25 GW.
- In April 2020, the 300 MW (1.750 crore) solar plant (USD $250.39 million) project bagged by Vikram Solar under the CPSU-II bid auction was carried out under CPSU II by the National Thermal Power Corporation (NTPC).
- Planning to become by 2025 the largest solar firm in the world and by 2030 the largest clean energy company.
- Through April-Dec. 2019, Investments in renewable energy by private player were made about Rs. 36729.49 (USD 5.26 billion).
- Shapoorji Pallonji and ReNew Power spend approximately Rs. 750 crore, in Uttar Pradesh's 150-MW floating solar power plant.
- In Rajasthan India launched its Bhadla Solar Park, the biggest solar project in the world with a power of 2255 MW in 2019.
- In 2020 December, Indian government announced to set up 300 GW Hybrid Renewable energy park in Gujarat's Kutch district build as the largest in the world developed by Adani Green energy, Saran Reality Limited, NTPC, Gujarat Industries Power Company Ltd and Gujarat State Electricity Corporation.

9. INITIATIVES BY THE GOVERNMENT OF INDIA

The Government of India is following many measures to improve the renewable energy industry in India:

- The PSU joint venture Energy Efficiency Services Limited (EESL) under the Power Ministery and DNRE. Department of Goa signed a memorandum of Agreement on 17 November to explore the introduction of India's first merge type project in the world.
- The government declared in October 2020 a decision to set up the NITI Aayog inter ministerial committee to lead analysis and modelling energy studies. The Indian Energy Modeling Forum, initiated in joint cooperation by NITI Aayog and the U.S. Agency for International Cooperation, will function along with the steering committee (USAID).

- The government revealed in August 2020 the intentions to provide solar plant construction firms with property near its ports.
- India aims to instal 30 GW of green energy in the west frontier, in the desert like that of Rajasthan and Gujarat.
- The state government of Delhi agreed to pack up the Rajghat thermal power plant and transform it into a 5 MW solar PV park.
- The Rajasthan govt., exempted from the electricity duty in Budget 2019-20 renewable energy and concentrated on solar pv power usage in its medical and agriculture sectors.
- For hydropower projects in the region, revised hydropower strategy for 2018 - 28 was drafted.
- The Indian government unveiled proposals for the launch of the US$ 238 million National U.S. U. Supercritical Advanced Technology Mission for Cleaner Coal Use.
- The MNRE decided to benefit from custom and excise duties to the rooftop solar industry which reduces installation costs and generates electricity, thereby boosting growth.
- Indian Railways is working hard to reduce pollution by 33 percent by 2030 with continued energy conservation initiatives and maximum renewable fuel usage.

By 2020 India has set an aggressive target of 175 GW of renewable energy. More than 55% of this, i.e. 100 GW of solar energy is produced. The hundred GW for utility and 40 GW for rooftop schemes is further split in 60 GW. Solar, which is economically feasible, simple to build, and low operational and maintenance costs, is dominated by the green energy sector.

In India, the market for modules, inverters and allied hardware is also growing with increasing solar energy usage. However, the imports from China, Vietnam, Europe and so on rely enormously. The boost from India would have a beneficial influence on our economy and will reduce our import dependence. In order to satisfy the high demand of qualified workers, manufacturing companies can build and provide work in this field. The Indian solar industry generated 1,15,000 jobs in 2018 and will continue to expand in the years ahead, according to the International Renewable Energy Agency (IRENA).

The time has come to act and help to live sustainably. Investment is a much greater return on solar goods than any class of conventional properties and savings, and the annuity saving of 25 percent over 25 years is continued in the project. Adopting every megawatt of solar reduces CO_2 by 31000 tonnes, i.e. 49,000 teak wood for every megawatt, over the project lifespan. India is an emerging country with massive growth prospects and an increased energy demand.

Considering commercial and manufacturing consumptions in tandem with domestic use in more than 20 Indian crore households – the demand awaits us for a trillion dollars. To further boost the solar system usage, ecosystems need to concentrate on few factors – sensitising and supplying customers with funding alternatives while relying on efficient technologies.

Solar energy adoption turns many problem areas into possibilities. This will drive economic development, improve India's mission and build jobs while greening the planet.

10. DEVELOPMENT AND DEPLOYMENT OF SOLAR ENERGY CHALLENGES

Large investment costs of photovoltaic technology also deter developers who do not invest in solar photovoltaic technologies. In the absence of an appropriate funding structure, the production of PV systems faces difficulties. Research reveals that the funding appropriate for PV facilities is attributed to several reasons relatively to developed countries. These factors also hinder the country's solar photovoltaic production. In developed countries, Dobrotkova et al. investigated the cost competitiveness of solar photovoltaic prices.

It was concluded that although low costs of photovoltaic plants are feasible, a number of variables, such as high performance, low supplementary equipment costs, low risk investments, etc., are important. Their investigation shows that experts are worried regarding the auction mechanism because they suspect that auctions can contribute to unreasonable rates that could lead to low project efficiency. Demand and price interdependence also drives developers to support ventures because of unforeseeable threats. While different exemptions on solar PV technologies are currently being introduced, taxation still remains an obstacle in producing low-cost solar photovoltaic systems. Imposed energy costs determine the energy costs generated by photovoltaic technology. The expense of PV cells, sizing of batteries, peak load ratings, strength factor etc. are taken into account in PV solar production economics. The customer has to endure these. These considerations also raise the costs of expenditure in the plant and thereby diminish customers' confidence in technology.

11. ROAD AHEAD

The State is dedicated to increasing the usage of alternative energy sources and already undertakes numerous large-scale programmes to support green energy. Renewable energy also has the potential to generate several jobs, especially in rural areas, at all levels. In order to grow 225 GW of renewable energy capacity by 2022, including 114 GW of solar, 67 GW of wind, organic and other energy sources, the MNRE (Renewable Energy Ministry) has set an aggressive goal. The renewable energy market of India could draw US$ 80 billion worth of investment over the next four years.

By 2040, renewables are estimated to produce about 49 percent of total energy, while more effective electricity is collected by more efficient batteries, reducing the cost of solar power by 66 per cent relative to present prices. Usage of renewable energies in place of conventional coal power can save Indian Rs.54,000/- crores (US$8.43bn) per year. By 2030, the overall installed power for renewable energies would constitute 55 percent.

12. CONCLUSION

While solar energy production has begun to pick up, technological advancements are therefore required consecutively to achieve the goals of solar PV systems. The phase of growth in India is accelerated by vigorous R&D, right policy enforcement and suitable financial strategy to cope with the question of financing photovoltaic installations.

Since the sun shines in large sections of India all 12 months, solar power is a strong solution to energy production. Renewable Energy generation does not contain green house gases, produces a safe atmosphere and is infinitely accessible this is because Indian Government is pushing this sector. Government of India is interested in generating unstrapped employment in the new renewable electricity sector so far.

The initiative taken by Indian government and ISA for India's renewable energy policies like financing, development and deployment of structure will boost Indian energy economy. Certainly it will add a new drive to India's renewable energy market in the 21st century.

REFERENCES

Chaurey. The growing photovoltaic market in India Prog. Photovoltaics Res. Appl., 9(3) (2001), pp. 235–244.

Centre for Renewable Energy and Environment Development, BITS Pilani. https://bits-pilani.ac.in/RandDcentres (last viewed on 30-01-2021).

Central Electricity Authority, Ministry of New and Renewable Energy, Media Reports, Press Releases.

E.A. Moallemi, L. Aye, J.M. Webb, F.J. de Haan, B.A. George. India's on-grid solar power development: historical transitions, present status and future driving forces, Renew. Sustain. Energy Rev., 69 (2017), pp. 239–247.

F. Ahmad, M.S. Alam. Economic and ecological aspects for microgrids deployment in India, Sustainable cities and society, 37 (2018), pp. 407–419.

Gulagi, D. Bogdanov, C. Breyer The role of storage technologies in energy transition pathways towards achieving a fully sustainable energy system for India, Journal of Energy Storage, 17 (2018), pp. 525–539.

H. Sharma, P. Kumar, N. Pal, P.K. Sadhu. Problems in the Accomplishment of Solar and Wind Energy in India Problemy z pozyskiwaniemenergiisłonecznejiwiatrowej w Indiach, ProblemyEkorozwoju, 13 (1) (2018), pp. 41–48.

International Energy Agency (IEA) CO_2 Emission from Fuel Combustion (2015).

International Renewable Energy Agency (IRENA) Quarterly Report: Letting in the Light (2016).

International Energy Agency (IEA) Report IEA-PVPS: Trends in Photovoltaic Applications (2018).

Lupangu, R.C. Bansal. A review of technical issues on the development of solar photovoltaic systems Renew. Sustain. Energy Rev., 73 (2017), pp. 950–965.

M. Mukherjee. Private Participation in the Indian Power Sector: Lessons from Two Decades of Experience, The World Bank (2014).

M.K. Hairat, S. Ghosh, 100 GW solar power in India by 2022–A critical review, Renew. Sustain. Energy Rev., 73 (2017), pp. 1041–1050.

N. Saxena, Solar energy as renewable energy systems: perspective and challenges in Indian context Int. J. Eng. Technol. Sci. Res., 5 (1) (2018).

N. Kannan, D. Vakeesan, Solar energy for future world:-A review Renew. Sustain. Energy Rev, 62 (2016), pp. 1092–1105.

Narula, K., Reddy, B. S., Pachauri, S., & Dev, S. M. Sustainable energy security for India: An assessment of the energy supply sub-system. Energy Policy, 103 (2017), pp. 127–144.

PLANNING COMMISSION of India, 2002, Indian Government Report.

P. Garg. Energy scenario and vision 2020 in India J. Sustain. Energy. Environ., 3 (1) (2012), pp. 7–17.

Ramachandra, T. V., Jain, R., & Krishnadas, G. Hotspots of solar potential in India. (2011).

Renewable and Sustainable Energy Reviews, 15(6), 3178–3186.

Rajput, Saurabh. SOLAR ENERGY - Fundamentals, Economic and Energy Analysis First Edition, 93 (2017).

R.M. Swanson. Approaching the 29% limit efficiency of silicon solar cells Photovoltaic Specialists Conference, 2005. Conference Record of the Thirty-First IEEE, IEEE (2005), pp. 889–894.

Shidore, Sarang & Busby, Joshua. One more try: The International Solar Alliance and India's search for geopolitical influence. Energy Strategy Reviews. 26 (2019).

School of Energy Studies, Jadavpur University. http://www.jaduniv.edu.in/ (last viewed on 21-01-2021).

Shahsavari, M. Akbari Potential of solar energy in developing countries for reducing energy-related emissions Renew. Sustain. Energy Rev., 90 (2018), pp. 275–291.

S. Teske, S. Sawyer, O. Schäfer, T. Pregger, S. Simon, T. Naegler, S. Schmid, E.D. Özdemir, J. Pagenkopf, F. Kleiner, J. Rutovitz Energy [r] Evolution-A Sustainable World Energy Outlook 2015 (2015).

Z. Dobrotkova, K. Surana, P. Audinet, The price of solar energy: comparing competitive auctions for utility-scale solar PV in developing countries, Energy Policy, 118 (2018), pp. 133–148.

The Colour Images

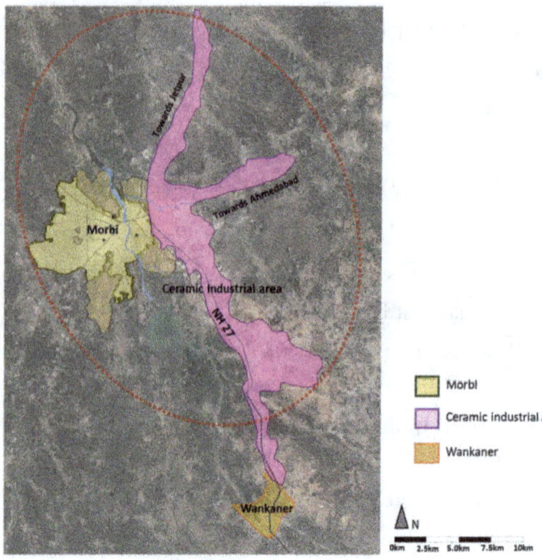

(This image appears on page 24)

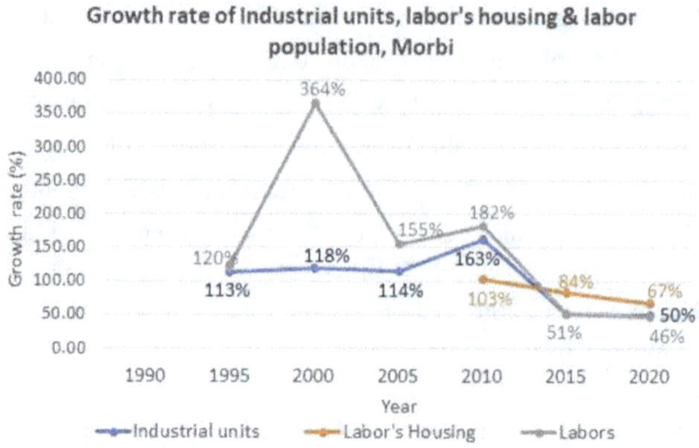

(This image appears on page 26)

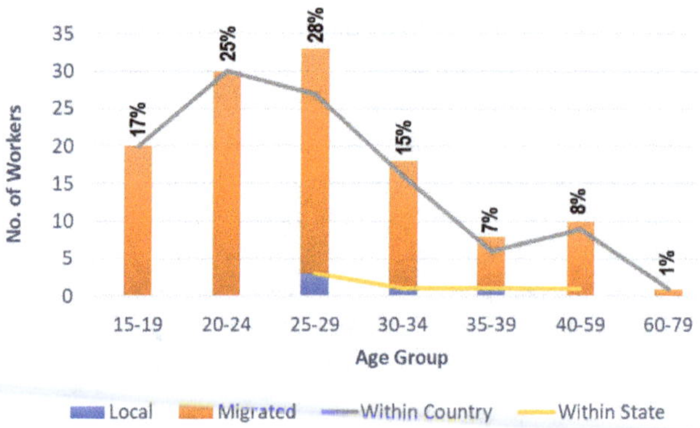

(This image appears on page 26)

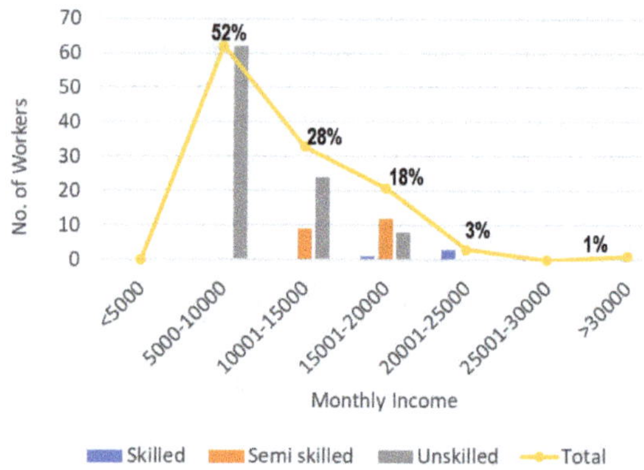

(This image appears on page 27)

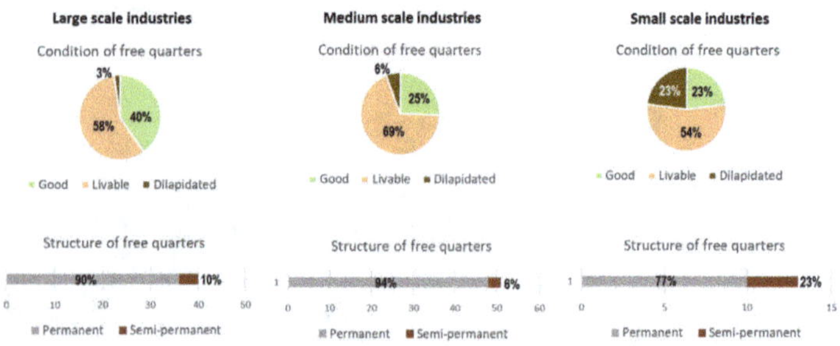

(This image appears on page 28)

(This image appears on page 29)

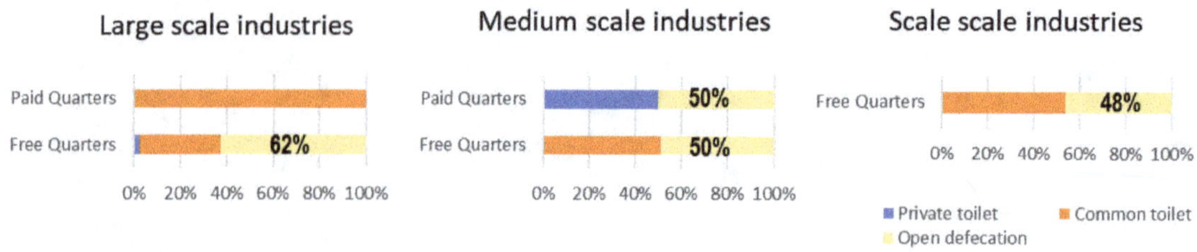

(This image appears on page 29)

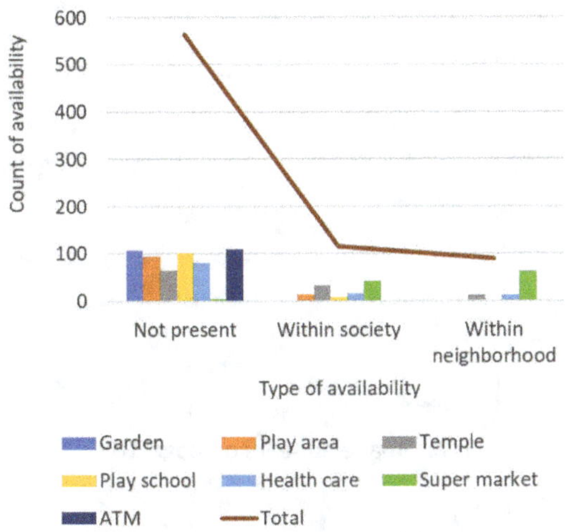

(This image appears on page 30)

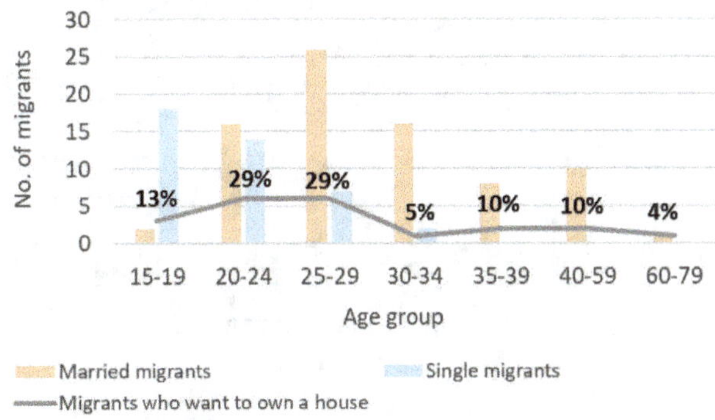

(This image appears on page 31)

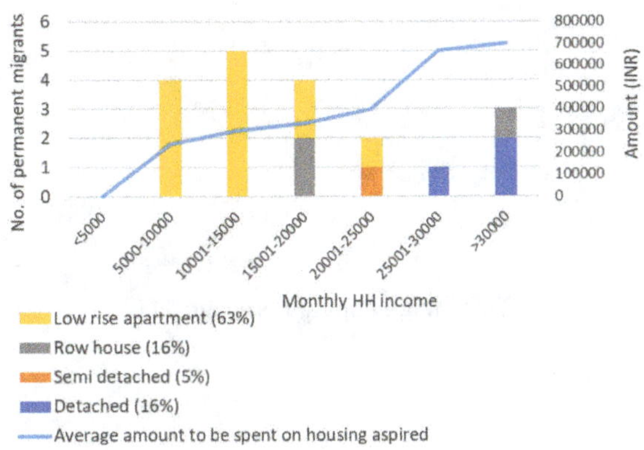

(This image appears on page 31)

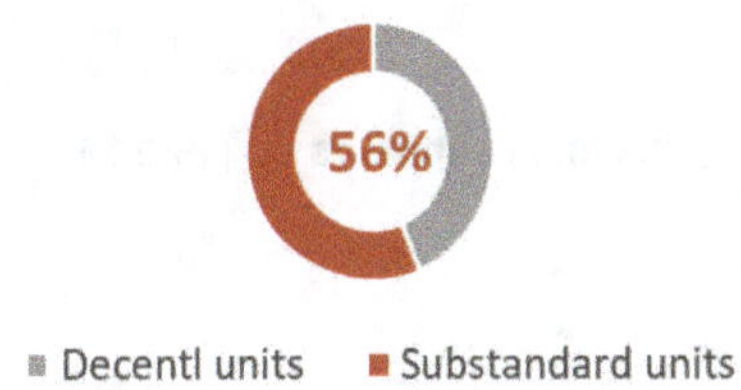

(This image appears on page 32)

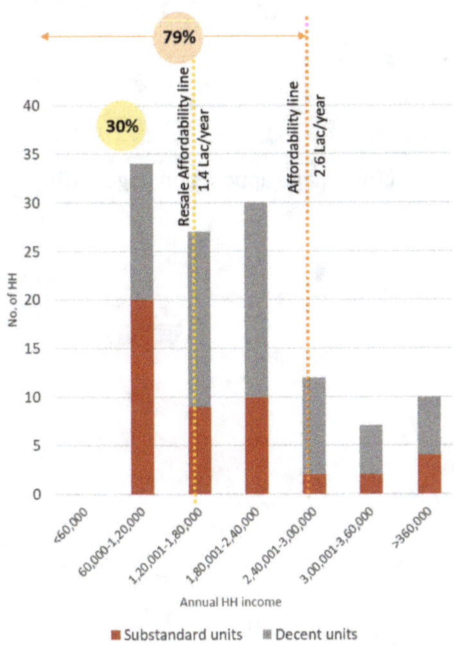

(This image appears on page 32)

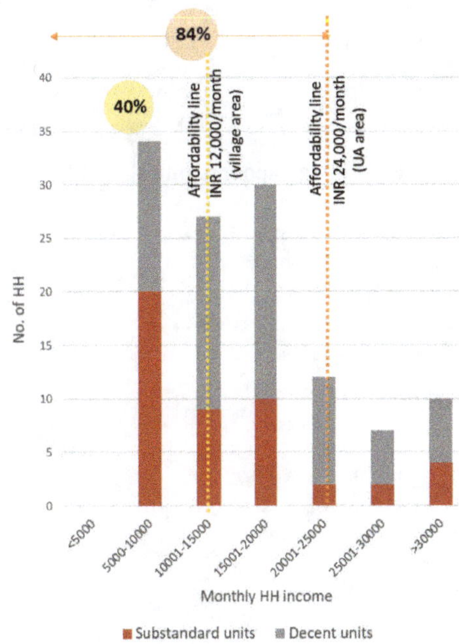

(This image appears on page 32)

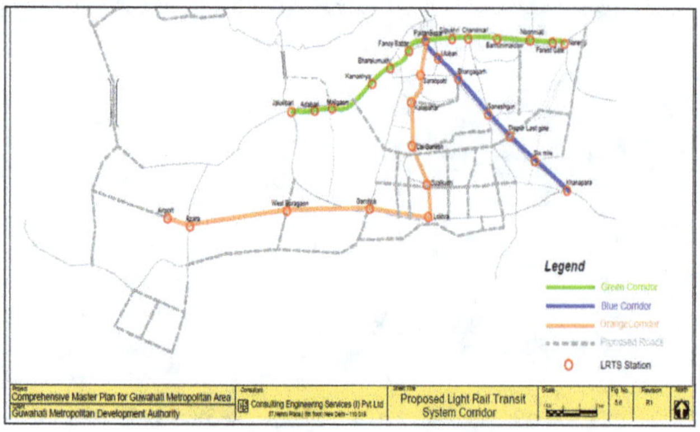

(This image appears on page 83)

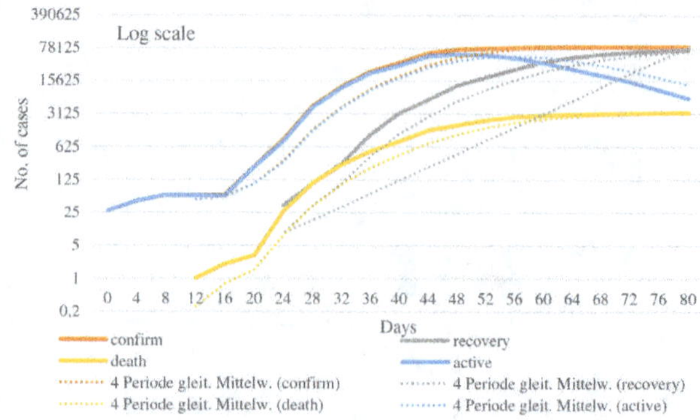

(This image appears on page 109)

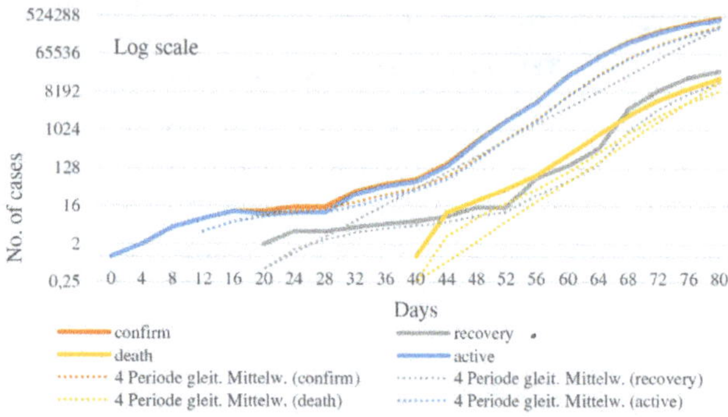

(This image appears on page 110)

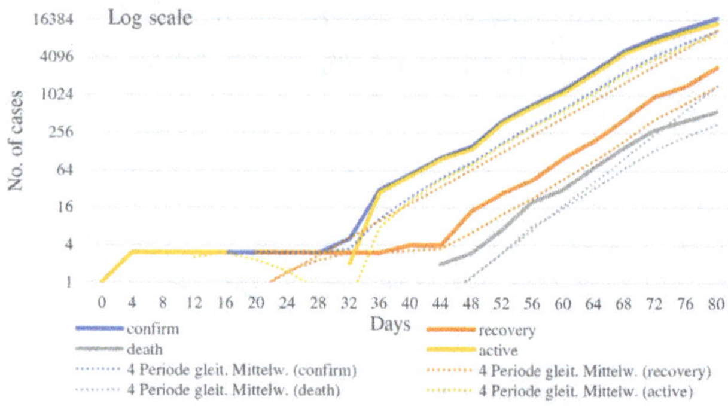

(This image appears on page 110)

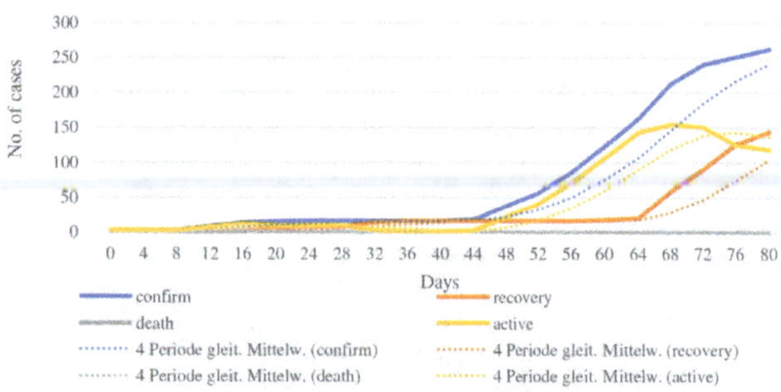

(This image appears on page 111)

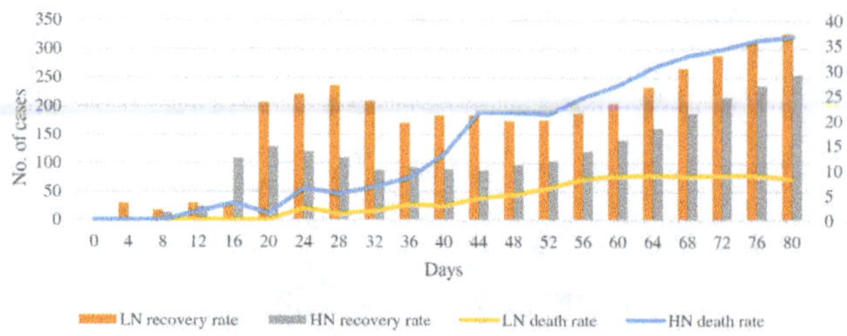

(This image appears on page 113)

For Product Safety Concerns and Information please contact our EU
representative GPSR@taylorandfrancis.com
Taylor & Francis Verlag GmbH, Kaufingerstraße 24, 80331 München, Germany

www.ingramcontent.com/pod-product-compliance
Lightning Source LLC
LaVergne TN
LVHW080546210926
848481LV00025B/2747
* 9 7 8 1 0 3 2 1 1 4 6 6 8 *